An Ecological View of History

JAPANESE SOCIETY SERIES

General Editor: Yoshio Sugimoto

An Ecological View of History

Japanese Civilization in the World Context

Tadao Umesao

Edited by
Harumi Befu

Translated by
Beth Cary

Trans Pacific Press

Melbourne

This English edition first published in 2003 by
Trans Pacific Press, PO Box 120, Rosanna, Melbourne, Victoria 3084, Australia
Telephone: +61 3 9459 3021 Fax: +61 3 9457 5923
Email: enquiries@transpacificpress.com
Web: http://www.transpacificpress.com

Copyright © Trans Pacific Press 2003

Designed and set by digital environs Melbourne.
enquiries@digitalenvirons.com

Printed by BPA Print Group, Burwood, Victoria, Australia

Distributors

Australia
Bushbooks
PO Box 1958, Gosford, NSW 2250
Telephone: (02) 4323-3274
Fax: (02) 9212-2468
Email: bushbook@ozemail.com.au

USA and Canada
International Specialized Book
Services (ISBS)
5824 N. E. Hassalo Street
Portland, Oregon 97213-3644
USA
Telephone: (800) 944-6190
Fax: (503) 280-8832
Email: orders@isbs.com
Web: http://www.isbs.com

Japan
Kyoto University Press
Kyodai Kaikan
15-9 Yoshida Kawara-cho
Sakyo-ku, Kyoto 606-8305
Telephone: (075) 761-6182
Fax: (075) 761-6190
Email: sales@kyoto-up.gr.jp
Web: http://www.kyoto-up.gr.jp

UK and Europe
Asian Studies Book Services
3554 TT Utrecht
The Netherlands
Telephone: +31 30 289 1240
Fax: +31 30 289 1249
Email: marie.lenstrup@planet.nl
Web: http://www.asianstudiesbooks.com

ISSN 1443–9670 (Japanese Society Series)
ISBN 1-8768-4308-X (Hardback)
ISBN 1-8768-4389-6 (Paperback)

National Library of Australia Cataloging in Publication Data

Umesao, Tadao, 1920–.
   An ecological view of history : Japanese civilization in the world context.
   Bibliography.
   Includes index.
   ISBN 1 876843 89 6(pbk).
   ISBN 1 876843 08 X.

   1. East and West – History. 2. Social ecology – Japan –
   History. 3. Japan – History. I. Befu, Harumi. II. Title.
   I. Title. (Series : Japanese society series).
952

Contents

Figures

Preface

In 1964, *Chūō Kōron* (Central Review), the premier and venerable intellectual journal of Japan, published a special issue for which its editorial committee and a special ad hoc committee selected eighteen articles appearing in intellectual journals in postwar Japan that the committee considered to be the most important and the most influential in shaping Japan's postwar thought. 'Bunmei no Seitaishikan Josetsu,' which constitutes the centerpiece of *Bunmei no Seitaishikan,* the book being translated here as *An Ecological View of History: Japanese Civilization in the World Context*, was among the eighteen articles.

In 1996 fifty-eight leading Japanese intellectuals in politics, government bureaucracy, business, and culture were asked to nominate the ten best books, fiction or non-fiction, published either before or after the Second World War. *Bunmei no Seitaishikan* placed fourth among all Japanese books, only after Shiba Ryōtarō's *Saka no ue no kumo* (Clouds over the hill),[1] Nishida Kitarō's *Zen no kenkyū* (Study of good),[2] and Natsume Sōseki's *Wagahai wa neko de aru* (I am a cat).[3] It was ranked ahead of, for example, Watsuji Tetsurō's *Fūdo* (The climate),[4] Tanizaki Jun'ichirō's *Sasameyuki* (The Makioka sisters),[5] Doi Takeo's *Amae no kōzō* (Anatomy of dependence),[6] and Nakane Chie's *Tate shakai no ningen kankei* (Japanese society),[7] just to name a few of the classics well known not only to Japanese but also among Anglophone readers. In the same survey, Umesao Tadao, the author of this book, was considered the tenth best known among all Japanese authors, surpassing such prominent writers as Mishima Yukio and Yoshikawa Eiji. Shiba, Nishida, and Natsume are all household names in Japan, and their works are read by millions of Japanese. To follow on the heels of works by these literary giants in 1996, some thirty years after its original publication, attests to the critical acclaim Umesao's book has enjoyed to this day. *Bunmei no Seitaishikan* is by now a veritable classic in the Japanese intellectual library. To understand the place of this important work in Japan's intellectual history, it is necessary to provide some background.

Ten years following Japan's defeat in the Second World War, Umesao joined a scientific expedition to Central and South Asia. What Umesao saw in Hindu Kush, Afghanistan, Pakistan, and India through his ecologically trained mind gave him a vastly different perspective on Japan from the conventional view. This experience led Umesao to a totally unorthodox interpretation of Japanese civilization. Out of this experience, his ecological theory of civilization was born. Umesao came to the conclusion that Japan's civilization is structurally the same as Western Europe's, not China's as one would normally assume. This is so, he argued, because ecological conditions are similar on both the western and the eastern fringes of the Eurasian continent. He contended that in the center of this continent, dry regions and deserts stretch from northeast to southwest, impacted by prevailing winds. On their outskirts, nomadic people have held power on vast plains, flanked by the empires of China, India, the Ottoman Turks and Russia. The Mediterranean Sea may be compared to the China Sea in this context. On the outer fringes are located Western Europe to the west and Japan to the east – with many parallel developments in their respective histories. This theory of likening Japan to Western Europe and dissociating with China was first published in 1957 in *Chūō Kōron* (Central Review), under the title 'Bunmei no Seitaishikan Josetsu.'[8]

The 1957 *Chūō Kōron* treatise occupies the core of the book entitled *Bunmei no Seitaishikan* published in 1967, to which other related essays by Umesao were added. In these essays Umesao demonstrated the centrality of ecology in understanding civilizations, this already in the 1950s and 1960s when an idea of this sort was totally foreign to those who worked in civilizational studies. He also presaged the view now quite current that Westerners are highly Western-centric in their conceptualization of the world. The present book is its translation with one important exception. We have added a translation of a paper Umesao has written recently, which expands his earlier theory and applies it to the ocean. After cogitating on Japan's dismal record of expansion on land and its unfortunate consequences, Umesao urges Japan to turn its attention to the ocean for its future. This addition demonstrates Umesao's continually evolving thoughts on civilization.

Some of the chapters in this book may seem overly descriptive. But such an observation is possible only with the hindsight of some fifty years. These descriptive chapters offer some of the empirical bases upon which Umesao's theory in Chapter Three and elaborated in other chapters is formulated. To understand inclusion of these descriptive chapters, it is also important to be aware that at that time, still poor and suffering from the devastation of the war, few Japanese had the resources to travel abroad. The currency exchange rate was then fixed at an unfavorable 360 yen to the dollar. Moreover, a severe limitation on the amount of currency that could be taken out of the country imposed by the Japanese government made foreign travel by the Japanese virtually impossible. Thus information about foreign lands as such was much missed and much welcomed by the Japanese thirsting for knowledge about the world outside Japan at that time, let alone his novel interpretation of Japan's place in world history. Umesao's reportage on Central and South Asia opened Japanese eyes to these parts of the world which were barely known to most Japanese. The popularity of the book, published in 1967, can be in part attributed to the eagerness with which the Japanese waited to discover what that part of the world was like. However, the book has continued to be popular and has been published in several editions, each edition going through numerous printings, the latest edition being published in 2002. The book in different editions altogether has gone through some fifty printings. This continued popularity almost half a century after the publication of his original thesis, when millions of Japanese travel abroad, cannot be accounted for by the readers' thirst for information about exotic lands. Rather, it is a clear indication that the book has demonstrated its lasting intellectual worth. Its significance in Japan's modern intellectual history goes without saying. It thus behooves those outside Japan to have an understanding of a book reputed to be one of the four most important books in modern Japan.

France, Italy, Germany, and China have already seen translations of a good portion of the book in their respective languages. But the Anglophone world has not had the opportunity to become acquainted with Umesao's far-reaching thoughts on civilization except through translations of a chapter of this book and a transcript of a conference lecture.[9] It is high time something is done about it.

Umesao is a preeminent figure in Japan's intellectual world, not only in anthropology, where he is most certainly acknowledged as the dean of the discipline in Japan, but more broadly as a leading intellectual with many honors bestowed upon him. His name is literally a household word. Most college graduate Japanese know at least something of Umesao's accomplishments: if nothing else, they know him as the author of *Bunmei no Seitaishikan.* But because he is surprisingly little known abroad, some space should be devoted to informing the reader of the intellectual background of this book and its author.

Born in Kyoto, Japan in 1920, from pre-collegiate days Umesao showed keen interest in unknown lands and climbed innumerable mountains in central Japan. As an undergraduate at Kyoto Imperial University (now Kyoto University), he had already explored Micronesia and Northeast China. Such expeditions to foreign countries in those days (1930s and 1940s) by an undergraduate were unheard of. His mentor was Imanishi Kinji, well known in the West for his pioneering work in primatology. As a graduate student in the midst of the war, he joined Imanishi's team and went to Mongolia to research the ecology of Inner Asia and Mongolia. Thus his postwar expedition into Inner and South Asia, which region he later came to call the 'Mediant' in contrast to the Orient and the Occident, was a natural continuation of a long career in exploring unknown lands. His pioneering 1957 essay was based on many years of eco-ethnological investigation in various parts of Asia. Umesao's interest in ecological field research continued throughout his life until he lost his eyesight in 1986. He was to spend a considerable amount of time in Africa, especially East Africa, studying ecological adaptations of pastoral peoples in that region.

Umesao's first academic appointment was at Osaka City University in 1949. In 1965 he moved to Kyoto University to succeed Imanishi at the Research Institute for Humanistic Studies. In 1974, when the National Museum of Ethnology was established, he was appointed its first Director General. This museum was long in the making, its history going back to prewar years, with many attempts in the interim. Umesao was involved in the creation of the National Museum of Ethnology from its initial planning and practically master-minded the shaping of this museum. The Museum is arguably one of the largest and finest ethnological museums in the world, boasting some seventy fulltime researchers and the latest technologies in research, display, storage, and curation, and a large library collection with subscriptions to thousands of journals. As a favored institution it receives a substantial budget from the Ministry of Education, Culture, Sports, Science and Technology.

In 1986 Umesao lost his eyesight literally overnight. An ordinary person would resign from a position of heavy responsibility, such as the head of a major research organization. But Umesao is no ordinary man. He served as the Museum's Director General for another seven years. Not only did he carry on this position of responsibility, he continued to be amazingly productive, undertaking lectures and publications. In 1989, he embarked on the compilation of his collected works in 23 volumes, taking four years to complete this effort.[10] Each volume, 600 to 700 pages long, was carefully edited and annotated, containing previously published books and articles on a given theme, such as 'Comparative Civilization,' 'Ecological Studies,' 'Japanese Studies,' 'Women and Civilization,' 'Ethnology and Museum,' 'Mediant Countries,' 'African Studies,' and 'Global Age.' It is significant that Volume Five: 'Comparative Civilization' was the first volume in the collection to be published. Even after the completion of this project, Umesao has been unceasingly productive.

Throughout his life Umesao has been showered with numerous awards and honors, both private and public, domestic and foreign. He is an honorary member of the Anthropological Society of Nippon, the Japan Association for African Studies, the Japanese Alpine Club, the International Association for Mongolian Studies, and the Japanese Professional Photographers Society. He is also an honorary citizen of Kyoto. From the Japanese government he has received the Medal with Purple Ribbon (1988), the Award for Dis-tinguished Cultural Merit (1991), the Order of Culture (1994), and the Grand Cordon of the Order of the Sacred Treasure (1999). He is a recipient of Palmes Academiques from the French government. The Mongolian government has honored him for his pioneering contributions to Mongolian studies, as well. No other anthropologist and few other intellectuals in any field in Japan have received as many distinguished recognitions as

Umesao. This is an acknowledgement not only of his academic accomplishments, but also of the broad-ranging intellectual impact he has had on Japanese society in the past half a century. Umesao is truly a man of phenomenal achievement.

Josef Kreiner
University of Bonn
Harumi Befu
Stanford University

Introduction to the English Language Edition

I first began to give serious consideration to the comparative study of world civilizations in 1955. It was in that year that, having completed my ethnological field research in Afghanistan, I returned to Japan via Pakistan and India. During this passage through the Indian subcontinent, I came in contact with two great civilizations: the Islamic civilization and the Hindu civilization. This exposure completely changed my views on the layout of global civilizations. I perceived that the region through which I traveled was neither East nor West; not Orient yet not Occident either. I began to think of it as the 'Mediant.'

When I combined my impressions from the South Asian trip with the knowledge I had gained in China during the Second World War – particularly the two years I had spent in Mongolia – I was struck by the extensive qualitative differences between Japanese civilization and the civilizations of those areas on the Asian mainland. Even though Japan is also located in the region we call Asia, our civilization seemed very similar to that of Western Europe, in comparison with the more typically 'Asian' ones. I further realized that the histories of Japan and Western Europe, from medieval times on, were also highly similar in their experiences of feudalism, revolution, and the development of modern societies. I was thus led to the interpretation that the nations of Western Europe and Japan had passed through parallel phenomena in terms of the history of their civilizations.

Since I began my scholarly life as an ecologist, it seemed natural to approach history from an ecological perspective. Hence grew my thought that the reason for the parallels between Japanese and Western European civilizations lay in the ecological structure of the Eurasian continent as a whole.

In the ten years following my return from South Asia, I published several articles concerning comparative civilization theory. One of these, 'An Ecological View of History: Japanese

Civilization in the World Context' (Bunmei no seitaishikan), attracted quite a bit of attention, and was taken up for discussion by scholars and journalists. Later, after my ethnological fieldwork in Southeast Asia during 1957 and 1958, I published an article entitled 'Travels in Southeast Asia' (Tōnan Ajia no tabi kara). This was in effect a sequel to 'An Ecological View of History,' containing a partial revision of my earlier theory.

In 1967, I was finally able to publish these two articles along with several others in volume form. This volume was named after the essay that had launched my enquiries: *An Ecological View of History: Japanese Civilization in the World Context (Bunmei no seitaishikan)*.

In the thirty-some years since its first publication, this work has garnered a large readership within Japan. It has been translated into Chinese, in addition to partial translations into French, Italian, and German. Until now, however, there has not been an English edition – although there were periodic proposals to translate it, in the end none were realized.

After my retirement in 1993 from many years as Director General of the National Museum of Ethnology, I was able to return my focus to writing. Once again it was suggested that an English language translation of *Bunmei no seitaishikan (An Ecological View of History: Japanese Civilization in the World Context)* be published. Dr. Harumi Befu, Professor Emeritus at Stanford University, was kind enough to advise me and shepherd the project to completion, as I know nothing about academic publishing in the West.

We were fortunate enough to conclude an arrangement with Trans Pacific Press, a publishing house in Melbourne, Australia. This was made possible with the strong support of Professor Yoshio Sugimoto of the School of Social Sciences, La Trobe University.

The Preface to the English language edition was kindly written by Professor Josef Kreiner, of Bonn University, and Professor Befu. For the translation, through Professor Befu's introduction, I depended on Ms. Beth Cary, a bilingual translator who was raised in Kyoto. In addition, Ms. Deborah Poskanzer, a specialist in modern Japanese history, edited the translation. Professor Befu has overseen the entire effort.

Several editions of *Bunmei no Seitaishikan* exist in Japanese. The edition used for this English translation is the revised Chūkō Bunko edition published in 1998. To this has been added the essay 'The Ocean and Japanese Civilization' (Umi to Nihon bunmei), published in 2000. Each of the articles has a Commentary in which I provide some background.

The Japanese edition included rather detailed endnotes giving bibliographic references on the various responses to my work. The discourse held internally in Japan may not be too meaningful for the English reading audience, but I have included these as endnotes for Chapter Three in the interest of being faithful to the original. The Japanese edition has a commentary by Tani Yutaka, Professor Emeritus of Kyoto University, which is also included in this English translation.

When this volume was originally published in Japanese, there was not yet an established academic discipline that covered my type of work. At the time, I chose to call it a 'comparative theory of civilization.' Nowadays, the field of comparative civilization is full of lively discourse, and there are at least two active research associations in the field, The Japan Society for the Comparative Study of Civilizations, and The International Society for the Comparative Study of Civilizations. This volume can be thought of as a precursor to these academic movements. I look forward to the development of more comprehensive and systematic discourse in the future.

I express my deep gratitude to Professor Befu and Professor Sugimoto for realizing the publication of the English language edition of this work. I also express my appreciation to Professor Befu and Professor Kreiner for writing the Preface. I would also like to thank Ms. Cary and Ms. Poskanzer for their work on the translation. Chūō Kōronsha, the publisher of the Japanese edition, graciously extended permission for the publication of the English language edition. This publication is supported by the Daidō Life Foundation. I express my appreciation to these organizations as well.

Umesao Tadao (June 2002)

Acknowledgements

Efforts to produce an English translation of Umesao Tadao's *Bunmei no Seitaishikan* began in 1999, when Professor Umesao approached me about the possibility of translating the book in its entirety. When the project started in earnest in the following year, the first order of business was to locate a publisher. Fortunately, Trans Pacific Press, headed by Professor Yoshio Sugimoto of La Trobe University, gladly agreed to publish it. He first read the book as a student and had been deeply impressed, along with a great number of other Japanese. We are grateful that he stepped forward to undertake publication of the book.

The next step was to find an able translator who could do full justice to the book. Here, again, we were fortunate in finding Ms. Beth Cary, translator of such well known works as *Inspector Imanishi Investigates (Suna no utsuwa)* by Matsumoto Seichō and *Sensō: The Japanese Remember the Pacific War* (edited by Asahi Shinbun; translation edited by Frank Gibney). Ms. Cary enlisted the aid of Ms. Deborah Poskanzer, a historian of modern Japan trained at Stanford University and Columbia University, to ensure the work conformed to English language standards of social science writing. Together they have done a meticulous job of achieving accuracy where accuracy was needed, and yet rendering Professor Umesao's work in lucid English. Our heartfelt thanks go to Ms. Cary and Ms. Poskanzer.

Chapter Three was originally translated by Ms. Sakamoto Rei, whose work served as a convenient basis for the final version. I wish to acknowledge Ms. Sakamoto's work in this connection, though in the present version, credit of course goes to Ms. Cary and Ms. Poskanzer.

The ultimate responsibility of overseeing the project, including checking the accuracy of the translation and negotiating with the publisher, fell on me, to whom Professor Umesao had entrusted the entire project. Therefore, the final responsibility for the execution of the entire translation rests with me. My ill health in the middle of this project incapacitated me for several months, causing much delay in its completion. I apologize to all those involved in the production of the book and to the readers who have been waiting patiently for its publication.

The translation here is based on the 1998 edition published by Chūō Kōronsha with slight modifications.

Harumi Befu
Stanford University

Note on conventions

A word should be said about the convention of Romanization of Japanese terms adopted in this book. Among the many areas in which Professor Umesao has been active, the Japanese writing system has drawn his particular passion. He has served on a national committee on the Japanese language. One of his special concerns is the state of Japanese orthography, which was and still is in dismal disarray. He joined the Japan Romanization Society and is a proponent of the ''99 Romanization system,'named after the year of its adoption. As current President of the Society, he very much wished to use the '99 system for this volume. Unfortunately, this system, despite its internal logic and consistent rules, is as yet unfamiliar to Western readers. We, and the publisher, feared that the perceived unconventionality of the system would be likely to hinder the pleasure of reading this important work. We therefore persuaded Professor Umesao to allow us to use the more conventional, modified Hepburn Romanization system, which is at this time the most widely used in Western countries. As President of an organization which promotes the '99 system, it goes entirely against his intentions to use the Hepburn system. It is thus with considerable reluctance and chagrin that Professor Umesao has consented to the use of the Hepburn system.

In this book we have followed the Japanese practice of writing the family name first, followed by the given name, with the exception of the author's name as it appears on the cover, title page, and the author name page.

1 Between East and West

Commentary on Chapter 1

In 1955 I spent six months, from May to November, traveling in Afghanistan, Pakistan, and India. At the time I was affiliated with the Faculty of Science at Osaka City University, and I joined the Karakoram-Hindu Kush scientific expedition, organized by Kyoto University, that sent a group to Southwest Asia. This was the first and largest scientific expedition sent abroad from Japan since the end of World War II. The group was led by Dr. Kihara Hitoshi, then professor in the Faculty of Agriculture, and included over a dozen specialists in plant biology, geology, anthropology, archaeology, linguistics, and medicine. The expedition was split into the Karakoram and Hindu Kush groups, which engaged in research in four countries: Afghanistan, Pakistan, India, and Iran.

Many people still recall hearing about this expedition, as it was covered in detail in newspapers of the time, and became the subject of a documentary film, *Karakoram*. Several members of this expedition wrote accounts and summary reports for the general public. *Sabaku to hyōga no tanken* (An expedition to deserts and glaciers),[1] edited by Kihara Hitoshi, is a collection of such accounts. The official academic report has been published in English; with the first volume issued in 1960, and the last, volume eight, in 1966.[2]

I was in charge of anthropological research for the Hindu Kush section of the expedition, which gave me ample material for several publications. The trip took place in three stages: the first from Karachi to Kabul; the second within Afghanistan; and the third from Kabul to Calcutta. My general travel diary is included in *Sabaku to hyōga no tanken* (An expedition to deserts and glaciers), published soon after our return. The second stage of my trip, an investigation of the Moghol tribe in the Golat region of Afghanistan, is detailed in the book *Mogōruzoku tanken ki* (An account of an expedition to the Moghol tribe).[3] My

1

observations on Afghanistan in general are in the volume *Afuganisutan no tabi* (Travels in Afghanistan), in text accompanying photographs.[4]

The essay below, 'Between East and West,' is based chiefly on my experiences during the third stage of my travels: it focuses on Pakistan and India, with little reference to Afghanistan. To be sure, my experiences in Afghanistan yielded valuable results. Yet, it was my travels in Pakistan and India that opened my eyes to the topic of comparative civilizations. In my essay I refer to two German-American scholars, H.F. Schurmann and E. Landauer. From Kabul onward, the three of us traveled together in a Volkswagen, and I gained a great deal from our discussions during this trip, particularly from talking with Dr. Schurmann.[5] This essay is an impressionistic piece rather than a travelogue. (Later, I also wrote a travelogue on this third stage of the trip, which is included in the series *Sekai no tabi* [Travels around the world] Volume 2.)[6]

My training was originally in the natural sciences, and at that time my affiliation with my university was in the Faculty of Science. I never dreamed that I would end up thinking and writing about matters such as art, culture, religion, history, and the other subjects I took up in this essay. And yet this was the first piece I published upon my return. This trip seems to have proved an intellectual turning point for me. I sent in my essay to the journal *Chisei* (Intellect), published at that time by Kawade Shobō. It appeared in the February issue the following year (1956).[7] The essay had a different title when it first appeared in the journal, but for this volume I have changed the title to the one I originally planned. Rereading it after ten years, I find that many of the points I intended to make were incompletely articulated. Nevertheless I have included it as the opening chapter in this collection because it provides grounding and acts as a prologue for several of the pieces that follow. I have reworked some of the passages I felt were awkward in the original, and have added sub-headings and rearranged the order of some sections. I hope the reader will find that this has clarified my meaning.

I A Difficult Issue

Japan: a northern country

I returned to Japan from India on November 11, 1955. It was half past nine in the evening when I arrived at Tokyo's Haneda International Airport. I had departed Dum Dum Airport in Calcutta at seven in the evening the previous day. While in flight, I traveled over fifty degrees in longitude. The distance was too vast to absorb – it seemed unbelievable to cover it at one leap. When I stepped off the plane into the darkness of Haneda Airport, I felt as if the humid tropical air mass that heavily blanketed Calcutta was lurking just nearby, bumping up against Tokyo's chilly night air.

My first impression upon returning to Japan was of a terribly cold place. Walking the streets of Tokyo the day after I landed, I was bewildered by the clothing of the people on the streets. It seemed that everyone wore the same somber, dark-colored overcoat. During the last six months, I had grown used to seeing lightweight clothing, either in white or brightly clashing colors. In contrast, the scene before me in Japan reflected a north country heaviness.

I thought of an occasion when I had seen color slides of someone's trip to Europe. The Tokyo street scene before me now looked like that of the Northern European towns in the slides. The trees lining the streets of the city were bare of leaves. In this chilly Tokyo scene, the sun was shining, but compared to the sun's glare in Karachi and Delhi, the light seemed weak. Tokyo was indeed a northern city, and I realized anew that Japan was a northern country.

Before this trip it had not occurred to me that Japan was a northern country – to the contrary, I felt that Japan's scenery and culture had more affinity with southern countries. It was only after I had traveled extensively in those southern regions that I became aware of Japan's northern personality. By going abroad, I discovered things I had not known about Japan. Traveling of course brings us a wealth of knowledge about the countries we visit, but it also gives us new perspectives on our own country. In this way travel is doubly valuable and doubly productive. Thus this impressionistic travelogue comprises two types of information: my observations of the Asian countries I visited, and my view of Japan through the lens of my travel experiences.

Europeans have written many accounts of their travels through Asian countries. I, however, am not a European but rather a Japanese attempting to describe these Asian countries. I want to describe how Asia appears, not from its western side, but from its eastern side. What is more, many Japanese have expounded theories about Japan, mainly in comparison to European countries. Yet in this essay, I am attempting to describe Japan as it compares to other Asian countries and not as it compares to Europe.

Crowds

Afghanistan is nearly twice as large as Japan, and yet its population is merely 12 million. While traveling in Afghanistan, I was amazed that, no matter where I went, there were so few people. This prompted me to reflect on the frightful population density of Japan. I recalled street scenes of Osaka and Tokyo, with their unceasing tides of people noisily ebbing and flowing. I was filled with gloom when I thought about the gravity of Japan's population problem and wondered about her fate. I felt envious of Afghanistan's small population.

After Afghanistan, however, I went on to Pakistan and India, and by the time I returned to Japan, my perspective had changed. Looking around me on the streets of Tokyo, nowhere did I see the hordes of people going to and fro that I had seen in my mind's eye while in Afghanistan. In actuality, I saw only a few people here and there. Had my mind arbitrarily created an image of the crowds in Japan that was much denser than the reality? The major reason that Tokyo seemed so thinly populated was undoubtedly because I had passed through India on my way home and had just seen the street scenes there. Still fresh in my mind was the extremely powerful image of the writhing throngs of downtown Calcutta.

Calcutta, with its population of 7 million, was an astonishing urban area. How could these overwhelming crowds of people live in this city with an area far smaller than Tokyo? The urban congestion was utterly chaotic. We gave up driving our car in the city, since it was impossible for outsiders like us to maneuver safely through the throngs of people, vehicles, and cows. We resorted to walking whenever we went around town, although it was not necessarily easy to walk either, as there were so many people on the sidewalks. We pushed our way through the crowds and skirted the peddlers of fountain pens, all the while shooing away beggars and keeping an eye out for pickpockets. The streets of Calcutta were literally packed with people. They slept on the streets. They slept at the edge of the roads, and on stairs, and on rooftops. One must be careful not to step on someone's body when one walks at night in Calcutta.

It was no wonder that Tokyo seemed thinly populated to me, having just returned from such a place. The crowds in Tokyo can hardly compare to the crowds in Calcutta.

Trial by water

While we were in Pakistan, we experienced a major flood. The water seeped over the Punjab plain, moving slowly south. I do not know how many villages in Punjab were flooded – it must have been several tens of thousands, while the victims numbered perhaps several million. I was ignorant of the exact numbers, but I wanted to understand the effects of such a disaster.

A doctor whom I had met in Lahore was a member of the flood area relief group, and I accompanied him on a visit to one of the affected villages. Evacuees who had been flooded out of their homes were lined up for several kilometers along a road just barely above the water level. Other than their flimsy beds, they had few if any belongings. These evacuees were poor to begin with, and now the flood had taken everything from them.

We went into a village where the water had receded a bit. We left the road and crossed a creek. When we arrived at the village area, we found nothing resembling a village. The peasants' houses had been made of earth, and when the water came they simply dissolved. The village had reverted to mud; the mud spread out over the plain. The peasants sat on the mud that had been their village and fixed us with their hopeless stares.

The peasants' grain had been completely soaked by the water, leaving them with nothing to eat. The gravity of the situation finally sank into my head. A few hundred or a few thousand flood victims might be managed, but what is to be done when hundreds of thousands or even millions of people have nothing to eat? The Punjab area, the region affected by the flood, had the highest population density in West Pakistan. Who was going to feed this huge population of starving peasants?

Our flood area relief group had gone out with some food loaded in a luxury automobile. In truth, this was nothing more than the kind of charitable act the rich carry out for the poor. Of course it is better to be charitable than not, but how effective is this type of small-scale effort in responding to such a major disaster involving large masses of starving people? What is needed, obviously, is not charitable acts on an individual basis, but effective relief measures on a national scale. Moreover, disasters are not unusual in this region. Each year flooding occurs somewhere along the five major rivers flowing through the Punjab plain. Each time this happens, tens of thousands of victims are affected, and the Pakistani government must struggle mightily to aid them. This is the kind of trial facing the newly formed nation of Pakistan.

A difficult issue

In India, as well, I saw a vast number of impoverished people. In this country with its surplus of human beings, those who have been squeezed to the margins of society must find what little work they can at miniscule wages, much like the 'dumping' of excess goods at below-cost prices. These people work for unbelievably low pay. In Japan we sometimes use the phrase 'India-like low standard of pay.' But an economist I met in Delhi was indignant at this description: 'What "India-like low standard"? People who say that have no idea about the reality of India's unspeakably low wages. Compared to here, Japan's so-called low wages would be paradise!'

As I traveled in India I came across absolutely unimaginable forms of employment. For example, the saris worn by women, which consist of one long piece of cloth, are not hung out on a line to dry. Instead, two men – each gripping one end – stand, holding the cloth in the sunshine until it dries. I also frequently saw men who were crawling along the side of the road, slapping the ground with their hands. These were road repairmen who, without tools, were placing bricks into the ground with their bare hands. Such are the dreadful consequences of the 'human wave' approach to solving problems.

India's population is nearly 400 million, making it the second most populous nation in the world after China. With some 100 million people, Pakistan is the sixth most populous country in the world. What is to become of these nations with such large populations and such dire poverty? Of course the problem of overpopulation is a relative matter. Ultimately, it depends upon a given country's production capacity. If a nation has adequate production power it can sustain even a huge population. But what can be done to raise productivity enough to pull such a large population out of poverty? This is the problem faced by the two newly established nations of India and Pakistan – without question, an extremely difficult issue.

In Japan we are similarly concerned about our overpopulation problem. Although they are both nominally the same population problem, I realized that our problems are really quite different, after seeing the situation in India and Pakistan. Our concern in

Japan is that when our children are grown they may face tough competition in finding employment. For the masses of India and Pakistan the challenge is just to stay alive until tomorrow, or even for the rest of today. The word 'overpopulation' may be the same, but the situation is entirely different.

When Japan began to modernize eighty years ago, we had no overpopulation problem. Yet India and Pakistan have been burdened with this serious problem since the day of their independence. I cannot help but be concerned about the severe difficulties ahead for these nations.

II After Partition

After Partition

Both India and Pakistan have been changing rapidly since independence. They are definitely no longer the India of the British Raj. Regrettably, I did not know India under British rule, so I cannot give exact explanations of what and how things have changed. It seems there are great variations in the amount of change, with some things that have changed greatly, or are about to, while others remain just as they were. I can cite instances to support either view.

My visit to Karachi, for example, gave me the impression that great change is afoot. There is much construction going on there, with many brand new buildings and brick houses being built. Karachi has a long history as a commercial port, but it was not a large town. Since becoming Pakistan's capital at independence, it has grown suddenly. Even to first time visitors, it is clear that this town is on the verge of a dramatic transformation.

Despite this, the following incident made me think that nothing has changed. Near Lahore, Pakistan, the policemen wore khaki uniforms, shorts, and turbans with red tassels. These turbans were so distinctive that it was impossible to forget them. But when we crossed the border and entered India, we were astonished to see that the policemen in India wore exactly the same uniforms as those in Pakistan. Since Pakistan and India are two separate nations, it might seem strange that officials on both sides of the border would wear the same uniform. This can be explained by the fact that both sides of the border were formerly part of the state of Punjab under British rule. With the 1947 Partition of India and Pakistan, the western half of Punjab came under the jurisdiction of Pakistan and the eastern half went to India. But the uniform of the policemen of the old state remained in use in both India and Pakistan.

In other words, this particular aspect of the former colonial empire persisted after independence. Moreover, though eight years have passed since Partition, neither nation had attempted to change the uniform. It was difficult for those of us with a Japanese sensibility to understand this. If it had been Japan, we would have immediately switched to new uniforms in the spirit of government reform. In this light, the fact that in India and Pakistan the term 'partition' is used rather than 'independence' or 'revolution' is significant. It seems to imply that the birth of these nations was the result merely of a division, rather than of a 'restoration' or 'renewal' as we say in Japan. The revolution may not be over yet.

The spinning top and the massive rock

The different attitudes towards change in India and Japan struck me again in the following episode. One day I went to a hotel restaurant in an Indian town. On the walls were many colorful tourist posters depicting landmarks in each region in India, with the title 'Visit India' in English. When I looked at one of these posters I noticed that it clearly depicted the Khyber Pass, with the caption 'The Northwest Frontier.' I was taken aback, as just a few days before we had gone over the Khyber Pass while crossing from Afghanistan to Pakistan. Khyber Pass and the Northwest Frontier where it is located are now part of Pakistan; and yet it was advertised as part of a 'Visit India' poster.

The India of 'Visit India' was the India of the British Raj. This poster had been printed when the Northwest Frontier, including the Khyber Pass, was still part of India – before Partition. For at least the subsequent eight years, through the major events of India's independence and the partition of India and Pakistan, this poster had continued to hang on the restaurant wall, regardless of political developments.

It warmed my heart to see this, as it suggested that both India and Pakistan were, after all, very stable societies. Certainly there were political changes after the Second World War, when Britain withdrew and transferred political authority. But I had to wonder whether there had been any change at all at the social level, in the lives of the Indian and Pakistani people. Or again perhaps preparations for such change are gradually taking place, but are not yet visible on the surface.

In Japan, by contrast, social trends never cease to change, making it seem quite unusual compared to countries where change is scarce. Japanese people seem constantly to embrace the new. They replace old things with new things for no particular reason other than that they have had them for a while – this is simply the way things are done in Japan. No matter how beautiful the tourist poster, in Japan it would be unthinkable that the same poster would hang on a hotel restaurant wall for eight years. In Japan, new tourist posters are printed every year.

The mere fact that a tourist poster is replaced annually does not necessarily mean that society as a whole is undergoing substantive changes. No matter how rapidly Japan changes on the surface, there is no question that Japan is overall a stable society. Compared to the stability in India and Pakistan, however, there are significant differences. India and Pakistan exhibit a massive, rock-like stability. Against this rock solid stability, Japan is like a stable, well-spinning top. It takes a lot of energy to overturn a massive rock, while a top is only stable for as long as it continues to spin.

Bureaucracy

Both India and Pakistan gained their independence after a long period of British rule. From the Japanese point of view it seems that these nations have inherited a great many things from the British system of government which they are in no hurry to change. My interpretation of the situation, although I am not confident of its accuracy, is that the people of the former British Raj absorbed British culture, including the value placed on strict adherence to old customs. The former colonial subjects have inherited their rulers' extraordinary attachment to past traditions.

Certainly I had not expected Britain to be so popular in India. I had assumed that Indians would be anti-British, given the long struggle against British rule, the independence movement, and the post-independence movement toward democracy. Instead I found a generally respectful attitude toward Britain. Independence does not seem to have brought about an upheaval of the value system. In this sense, Britain's withdrawal was superbly accomplished.

Meanwhile the Indian bureaucracy seems to have a negative reputation. Anyone who visits India can cite some vexing encounter with the bureaucracy. Is this also a legacy of British rule? I myself had many amusing – or perhaps not so amusing – experiences with Indian officials. For example, before I left the country I noticed that a section of my vaccination records had expired, and I attempted to bring my vaccinations up to date. I was sent from one government agency to another for an entire day, without being able to get a vaccination. What was most astounding was that, until I discovered on my own that I did not need this vaccination in order to leave India, none of the Indian bureaucrats informed me of this.

In India one often encounters various aspects of bureaucratic behavior – bureaucrats who are irresponsible, unaccommodating, perfunctory, and inefficient. It would be easy to just criticize the Indian tendency to bureaucratism, but I suspect that this is part of an inevitable legacy. These people had been under British rule for a long time. In a society where the results of one's decisions and efforts did not benefit oneself, who would work with energy and vigor? It has been a mere eight years since Indian independence. It will take more time to get over the psychological distortions of the colonial period. In fact, I met many extremely able government officials in India. They dealt with the rather troublesome matters that I brought to them in a responsible, polite, and timely fashion.

Colonies and English

The university where I work is located in Osaka's Ōgi-machi. On my way home to Kyoto, I must pass through Umeda train terminal. It is impossible to avoid seeing the large neon sign rising above the Japan National Railway station, flashing 'OSAKA STATION' in English. Atop the Central Post Office building next door is a sign reading 'POST OFFICE,' also in neon lights. Before my trip to South Asia, I used to take offense every time I saw these signs. Since the train station and the post office were for the citizens of Japan, what was the point of placing English language signs on the buildings? I was also annoyed at the names of Japanese cigarettes. Why should a Japanese cigarette be called 'PEACE'? My irritable reaction to this meaningless deluge of English was that we Japanese should stop acting as if our country were some kind of colony.

When I returned to Japan from my travels, however, I was astounded to discover that my perception was completely different. Now, I saw Japan as a nation with very few English signs. It wasn't that Japan had changed: the neon signs at Osaka Station and the

Central Post Office were still there. But to my eyes, which had just seen the flood of English language and English letters in India and Pakistan, the amount of English in Japan seemed insignificant.

Of course indigenous languages are used in South Asia. Indians write in Devanagari and Bengali, and Arabic script is used in Pakistan. Indians and Pakistanis write in their own languages. But English is so prevalent that in an average town it is hard to determine which is more visible, English or the indigenous language. In areas like Calcutta's business districts, English is overwhelmingly more visible.

As I cast fresh eyes around the Umeda area, everywhere a multitude of written figures danced on signs, on walls, and on posters. I made a tally of the signs using foreign letters (including Romanizations of Japanese words) and discovered there were actually very few. The OSAKA STATION sign was among the exceptions. One might conclude from this that only governmental agencies, such as the national railway, the post office, and the public tobacco corporation, have absorbed colonial attitudes, while the attitudes of the citizenry remain quite healthy.

The difference in the prevalence of English between Japan and South Asia is doubtless due to the long period during which India and Pakistan were ruled by an English-language nation. It seems I have been able to learn even from the language of signs just how deep the influence of the colonial experience is on the lives of the citizens.

The problem of national language

Even since independence, the English language enjoys an extraordinary power in India and Pakistan. English is the administrative language, and on a practical level, it is the only common language. One cannot hold public office in either of these nations without knowing English, nor can one be treated as an educated person. It seems that English is so vital here that for all intents and purposes one might as well define being educated as knowing English.

In this situation of absolute English dominance, the Pakistani and Indian governments are making valiant efforts to abolish the use of English as the administrative language. Pakistan is trying to make Urdu, written in Arabic script, its national language, while India is attempting to do the same with Hindi, written in

Devanagari. These countries are struggling against nearly insurmountable obstacles as they try to formulate new policies regarding the problem of national language. Should they succeed in reducing their reliance on English to a degree similar to that of Japan, it would be an astounding achievement.

Compared to the situation in India and Pakistan, Japan's national language problem is minor. I now think that my complaints about Japan's 'colonial culture,' and my frustration with the Japanese fashion of affecting a small amount of English, were petty and overly purist. Nevertheless, when I returned to Osaka and saw the bright neon signs flashing English words, I still felt it was nonsensical. And when I found out that the tobacco monopoly has just come out with PEARL, yet another English-named cigarette, I felt I must protect my beloved Japanese language. A new spirit of determination welled up within me.

India is India; Japan is Japan. The conditions of these nations differ greatly. It might have been a mistake to make facile comparisons and leap to conclusions.

Windows

I would like to examine another, slightly different issue with regard to written figures.

Travelers to India and Pakistan can get by if they know English. There are people who understand English in all sorts of places, and most road signs and shop signs are in English or at least in the Romanized alphabet. Since I cannot understand Urdu or Hindi, nor can I read Arabic or Devanagari, I relied on English and Romanizations. English is a window that opens up India and Pakistan to foreigners. This is true for those like myself who are not even native speakers of English. Only through English were we able to understand something of the lives of Indians and Pakistanis.

During our trip by automobile through India, we sometimes stopped to read road signs. If the place name was Romanized we had no problem, but when it was written only in Devanagari letters, we would exclaim 'Drat! It's in Sanskrit!' Of course it was our mistake to refer to it as Sanskrit; we should have called it Hindi. But when Devanagari script was used, it seemed to us that it was as incomprehensible and mysterious as Sanskrit. When we came across that non-English writing, it was as if our window into India had been slammed shut, leaving us helpless. There was no doubt a rich spiritual life that Indians engaged in using that other language, one that we had no way of understanding.

If English were abolished and Hindi became the only official language of India, it would be as if India were closing its windows to the rest of the world. Through English, India allows the peoples of the world free passage into its world. With the absence of English, this would no longer be possible.

Japan is just such an example of a country with 'closed windows.' When I returned to Japan, I reconsidered the very limited use of English in Japan from the perspective of a visiting foreigner. I remembered that in India, English was used in a very practical manner, whereas the English used in Japan was not practical at all. When English does appear in Japan, it is often a form of decoration or embellishment. It is not used where it is actually needed. It was strange and ironic to realize that foreigners in Japan were feeling the same frustration that I had felt on seeing 'Sanskrit' in India.

Since Japan has heartlessly closed its 'windows' against foreigners, a majority of our foreign friends must abandon their attempts to become familiar with the inner life of Japanese. This may be one reason that, despite the large number of foreigners in the country, Japan is not well understood. This is not to say that I am advocating the combined use of English and Japanese in order to open Japan's windows to foreigners. I have only commented on the depth of frustration that can result from impenetrable differences in letters and signs.

III Local color

Local color

India is an ethnographically interesting country, home to diverse peoples with different customs.

It was fascinating just to see the variations in women's clothing as we traveled: Punjab-style dresses over slacks, Indian saris, and, in places, pleated skirts. The forms of houses also varied according to locality, ranging from flat roofs to tiled gables. Had I allowed myself to delve into each locality, collecting legends and folktales, I would never have been able to pull myself away.

It was amazing to see the wealth of local color, not only in traditional manners and customs of clothing and shelter, but also in material culture of much more recent derivation, such as machines and tools. For example, every town had pedicabs and horse-drawn carriages. The bodies of these vehicles were usually of sheet metal adorned with designs or illustrations, which varied according to locality. If it had been Japan, such machinery would have been mass-produced in a factory, perhaps in Nagoya, and would be sold through a nationwide sales network. This is why the machinery and tools in Japan are standardized throughout the nation and not at all interesting. In India these kinds of machines and tools seemed to be made locally.

Overall, it appeared that each locality in India had a strong sense of economic self-reliance. The degree of self-sufficiency was high, meaning that each region could exist without borrowing strengths from other regions. It appeared that the organizational system of the nation as a whole was not yet well developed. In contrast to India, each region in Japan is so closely linked to every other region and so tightly organized that if one locality is hit hard it will quickly affect the entire nation.

Metaphorically, Japan can be likened to a small vertebrate with a highly developed central nervous system. It is nimble and often regenerates itself, but an injury to one location can prove to be fatal. In contrast, perhaps one could liken India to a kind of gigantic worm, with a body of loosely connected segments. In case of injury, each segment retains the ability for self-support. It seems to me that the physiologies of Japan and India are based on different fundamental principles.

Localism

Language vividly displays the local color of provincial regions. In the case of Japan, I am not in favor of the standardization of the Japanese language. I worry that local dialects, which are used with such vibrant liveliness in daily life, may be replaced by the monotonous and mechanical 'standard' Japanese. I consider it beneficial for Japan to retain some degree of cultural localism through the continued use of dialects and other local customs.

The situation in India, however, seems to differ in that localism predates and outstrips uniformity. Strong localism acts as a centrifugal force hindering the concentration of regional power into a unified Indian state.

The problem of language in India is also quite pernicious. To us Japanese, it is astounding that in the nation of India there is no single 'Indian language.' Instead there are the myriad 'local languages' of each region: reference books number these at several hundred. There is an Indian saying: 'Travel for twelve miles and the language will be different.' The situation is critical because the various regions refuse to relinquish their right to keep their own local languages.

As an example of linguistic diversity, consider the areas through which we traveled: from Pakistan we entered a region using the Punjabi language, then we went to an area using West Hindi, followed by East Hindi. We ended in the Bengali-speaking region. These were all Aryan languages with some commonality, but they are an entirely different language family from the Dravidian languages widely used in South India.

The government of the Republic of India is attempting to make Hindi the common language of all India and the future administrative language of the republic. So at least a common language has been designated. When I went to a bookstore to buy an Indian language textbook, it was of course in Hindi. But, in actuality, this supposed common language does not seem to be widely disseminated. There are vast numbers of Indian citizens who do not comprehend this common language.

When we were in the state of West Bengal, we noticed that even the lettering on the shop signs was different. We had entered the Bengali cultural sphere, where Bengali writing was used. At one point I saw a man making a speech at the side of the road, and asked a Bengali youth I had met to interpret for me. The youth replied, 'He is speaking Hindi. I can't understand a word!' His defiant attitude of refusal to understand the common language was a point of pride for him.

I said above that Japan should allow a bit of localism to remain, once the establishment of a common language has allowed free communication among all citizens. But the case of India falls entirely outside this philosophy. In India, the precondition for unification of diversity within the nation has not yet been established.

The central kingdom attitude and the frontier tribes

Despite India's many years as a British colony, it seemed to me that it held a kind of 'central kingdom attitude,' not unlike that of China. India has been invaded many times, and yet it has maintained a confidence that all invaders will eventually be assimilated. The British were a case in point: they invaded India but did not assimilate, and in the end had to withdraw. China is the classic example of a central kingdom mentality, even referring to itself as the 'Central Kingdom.' Yet it appeared to me that India's display of central kingdom attitude was often even more overt than China's.

Indians have an extremely strong sense of self-respect, which they themselves would be the first to acknowledge. I was warned by many people that I should not criticize India to Indians. Of course as a traveler, I knew it was not my place to utter criticisms. But at times I did come across examples of arrogance, such as the belief by Indians in the complete superiority of their culture, especially their spiritual culture.

This is another characteristic that is very different from Japan. Japanese have a sense of self-respect, but at the same time they are haunted by a certain sense of cultural inferiority. This shadow dominates the psychology of all Japanese people, unrelated to any objective evaluation of the cultural level actually held by Japan. It is a sense that real culture is created somewhere else and that Japan's culture is somehow second-rate.

I think that this psychological difference between Indians and Japanese is the difference between a people who have, from the beginning, developed a civilization with themselves at the core, and a people who originated on the frontier of a major civilization. China and India are countries that developed major central civilizations, whereas Japan was in origin merely one of the countries on the Chinese periphery. The Japanese really were, as the Chinese dubbed them, the 'eastern barbarians.'

In India I met some Tibetans on a visit to Kalimpang, at the foot of the Himalayas. Tibetan culture is of a fairly high level, but compared to Indian culture it is quite primitive. I said to my traveling companion, Dr. Schurmann, 'We Japanese are a frontier people, so we resist the central kingdom mentality and feel affinity toward other frontier cultures.' Dr. Schurmann, a German-American, laughed and replied, 'Germans are the same way.' The

Germans originated as Germanic barbarians who lived outside the civilization of the Roman world.

Self-admiration

In India, when I read newspapers and other publications, I often felt that the overall tone was one of self-admiration. Even the anti-government newspapers never put the Indian nation in a bad light. They praised India's successes in international diplomacy and its progress in domestic affairs. Perhaps this was only natural, but I thought that the attitude of Indian journalism was very different from what one finds in Japan.

In Japan, the journalistic tone is entirely self-critical. This tendency is usually even more pronounced among the more 'progressive' newspapers. At times it seems like self-abuse. I gather that in Germany the journalistic tenor is also quite self-critical.

Without passing judgement on the merits of either attitude, I found the contrast between self-admiration and self-criticism interesting. I wondered if this difference could be attributed to the distinction between a central kingdom mentality and a frontier mentality. Perhaps that was one cause, or again it might also stem from the difference in the status of the national government. In countries with a strong national leadership, the tone of journalism is more likely to become self-admiring. China and the Soviet Union are led by strong governments, and are definitely self-admiring. Wartime Japan shared this trait, and present day India also has a strong government.

IV The sacred and the secular

Beauty and religion

During my South Asian sojourn I looked at many places of worship. In the Islamic nations of Afghanistan and Pakistan I saw many mosques, while in India I visited Hindu, Jain, and Buddhist temples. To be candid, I was not impressed by any of them.

There were structures that I was drawn to because of their massive scale or intriguing shape, but even in these cases I disliked the color. Beyond the external architecture, I remained unmoved by religious paintings, Buddhist statuary, or indeed any work of interior ornamentation. I was perplexed as to why the people of such a great civilization were creating such unimpressive works. Certainly, the museums were full of brilliant pieces created in olden times. But the newer work filling the places of worship nowadays was not of comparably high quality. In the Buddhist temple at Sarnath there was a large mural – painted by a Japanese artist – which drew a lot of popular attention. In the context of present-day India I suppose the piece was worthy of admiration, but in terms of the tradition of Japanese art, it did not appear to be of significantly high quality. Did this region of Asia lack the necessary conditions to nurture an advanced sense of aesthetics?

Hearing my mutterings that the temples were dull, my companion Dr. Schurmann laughed. 'According to you Japanese, everything in the world is dull. Your aesthetic standards are too high.' I granted the point. There is something very exacting in the Japanese attitude toward aesthetics. Dr. Schurmann was familiar with this trait, having spent some time in Japan.

Meanwhile I engaged in a bit of self-criticism, trying to re-evaluate my judgements, to wit: 'This is a temple. A temple is a place of worship, not a work of art. It is a mistake to evaluate a site of religious experience from a purely aesthetic perspective ...'and so on.

We Japanese may be guilty of trying to measure everything with the yardstick of aesthetics. Or perhaps artistic feeling itself is the motive force behind all our other actions. In any case, we cannot conceive of a religious experience that is not accompanied by beauty. In Japan, we even tend to understand science as a type of aesthetic experience. It often seems that mathematicians or scientists pursue a theory for the sake of its beauty rather than for the sake of the theory itself. For Japanese, science can be a type of art.

At one temple I saw a painter who was earnestly copying a mural. To my eyes it seemed lacking in artistic qualities, but the painter himself no doubt thought it was a fine mural. Just as we Japanese commit an error when we measure religion with the yardstick of art, this painter may have been making the mistake of measuring art with the yardstick of religion. It would be interesting to find out whether Indians have a religious feeling about science.

In the end, it may be that we Japanese simply have no understanding of what the Indians mean by religion. When touring a temple in Japan, one usually hears an artistic commentary on the Buddhist statuary or paintings. This consists of explanations of the artist, the school of painting he was affiliated with, whether the work is a national treasure or an important cultural property, and so on. No one would listen to a long disquisition on the religious meaning of the painting. In India, however, one is far more likely to hear religious commentary rather than artistic commentary. The primary concern is for the spiritual teaching portrayed in the painting. The explanation of a work of art can often seem like a difficult philosophical discourse. This is something Japanese cannot comprehend – perhaps that was why I found the Indians' attitudes toward their religious sites so different.

On being a Buddhist

One of my traveling companions, Dr. Landauer, was due to depart for Japan before the rest of our party. In preparation, he was eager to learn as much as he could from me. But when he asked me about the religious life of the Japanese, I was hard pressed for an answer. I said something to the effect that asking Japanese about the religious life they engage in was extremely silly. This response astonished poor Dr. Landauer.

In fact, this was not the first time I had had such an encounter. Throughout my travels I was queried about my religion. It was dangerous to answer that I was irreligious, or worse yet an atheist, as this could be taken as a provocation. My interlocutors all believed in some kind of god and thought of religion as an essential part of human life. Displaying an overt indifference to religion could cause trouble.

I decided that the simplest thing was to say that I was a Buddhist. This made me feel a bit awkward, but it was not strictly a lie. I am not a Christian, and I am certainly not a Muslim. I am not so religious as to start a new religion, nor do I feel moved to forcefully deny religion by proclaiming my agnosticism or atheism. Having been brought up within a Buddhist culture, I do feel some affinity with Buddhism. So I must be some kind of Buddhist, although certainly not a devoted one. As my trip proceeded, I gradually recognized that I was taking some pride in identifying myself as a Buddhist. After all, Buddhism is one of the great religions of the world, well established and with a long and worthy history. My answer was accepted everywhere without further explanation.

This was another instance in which I discovered something new about Japan by going abroad. I realized two things: first, that many Japanese, including myself, are entirely indifferent about religion in their daily lives. It is extremely difficult for people in other countries to understand this. And secondly, that despite our general indifference to religion, when pressed we fall back upon Buddhism. The fact is that the Japanese are Buddhists after all.

As for Dr. Landauer, however, he remained dissatisfied by my attempts to answer his question. I finally realized how difficult it was to explain the religious life of Japanese.

The sacred and the secular

Compared to the peculiarity of the religious life of the Japanese (or rather the lack thereof), the importance of religion for the peoples of India, Pakistan, and Afghanistan is extremely clear. They unequivocally pronounce themselves 'very devout' believers in their respective religions. In Afghanistan and Pakistan, Islam is the dominant faith, while most Indians are Hindu. I was already aware that Islam was an intense religion, so powerful that it permeates all aspects of human life with Islamic beliefs. Before my journey I had not thought much about Hinduism, but I found it was a similarly powerful faith. No less than in Afghanistan and Pakistan, religion in India was also highly charged. The followers of the different religions in South Asia hold in common their high degree of religiosity, which is what sets them apart most strikingly from the Japanese people.

I expected to find that Muslims often had given or family names reflecting Arab and Islamic glories, such as Mohammed or Kuraish. But I was surprised that many Indian names too were taken from those of the gods, such as Lakshmi, Krishna, or Durga. The Islamic world forbids idolatry, so it is rare to see representational paintings there. But in India it was common to see paintings of the gods, sculptures of the gods, and dances purportedly 'of the gods.' Administrative offices were closed in conjunction with celebrations for the gods, and market areas were associated with patron gods. To state it in the extreme, in India all societal phenomena were religious phenomena. Here the sacred and the secular were so deeply fused they could not be separated.

In terms of the degree of religious devotion and the inextricable connection between the sacred and the secular, the worlds of Islam and Hinduism may resemble the Christian world somewhat. I am not that familiar with Europe, but extrapolating from my fragments of information it seems that, compared to Japan, the Christian world of Europe is again far more strongly related to God, with closer ties between the sacred and the secular. It may be inappropriate to compare the three great Semitic-origin monotheistic religions – Judaism, Christianity, and Islam – to a polytheistic religion such as Hinduism. But there appear to be common points with regard to the societal role of each religion. I am not sure whether this is due to common characteristics among the religions or among the societies. Regardless, it appears to us in Japan that India is more a country of the West, or the Occident, than of the East, or the Orient,[8] at least in terms of religious practice. I would not go so far as to say that India is an Occidental country. Nor am I prepared to expand my theory to claim that the likenesses between India and the West derive from their common origins in the primitive Aryan tribes. Nevertheless, the similarities that I did observe seem to suggest there is a social anthropological question waiting to be teased out and analyzed.

In prewar Japan, there was a politician who advocated the 'unity of church and state,' but he was the exception that proves the rule. The common arrangement in Japanese society has been the separation of the sacred and the secular, and the dominance of the secular over the sacred. Japan is a thoroughly secular nation as well as a pragmatic one. In terms of religion and society, we most closely resemble our next door neighbor China.

Christianity, Islam, Hinduism

Christianity and Islam do not have a history of peaceful co-existence, as we know from many past incidents. But speaking as a Japanese 'heretic' who is completely outside the fold, the tenets of these two religions seem quite similar. For example, in terms of structure, each has only one almighty God; each has prophets; and below them are ordinary humans. In both religions, followers pray to God, whereas we Buddhists worship Buddha rather than pray to him. To be honest, it is hard for us to understand what praying to God is about.

If one takes the route from Europe through Turkey and Iran to India, all of the countries one passes through are monotheistic, either Christian or Islamic. Once one crosses the border from

Pakistan into India, however, one enters the polytheistic sphere. While traveling through the Islamic areas from Afghanistan onward, the strict monotheistic atmosphere with its injunction against idolatry gave me a sort of spiritual fatigue. I must admit that I felt relieved upon entering the Hindu world with its lively idols. I felt that here I could communicate with people. We Japanese are, after all, idol worshippers.

The relationship between the religious cultures of India and Japan is complex. On one hand is the apparently great difference in our religious attitudes, since the Indians are devout believers and we are not. On the other hand, we Japanese feel a sense of familiarity because the religions of India and Japan have a common lineage: Buddhism can be considered an offshoot of Hinduism.

I visited the Birla Temple in Delhi, so called after the wealthy patron who built it, although its true name is Lakshminarayan Temple. It is obvious from the name that it is a Hindu temple. And yet there is a Buddhist temple within the grounds, a fine example of Hinduism including Buddhism. Hinduism embraces universality; it is able to contain everything within it. It may be that Hindus regard Buddhism, Jainism, and Sikhism as sects within the great Hindu tradition. That viewpoint is certainly understandable, as there are indeed connections among these religions.

The prophet Buddha

Before my visit to India, I thought that even in the present age, Buddhism might still be a tie that spiritually binds Japan and India. We Japanese often associate India with Buddhism: we tend to think that Japan and India are part of a common cultural region, and in some respects we look to India as a point of origin for our culture. Both historically and currently, numerous Japanese Buddhist monks and priests have gone to India to study Buddhism. Nowadays their numbers are not as conspicuous, as some youths go under the guise of study abroad, but many of the Japanese students in India are those who have entered the priesthood. I myself met a number of these Japanese during my travels.

Unfortunately, this sense of familiarity and closeness is unwarranted and can lead to disappointment. The fact is that contemporary India is a nation of Hindu believers, where Buddhism barely exists. I thought I knew this, but when I actually traveled around India and learned that Buddhists account for less than 0.1 per cent of the population, I realized I needed to further modify my thinking. Although Buddhism is thriving in Ceylon, Burma, Thailand, Tibet, and even in distant Japan, it has become nearly extinct in India, its place of origin. There are no grounds to suppose that Buddhism might provide a special spiritual connection between Japan and India. Our special feeling toward India is somewhat akin to a case of unrequited love.

Buddhism has not disappeared entirely from contemporary India. There remains a tiny minority of Buddhists, who have recently become active as part of a religious revival movement. However, their form of Buddhism is quite unlike that in Japan. As I am a casual Buddhist at best, my knowledge of Japanese Buddhism may be suspect, but something seemed different in the practices I observed. For one thing, in Indian Buddhism the Buddha himself seemed very important. The only statues in Indian Buddhist temples were those of the historical Buddha, Shakyamuni. Logically speaking, this should make sense, since Shakyamuni is the historical incarnation of the Buddha, and Buddhism is, after all, Buddha's religion. Nevertheless, something was amiss to my Japanese sensibility. It seemed as though Buddha stood as the intermediary between the world of the gods and the world of human beings. In Indian Buddhism, Buddha appears to take the role of a prophet of Buddhism, just as Christ does in Christianity and Mohammed in Islam.

The theology of Buddhism in Japan is different. We do not believe that the Buddha existed only, or even primarily, as his historical incarnation Shakayamuni, nor do we think that the Buddha is the only bodhisattva. Indeed, such an idea would be quite disconcerting. To us, Buddhist statuary takes many forms besides that of the Buddha himself, and Shakyamuni is but one among many bodhisattvas. In our practice Kannon, Nyorai, Bosatsu, Bishamon, Benten, Niō, our ancestors' funerary tablets, and Oshōraisama are all categorized as bodhisattvas. I was struck by the great differences, and troubled over which was the 'true' Buddhism – Japanese or Indian.

Religious recharging

The contrast between Japanese and Indian Buddhist practices may be no more than the difference between the Mahayana and

Theravada branches of Buddhism. Our Buddhism came to us from
the north one and a half millennia ago, after having traversed
Central Asia. Present-day Indian Buddhism is a re-imported revival
that came to them from the south. That would account for some
of the differences. But in fact I think that the 'original' Buddhism
established long ago in India was probably closer to current Indian
Buddhism than to Japanese Buddhism. Before reaching the present-
day Buddhist temples of India, I had a chance in Pakistan to visit
the museums in Taksila and Peshawar, which contained many
artifacts dug from ancient Buddhist ruins. These artifacts also
strongly asserted the primacy of the Buddha, to the extent of
suggesting a nearly monotheistic belief. This made me think that
Buddhism originally grew in the form of a monotheistic religion,
to differentiate itself from the polytheism of Hinduism.

The Buddhism that reached Japan was not like this. Along its
route to Japan, ancient Buddhism was reshaped by the influence of
the folk beliefs with which it came in contact. Perhaps one could
even say that because of these ancient folk practices, Japanese
Buddhism ended up more like Hinduism than like Indian Buddhism.
As I have styled this piece as an impressionistic travelogue, I could
just spread my wings and continue on this flight of fancy. For
instance, I wonder if the horse-headed Kannon is the counterpart
of the elephant-faced Ganesh? But perhaps it is best to stop this line
of speculation, unsupported by any actual knowledge on my part,
before I crash to the ground.

I am not the only one to have felt the effect of India's religious
atmosphere. One of the scientists who went to Nepal on the
Manaslu mountaineering expedition, Mr. Kawakita Jirō, became
fervent about religious theory upon his return to Japan. His
colleagues teased him about this, but I empathize, as I too have
begun to discuss religion since returning from India. The
fascinating nation of India is an excellent place to recharge one's
religious batteries.

V The 'Mediant'[9]

Arya Dharma

As I stated earlier, we Japanese feel a kind of cultural solidarity
with India, however imaginary that may be. But it is doubtful that
the feeling is reciprocated. Our sense of cultural solidarity with

India owes much to Buddhism, but Buddhism has been exported from its country of origin, leaving hardly a trace. Meanwhile there have been no cultural imports into India from Japan.

Based on various experiences during my travels, I gathered that India feels more cultural solidarity with the western world, particularly with Europeans, than with the countries to its east. Even aside from the fact that India was steeped in British culture during British rule, it may be that connections to Europe existed from the time Indian culture originated. The accepted theory of the origins of the Indian people is that they were the result of a union between the native Dravidians and the Aryans who migrated to India from the north or northwest. The Aryan language was clearly part of the Indo-European linguistic family, distantly related to English, German, and Russian.

I mentioned earlier my visit to the Lakshminarayan Temple in Delhi. Here foreign visitors are handed a descriptive brochure, written in English, which states that the doctrine supporting the temple is a kind of Aryanism. It notes that Hinduism is regulated by 'Arya Dharma' (or Aryan law), and that the protection and preservation of the Arya Dharma is the responsibility of Europeans and Americans, as well as of Indians, since these peoples share a common descent from the Aryans. This brochure must have been created for English-speaking people, but in this case I, a non-Aryan Japanese, was the recipient. It did not make any reference at all to other Asian peoples such as the Chinese or Japanese. As I read it, I realized all the more that the people of India face westward. And yet, at the end of the brochure was a description of the gammadion or swastika symbol (卍), used in Japan as the Buddhist symbol *manji*, noting it to be the basis of all Aryan letters. Included among examples of Aryan-derived writing were Roman, Greek, and Japanese letters. This seemed to indicate that Japanese might be included among Aryans.

Racial theories

The concept of pan-Aryanism does not exist solely in India. It is possible Pakistanis might think the same way, as they are ethnically the same as Indians, although in fact I did not see any instances of Aryanism while there. In Afghanistan, however, the idea of Aryanism was overtly expressed. For example, Afghanistan is also called Aryana (meaning Arya nation) – not just as a colloquial expression, it is also noted in government publications – and the Afghani airline is called Aryana Airlines. This can be seen as a profession of cultural identification with all Indo-European peoples. Even further, it expresses a consciousness of belonging: an assertion that the Afghanis are indeed part of the mainstream of Aryans.

The idea of pan-Aryanism, however, cannot be of very long standing, since the advances in linguistics and anthropology that led to the concept of the Indo-Aryan people are relatively recent. This convenient application of scientific discoveries is an example of modern racial nationalism.

Perhaps it is natural that racial nationalism prevails in Asian nations. When the purpose of such an ideology is to emphasize cultural solidarity within a nation it does not trouble me, but some aspects of the pan-Aryanism I encountered during my trip gave me concern. The statements I heard from various people in support of Aryanism had a whiff of racism that seemed stronger than the idea of cultural solidarity among Aryan peoples. If most of the comments I heard had remarked upon the connections among the Indo-European family of languages – for example noting the similarity between the English word 'mother' and the Farsi 'modar' – that would have been a positive indication of cultural solidarity. But in fact I more frequently encountered statements such as 'Our noses are large just like those of the Europeans,' which stressed a racial solidarity based on physique and facial features. This attitude reminded me of the Nazi ideology of Aryan racial superiority.

If this new Aryanism influences the shape of nationalism in these recently established Asian nations, the implication for the attitude toward non-Aryan citizens is a major issue. There are numerous ethnic groups in India and Afghanistan, which include many non-Aryans. For example, south Indians are mainly Dravidian, and northern Afghanis are mainly Turkish.

Aryanism may also give rise to awkward interactions with people of other nations. I imagine a scene in which someone – perhaps a Japanese – expresses his sense of familiarity and solidarity with India based on his status as a 'fellow Asian.' The believer in pan-Aryanism is bewildered, replying, 'But we are Aryans!' The Japanese can do naught but pull back, murmuring, 'Ah yes, is that so....' Then again, what kind of reaction will the Indian advocate of western-facing Aryanism encounter when he actually goes to the West to make direct contact with Europeans? The Europeans may feel just as bewildered by these Aryans from Asia.

Where does the Orient begin?

I realize that the analysis of racial features is a dubious basis for theories of cultural identities and differences. But as I spent many months among peoples with such a variety of features, I felt compelled to think about race at frequent intervals.

The peoples with whom I came in contact over the entire course of my travels were of mixed racial heritage, but they were mostly Caucasian. They had high noses and sharply etched facial structures. In this respect they were similar to Europeans, but the color of their skin was not pale; it was, for the most part, darker than the Japanese.

It was interesting to observe regional variations among the Caucasians I encountered. For example, the Pashtuns of Afghanistan were quite distinctive. At the ferry dock in Calcutta, I was blankly gazing at the crowd of people disembarking when I saw two Pashtuns. I cried out with surprise and recognition because they stood out so conspicuously from the Indians surrounding them. Afghanis and Indians may both be Caucasians, and they may both espouse their Aryan heritage, but their racial features are strikingly different.

It was in Calcutta that I first began to feel that we were approaching the Orient. Now amongst the jumble of faces a large number of apparently Mongoloid people appeared, most likely Chinese or Burmese. I don't consider myself to be a racist, but when I reached Calcutta, I felt pleased to be closer to the world where people of my own race lived. It was also a confirmation of the distinct divide between Eastern races and those to the west of India. There was an expression used by European travelers approaching Calcutta from the west: 'The East begins in Calcutta.' Now I could understand that feeling.

The mingling of races is even more obvious in the Himalayas. I made a side trip as far as Kalimpang, an outpost for trade with Tibet. Kalimpang is technically within the Indian state of West Bengal, but many Tibetans, Nepalese, and Bhutanese live there. They are all Mongoloids with Oriental faces. One thinks of the 'East' as beginning just north of the Himalayas, but these people had crossed over to the southern side of the range, overflowing like a waterfall.

When I returned to Japan I was surprised to hear that the Himalayan tribe of the Lepchas was mentioned prominently in Yasuda Tokutarō's bestselling book *Man'yōshū no nazo* (The mystery of the Man'yōshū).[10] According to this author, the Lepcha people look very much like the Japanese and speak a language similar to ancient Japanese. When I visited Kalimpang, I did see some Lepcha people whose faces were indeed similar to the Japanese. But in the Himalayan region they were hardly unique in that regard. The faces of the Tibetans and Bhutanese were also indistinguishable from ours. This simply indicated that we are all of the Mongoloid race. Naturally, none of them spoke Japanese.

India and the West

Leaving aside for now the difficult issue of racial identity, let us discuss India's cultural and historical connections to the West. These have certainly formed the basis for a deeper relationship between India and the West than the East. On my journey I entered India from the west, traveling from Afghanistan to Pakistan, and then on to India. Pashto, the language of Afghanistan, is a member of the Persian language family, very similar to the Farsi spoken in Iran. In Pakistan, the national language is Urdu, but it is intermixed with many Persian words; and in the Punjab region Persian is often understood. Hindi, the national language of India, uses different lettering from Persian or Urdu, and is of course a separate language. But in terms of linguistic origins its derivation is basically the same as Urdu. To a great extent, if one starts off knowing the Persian languages, one can manage all across the South Asian subcontinent. I was able to use the Pashto I learned in Afghanistan, which was the westernmost point of my travels, all the way to Calcutta, my eastern terminus.

India's history is full of dealings with the West rather than with the East, the primary example being the many invasions by forces from the west. The Aryans themselves were originally invaders from the west, followed by Persians, as well as Greeks. Timur and Emperor Babur, the founder of the Mogul Empire, claimed they were descendents of the Mongols, but in fact they were invaders from the west, unrelated to the Mongolians of East Asia. India was also repeatedly conquered by a succession of Afghani dynasties.

The route that I took from the Afghani capital of Kabul over the Khyber Pass to the Punjab plain was the well-worn historical route of these invasions. It is said that present day Urdu and Hindi are languages born of the mixture of the conquerors' Persian and the languages of the indigenous peoples. It was no wonder that I was able to use the Persian I had learned.

In recent history, the proportion of the Islamic population in India has decreased, but this is an artificial political creation resulting from Partition. The traditionally Islamic regions have become the nation of Pakistan. This does not negate the fact that the historic region of India had a deep connection to the Islamic faith that had spread from the West. It was ruled for a long time by the Islamic Mogul dynasty, which left a deep influence on every aspect of society and culture. Even now there are numerous Islamic mosques. The Taj Mahal, the most famous site in India, is said to represent the pinnacle of Indian architecture, but in fact this large, splendid marble structure is built in the Islamic style. The mosque in New Delhi, India's capital, is one of the three main mosques of the Islamic world. Modern India is not an Islamic nation, but it shares much of its history with the Islamic areas to its west.

The 'Mediant'

In conclusion, I can firmly state that India is not part of the Orient. Its cultural tradition is fundamentally different from that of the East Asian countries that developed around the core civilization of China. India shares its history with the Islamic world to its west. But if India is not part of the Orient, it is equally true that it does not belong to the Occident, that is, to the European world. As I was puzzling over how to denote an India that was neither Oriental nor Occidental, I met a Japanese student in New Delhi who used a very clever term.

'India is part of the "Mediant".'

I was so impressed with this term, I decided to employ it. I felt deeply ashamed that I had not previously understood that India and the Islamic world need not be classified as either Oriental or Occidental. I don't wish to shift blame to others, but I thought that my ignorance was due at least in part to the negligence of the Japanese education system, which taught us almost nothing about the middle world. My memory is that my prewar middle school Eastern History textbook contained perhaps one page on India. This kind of education, among other things, has led to the tendency among Japanese intellectuals to divide the world into an East-West paradigm, focused on comparing the Orient and the Occident. I was conditioned to think in this way, but I have come to realize that this concept of the world is not valid. We must include the Mediant along with the Orient and the Occident.

The Mediant is a huge expanse. Flying from the Orient to the Occident, one spends nearly an entire day in the skies over the Mediant countries. It is important to remember that as we do so, we are not crossing a barren spiritual desert.

VI Japan: an unsuitable model for Asian modernization

The flow of history in India, Japan, and Western Europe

At a bookstore in India I picked up a book on the history of Indian thought, and was amazed to see that more than half of the book was devoted to the ancient period. This emphasis seemed to be part of a general tendency in the treatment of Indian history; I saw other works that also devoted a large proportion of their pages discussing ancient times. In Japan, history books have greater focus on more recent periods. Indian culture is full of wonderful stories about the events of two thousand years ago. But no matter how old the country's culture, is it really possible that there have been so few significant developments since then?

I thought that we should consider whether the flow of history in India is entirely different from that in Japan or other nations. Although I had not studied Indian history in particular, it seemed to me, even from my limited knowledge, that the history of India was very different from Japan's. Meanwhile, that striking contrast made the differences between the histories of Japan and the Occident (especially Western Europe) seem insignificant in comparison. Indeed, it began to seem that Japan and Europe had experienced very similar historical development in some basic ways.

As I mulled over these ideas during my travels, I thought back to the debates amongst my colleagues in Japan. The focus of these discussions seemed always to have been on the differences between East (the Orient) and West (the Occident), or between Japan and the West. India did not even enter into it, which in retrospect seemed a pity. But now on my journey I had the great good fortune to have companions with whom I could consider these issues. I was particularly fortunate to work with Dr. Schurmann, a historian from the United States who was originally from Western Europe. The living presence of India in full frontal view enabled us to advance our discussions with concrete examples. How fitting that a close relationship between a Japanese and a Western scholar was brought about by a country of the Mediant.

Among the many interesting topics that came up as we compared Japan, Western Europe, and India was the issue of colonialism. India was of course the colony of a European country, whereas Japan was never colonized. Japan itself colonized parts of Asia, as did the Western European nations.

The function and nature of revolutions also attracted our attention. Japan and many of the Western European nations experienced various revolutions, which enabled them to surmount old inconsistencies or contradictions, leading to a new period of rapid progress. These historical events were for the most part the result of forces within the nation. In contrast, India seemed not to have experienced revolutions. Instead, it was the object of invasions and destruction by external forces. Its history seems to have been pushed along mainly by events originating outside of the country.

Yet another topic was feudalism. Japan and Western Europe both had feudal systems. Moreover, in both places the feudal period came to an end as the result of a bourgeois revolution. In India, however, there was neither a feudal system nor a bourgeois revolution that overcame it.

Other Western European historical phenomena, such as free cities, peasant wars, and religious reformation, also have their counterparts in Japanese history. Even if there are differences, at the very least Japanese historians can refine their theories by comparing Western European and Japanese history. But this cannot be done with Indian history. In order to understand Indian history, it seemed to me that it was necessary to employ an entirely different way of thinking.

Conditions for modernization

In addition to historical development, sociological and anthropological issues also commanded our attention. The trip provided my first opportunity to observe in person the social systems of Islamic countries. I found the system of equal inheritance especially fascinating. India too, although not primarily Islamic, practiced equal inheritance. I already knew that equal inheritance was the practice in Chinese society as well. In complete contrast, the traditional system of inheritance in both Japan and Western Europe was primogeniture. This was no doubt related to the development of feudalism shared by these two areas. Dividing up the land among the heirs would have undermined the foundations of the feudal system.

I was also prompted to reconsider the system of polygamy. In Islamic countries men are allowed, by Islamic law, to have up to four wives. In India and China it was not a matter of religious law, but in any case they were traditionally permissive with regard to polygamy. In Japan's case, however, polygamy was not officially approved of, at least among the common people. Mistresses of course existed but were considered social outcasts. This was despite the absence of the religious prohibitions one found in the Christian nations.

Back in Japan, I had generally accepted the received wisdom that, due to its great difficulties in modernizing, Japan still retained many pre-modern characteristics. But once I saw a country like India, my thinking changed. I began to realize instead that Japan's modernization was actually a natural and inevitable process, and was accomplished far more easily than in a place like India. India and other nations like it are heavily burdened with obstacles to modernization that Japan and Western Europe did not have to face. Among the many problems are the caste system, polygamy, overpopulation, poverty, starvation, lack of capital, colonial-style domination by foreign countries, illiteracy, and religious oppression. My impression was that given these conditions, a normal course of modernization would be hard to carry out.

Japan, the unsuitable model

All of this thought and discussion brought me to a curious conclusion. As I have outlined above, comparisons of world civilization should involve three parties, the Orient, the Occident, and the Mediant. In my theories, these were most often represented by Japan, Western Europe, and India. Furthermore I have stressed the importance of the Mediant as a region distinct from the Orient and the Occident. Yet I noticed that when I brought up aspects of Japan and Western Europe to contrast them with India, these characteristics were quite specific to Japan and Western Europe, but not necessarily common to all of the Orient or the Occident. The picture is not simple, since China in the Orient has similarities to India in the Mediant, while within the Western sphere, Western Europe is but one particular region. Eventually, I came to realize what a very particular case Japan is among the Asian countries.

During my travels through Afghanistan, Pakistan, and India, I was repeatedly asked the same question. 'Japan has modernized so rapidly. Can you teach us your secret?' But frankly I do not think there is a secret. In those countries I saw conditions that were so vastly different from those in Japan that it would not be possible for them to emulate our experience. The people in those countries thought of Japan as a model for modernization, and some Japanese think so as well, but I believe this idea is gravely mistaken. Japan cannot be a model for the modernization of Asian nations.

The fact remains that, regardless of Japan's suitability as a model, Asian nations must modernize. They are, in fact, making steady efforts at modernization. Even if our country cannot be a model, we ought to offer help for their efforts in the form of technical and other aid. But we must not forget that Japan's position relative to those nations is one of singularity, not one of the *primus inter pares* in a group of similar nations. Japan's development was an exceptional case.

Asia and Japan

It seems that in terms of social structure and function, Japan more closely resembles Western Europe than other nations of Asia. But this does not mean that the nations of Western Europe would recognize Japan as one of their own. This is because the cultural lineages of Japan and Europe are completely different, no matter how similar the social structures. Japan is not part of Europe.

However, it is with good reason that Japanese intellectuals, especially social scientists, have tended to skip over Asia and to look to Western Europe in their search for comparative material. I once thought that this tendency stemmed from the weakness for all things Western prevalent among Japanese intellectuals since the Meiji period (1868–1912). But I see now that there may be a more well-founded cause, namely, that comparisons with Western

Europe can be easily drawn, while comparisons with Asian countries are difficult to establish.

We Japanese consider ourselves to be an Asian people. Moreover, we often think of ourselves as representative Asians. Thus when we hear Westerners speak about Asia or the Orient, we assume they are talking about us. But this is a dangerous misconception. If one perceives Asia or the Orient as a monolithic whole, one is embracing an Occidental bias. From a truly Asian perspective, we should see that it is not that simple. Each Asian country has its own unique characteristics, none more so than Japan. Thus the problems we face are very different from those faced by other Asian nations.

Recently one hears the expression 'Japan is Asia's orphan.' Upon reflection, this is nothing new. Already a few hundred years have passed since Japan first set out on the path to a destiny different from that of other Asian nations. I do not mean that it is desirable for Japan to continue too far along that path. Indeed, we must create many pathways for mutual understanding and cooperation between Japan and other Asian nations. But as we do so, it would be a mistake to rely on a simplistic, vague sense of unity or Asian solidarity. If, out of a misguided sense of identity, we thrill to the heroic struggle of Asian nationalism versus Western colonialism, it is no more than the enthusiasm of a spectator at a *sumō* match. It is only when we engage in our own *sumō* match that we truly face the substance and subtleties of our problems.

In the postwar period we have heard increasing calls for a Japanese rapprochement with Asia, but it seems to me that these calls lack substance. Our actions should be based on calm, rational observation, and objective research.

(February 1956)

2 Culture of the East, Culture of the West

Commentary on Chapter 2

The following article represents one of the many short pieces I wrote for magazines and newspapers in the year following my 1955 travels. The original article appeared in the science section of the daily newspaper *Mainichi Shinbun* on February 13, 1956, under the title 'Afuganisutan no yūbokumin' (The nomadic tribes of Afghanistan),[1] but here I have renamed it 'Higashi no bunka nishi no bunka' (Culture of the East, Culture of the West). I do not mean to propose a theory of cultural comparison between East and West, but rather to accurately convey that my focus was on tracing the lineages of regional 'culture.' It was a somewhat unusual direction for me, as my general interest tended more towards the analysis of 'civilization.'

Carrying

When I was traveling in Afghanistan and Pakistan last year, I naturally expected that the cultures of those countries would be different from Japanese culture. Language, clothing, food, and shelter were indeed entirely different, but my curiosity was most piqued by the local body language. Demeanor, bearing, posture, mien, and everyday actions were also very different from our own. For example, when I encountered a nomadic tribe living in tents in a valley of the Hindu Kush, I was surprised to see how they carried their children. Rather than bearing a child 'piggy back' as we might, they carried a crying child horizontally across the back. The child faced backwards, with his head and legs pinned by the crooked arms of the adult – he could not wriggle free. I had never seen the method in Japan, but it seemed a useful way to treat a flailing child.

Shortly after my return to Japan I happened to see the film *Sanga haruka nari* (the title in Japanese meaning 'The distant mountains and rivers'). In this story of European war orphans, there is a scene in which an American soldier gathers up orphans trying to run away among the war-ravaged ruins. I was amazed to see that the way in which the children were carried was exactly the same as the Afghan nomads.

This carrying method seemed most likely to have derived from the practice of animal husbandry. It was the most pragmatic way of carrying a small domesticated animal such as a sheep. Water bags made from the skin of domestic animals were also carried in this fashion in Afghanistan. It certainly seemed possible to me that this custom might be a very old cultural trait common to the entire region spreading from Western Asia to Europe.

Nowadays we tend to think of Islam and Christianity as very different religions, but upon closer consideration we find that they share many common concepts. Similarly, Western Asia and Europe may appear at first glance to be quite different, but closer investigation would probably yield many features common to these cultures derived from farming and animal husbandry.

Greeting

I had similar thoughts regarding customs of greeting. During my sojourn in Afghanistan I generally shook hands in the 'Western' fashion, but as I was unaccustomed to this, it felt awkward to me. The rural Afghanis were much more at ease with the handshake than I. For Japanese, the handshake is a custom transplanted from Western culture; but the Afghanis seemed to have their own indigenous style of handshake, differing slightly from the European custom. They grip each other's right hand, and then place the left hand on top of the other person's right hand, making what appears to be a two-handed handshake.

The Afghanis also embrace when greeting. Friends meeting after a long absence hug each other and brush cheeks three times back and forth. I also saw bearded men kissing each other's cheeks, in much the same gesture as one sees in Russian films. These forms of greeting may be another basic cultural trait in common with Europe. The handshake and the kiss are commonly thought to have derived from European chivalry. But from what I saw in Afghanistan, which did not share the chivalric heritage of Western

Europe, one might conjecture an entirely different cultural origin, far older and more deeply ingrained.

Bowing and Praying

Leaving aside Western cultural traits, in Japan we have many curious behaviors and demeanors of our own. What, for example, is the origin of the bow? There are those who assert that bowing derives from the practice of Japanese feudalism, but I think that the link between bowing and feudalism, much like the link between the handshake and chivalry, is specious. This is evidenced by the widespread custom of bowing in Asian countries that did not pass through a feudal period.

What is the significance of our typical gesture of prayer? When we worship at a Buddhist statue, we press our palms together in front of our chests. In India, people use this gesture as an everyday greeting, not just as a prayer pose. The Japanese prayer pose is most likely related to Indian practices. It is easy to jump to the conclusion that the pressing of palms is a sign of Buddhist influence on Japan, but even if one traced its origins to Buddhism, that would not be a sufficient answer. The real question is how Buddhism came to adopt this style of worship, as it seems to be a fundamental and pre-existing cultural trait of the East.

Although there is a great deal of comparative work on the cultural differences between East and West as expressed in high literature and art, it seems to me that the comparative anthropological examination of everyday behaviors of common people has been neglected. With more effort at this kind of comparative anthropological research, we could tap into the deep vein of human culture that courses underground through the ancient world. Thus were my thoughts as I wandered through Afghanistan awkwardly shaking hands.

(February 1956)

3 An Ecological View of History: Japanese Civilization in the World Context

Commentary on Chapter 3

The following article, which originally appeared in the February 1957 issue of the monthly *Chūō Kōron*, was written exactly a year after I returned from my 1955 journey to Afghanistan, Pakistan, and India.[1] As I mention at the beginning of the piece, Professor Arnold Toynbee was visiting Japan at that time. He attended my lecture on the Moghol tribe of Afghanistan at a joint conference on anthropology and ethnology in the autumn of 1956. Professor Toynbee's visit to Japan happily gave me the impetus to publish this piece.

In my article I borrowed certain terms, such as 'challenge and response,' from Toynbee's *A Study of History*. Thus the advertising copy at the time trumpeted my work as 'a unique perspective on world history developed in response to Toynbee's challenge.' In point of fact, however, my thoughts were not particularly related to Toynbee's theories. As I note at the end of the piece, it was primarily the fruit of my journey of the previous year – an attempt to refine and impose some theoretical order upon my travel notes, along with some additional material and related reading. Perhaps it was surprising to the reading public that a figure previously unknown in the media would suddenly publish such a work, but from my perspective as the author, there was nothing sudden or impulsive about it. The kernel of my ideas was already present in 'Between East and West,' which had been published the year before. 'An Ecological View of History: Japanese Civilization in the World Context' is a direct linear descendent of the earlier article.

The title 'An Ecological View of History: Japanese Civilization in the World Context' (Bunmei no seitaishikan) has a history all its own. When the article appeared in *Chūō Kōron*, it was entitled 'An Introduction to An Ecological View of History: Japanese Civilization in the World

Context' (Bunmei no seitaishikan josetsu). My own title had been 'An Ecological View of History: Japanese Civilization in the World Context' without the words 'An Introduction to…,' but for various reasons the editors saw fit to add the 'introductory' phrase. This ended up causing me some trouble, since people who read it thought it was in fact an introduction, and kept asking me when the main article would appear. No matter how short or simple it may be, this article stands on its own and is not an introduction to another thesis. Complaints that I wrote an introduction but never completed the main body of the thesis are without merit. It might have been better to title it 'An Outline…' rather than 'An Introduction…,' and perhaps I could still write some more detailed articles to fill in the outline or give more examples to elucidate the overview.

The publication of 'An Introduction to An Ecological View of History: Japanese Civilization in the World Context' evoked considerable reaction in the critical world, no doubt because it introduced a number of unfamiliar arguments. The commentary ranged from supportive to severely critical, sometimes with such gross misunderstandings and misreadings that they were not even worthy of rebuttal. I realized the great difficulty of making oneself understood. I would like to note below several of the major streams of discourse that flowed from the publication of the article. There is much I could say about these opinions and articles, but I will try to refrain from editorializing.

Just a month after 'An Introduction to An Ecological View of History: Japanese Civilization in the World Context' appeared, *Chūō Kōron* published Katō Shūichi's 'Kindai Nihon no bunmeishiteki ichi' (The place of modern Japan in the history of civilization).[2] I participated in a roundtable discussion on the theory of civilization with Mr. Katō and Mr. Hotta Yoshie.[3] Soon the people at the Japan Cultural Forum (Nihon Bunka Fōramu) took up the concept of 'ecological history.' The journal *Kokoro* hosted a roundtable,[4] and Mr. Takeyama Michio published an article on the topic in the journal *Shinchō*.[5] A symposium was held focusing on this work, and its transcription was later published as a book.[6] This debate itself became a target of discussion, in which my work was sometimes referenced. While there were similarities between the ideas of the Cultural Forum group and my own, there were also fundamental differences, as discussed by Takeuchi Yoshimi.[7]

Ueyama Shunpei wrote several articles on the significance of 'ecological history' as historical theory, comparing it to the Marxist approach.[8] Representing a Marxist analysis of my work were articles by Ōta Hidemichi and Kawane Yoshiyasu.[9,10] There were also several discussions on the position of 'ecological history' within the history of postwar thought.[11]

The joint research team in social anthropology at Kyoto University's Research Institute for Humanistic Studies placed my theory upon the cutting board and thoroughly dissected it. This resulted in many important advances and refinements. I am still considering the need to write a more systematic study based on the results of the joint research team discussions. Unfortunately the results of the study group were never published in a unified format. Some pieces were included in *Jinbun Gakuhō* Vol. 21: *Shakai jinruigaku ronbunshū* (Collected works on social anthropology)[12]; and others were introduced in the work of Ueyama Shunpei.[13] Still another portion appeared in *Imanishi Kinji hakase kanreki kinen ronbunshū* (Collection of essays in honor of Dr. Imanishi Kinji on the 60th anniversary of his birth) in *Ningen,* Vol. 3.[14]

'An Introduction to An Ecological View of History: Japanese Civilization in the World Context' was included under its original title in the October 1964 special issue of *Chūō Kōron,* 'Representative Articles that Created Postwar Japan,' with commentary by Ueyama Shunpei.[15] In retrospect, the article was the starting point of my theoretical development, and no longer fully represents my thoughts. Nevertheless, I am including it here as it originally appeared.

Challenge and response

The noted historian Arnold Toynbee recently visited Japan. Among his works translated into Japanese, I have read two: an abridgement of *A Study of History,*[16] and *Civilization on Trial.*[17] While I find them fascinating and full of profound theories, I am not completely persuaded. His arguments have not succeeded in undermining a theory I had formulated on my own. In particular, I disagree with his discussion in reference to Japan. Thus, despite my admiration for his work, I have not become a convert.

When Westerners relate the history of the world, they usually neglect Japan, mainly out of complacency and incorrigible ignorance. In contrast, Toynbee's theory does recognize Japan as a part of the independent civilizational sphere of the Far East, albeit lumped together with Korea as an offshoot of this civilization. His theory is at least redeeming in this respect, but then he goes on to state that five of the remaining six civilizations on earth are in the process of disintegration, including Japanese civilization. He asserts that Western civilization is the only one that remains healthy and free from decline. Fortunately Toynbee did not predict that Japanese civilization will disappear overnight, so we need not be overly concerned. Nevertheless his theory is not very encouraging.

The disproportionately grand scale of Toynbee's ideas is problematic. His theories are oversized both in terms of scope and in terms of standards of measurement. When he measures the history of the earth or the history of life, he considers the past several millennia as if they were one historical era. For example, he believes that in the twelfth century Japanese civilization had already started down the road to disintegration. Such an oversized scale leaves us feeling confused and helpless. It is much the same as being told by astrophysicists that the universe is expanding at an incredibly fast rate: it may indeed be true, but such a fact is difficult to relate to our daily lives. I do not think that the small changes that occur over a few years are necessarily significant. But in order to understand our history and our world, would it not be better to replace such a cosmic scale with a somewhat more human-sized yardstick?

However, my main purpose here is not to criticize Toynbee's theories – in any case, other scholars will no doubt be voicing their own opinions. I began by citing Toynbee because his visit to Japan inspired me to write this article. I considered his visit and his theory of civilization to be a challenge from the West. I felt that Toynbee's theory was quite Western-centric, and that as an Asian or as a Japanese, I could come up with something rather different. The rough and premature sketch of the world given below is not directly linked to Toynbee's theory, but still it is my response to his challenge.

Japan's site in the world

I mentioned earlier that I would write about 'the world,' but in fact I have not formulated a coherent theory of the New World. For now I would like to set aside the Americas, Oceania, and sub-Saharan Africa, and focus on what one might call the 'Old World' of Asia, Europe and northern Africa. To understand how we conceptualize space in these regions, we might begin by considering the site of Japan. What are the coordinates of Japan in today's global space? I am not using the word 'space' in a physical or geographical sense – obviously we can give precise latitudes and longitudes for that.

To illustrate, naming Japan as an East Asian nation is a way of indicating its site. Here Japan is grouped as one of the nations of East Asia, and its narrative is interpreted in contrast to those of Western nations.

Thus, calling Japan a nation of the East, or the Orient, is more than just specifying its longitude and latitude: the very concepts of East and West, Orient and Occident, are historically cultural constructs. Classifying Japan as an Eastern nation goes beyond geographical description, it also situates Japan within a cultural and historical space.

Orient and Occident: East and West

Classifying Japan as a nation of the East, however, is clearly insufficient as an interpretive tool. There have been numerous attempts to understand the various problems faced by modern Japan by referring to inter-linkages between East and West, or between Oriental and Occidental cultures. I do not subscribe to this approach, as the use of such positioning coordinates seems overly simplistic. It is merely an exercise in classification to say that Japan is an Eastern nation, or that Japanese culture is one type of Oriental culture. It gives us no suitable yardstick with which to examine specifics. Since Japan is not a typical case in the so-called East, we must address the differences that set it apart from the rest of that region. Upon examination, we may find surprisingly large differences.

Even more importantly, the practice of dividing the world into 'the East' and 'the West' is in itself nonsensical. As an intellectual schema, creating theories of the world by comparing East and West has an appealing neatness to it. But in reality, one is simply leaving out the parts that do not fit into either East or West. One example is the so-called Islamic world: the several hundred million people living in the vast expanse from Pakistan to North Africa. Is this part of the East or the West? The people in Western Europe may call this the 'Orient,' but in Japan we view it differently. When we Japanese visit the region, we in fact encounter many elements that seem strongly reminiscent of the West. But if we were to classify this region as part of the West, Western Europeans would no doubt be astonished.

'East' and 'West,' or 'Orient' and 'Occident,' are convenient words when referring vaguely to position or characteristics. When we try to introduce a little more precision into an argument, these terms are no longer useful. In particular, this method of classification cannot accurately pinpoint Japan's position in the world.

Modernization and Japanese culture

The influences which originally shaped Japanese culture were undeniably Eastern. Succumbing to the convenience of vagueness, I too have used the term 'Eastern,' although a more precise term would be 'Far Eastern.' Japan obviously shares numerous characteristics with the areas located on the eastern edge of the Asian continent. When we trace back the elements of Japanese culture, in most cases we can locate their origins on the Asian continent. So it was not unreasonable for Toynbee to place Japanese civilization as an offshoot of a Far Eastern civilization with China at the core. However, the picture is more complex, as many of Japan's Buddhist and artistic influences came from even farther west, all the way from India by way of Central Asia.

If it were only a matter of considering the balance of influences from Far Eastern and Central or Southern Asia, it would still be comparatively easy to pinpoint Japan's site in the world. It would be enough just to clarify the differences between Japan and other parts of Asia. The analysis of Japan's site, however, is rendered even more complex by the fact that a great many of the elements that make up modern Japanese culture have come from the West. These elements have been flooding in on the tide of modernization since the Meiji period (1868–1912), and their presence can no longer be ignored.

Today, a key issue in the analysis of modern Japanese culture is the treatment of these Western elements. One school of thought sees 'Westernization' as superficial, claiming that no impact has occurred at a fundamental level. This argument is an exaggeration. On the other hand, Toynbee believes Japan has converted from a Far Eastern civilization to a Western civilization. This argument is also an overstatement. There are a number of non-Western cultural practices that endure in Japan. Our supposed conversion has not gone so far that we would smash our household altars as vestiges of outdated beliefs.

The writer Katō Shūichi sees Japan as a 'hybrid culture,'[18] which I think is a very apt term. This is not to say that modern Japanese culture is a product of grafting Western imports onto Japanese roots, but rather that an entirely new hybrid plant has been created through crossbreeding. This is a fine way of describing Japan's site in the world, and I find Katō's ideas interesting. Even so, he fails to distinguish Japan from other countries. Countries such as China and India appear to be very different from Japan, but what exactly are those differences? Why have those cultures not become hybrids? Based on their histories of influxes from the West, one might have expected them to be even more hybridized than Japan.

Genealogy and functionalism

Until now, various theories have sought to assign coordinates to Japan's site in the world based on where its culture originated. Alternatively, there have been attempts to explain the condition of today's Japan by focusing on the genealogy of the many elements that constitute its culture. In Katō Shūichi 's 'hybrid culture' thesis, culture is examined in terms of lineage.

However, I believe that we can attain a more precise analysis by employing a functionalist perspective. The key question is how the various cultural elements are assembled, and how they operate together. This approach has nothing to do with where the elements of culture originated. Taking architecture as an example, the question of whether Douglas fir or Yoshino cedar is used as a building material is a matter of genealogy, while the question of whether the finished structure is a house or a school involves functionalism. The issue here is not what pieces make up the culture, but how the culture is designed to operate. To be more precise, it is an issue of the way of life of a community, which is, after all, what bears a culture forward.

To employ another analogy, imagine the culture of a given community – say the citizens of a country – as a box. A genealogical analysis of cultural elements would involve discussions about the color of the box. In contrast, the functionalist approach would examine the shape and size of the box. One might also imagine the culture of a community as a set of multi-colored building blocks. Although the blocks vary in color, that has no bearing at all upon the size and shape of the finished structure.

Modernization and Westernization

The issue of genealogy versus functionalism has great bearing upon our interpretation of Japan's so-called 'modernization and Westernization.' It is without dispute that Japan has managed somehow to construct an advanced modern civilization. However, to think of this as purely the result of Japan's modernization and Westernization is questionable. The litany that modern Japanese civilization is merely a copy of the West has gnawed at the self-esteem of Japanese intellectuals who have lived through this process of modernization. This rhetoric still carries considerable weight today. I believe, however, that we need not give so much credence to this kind of simplistic genealogical argument. In functional terms, our overall way of life has been adapted to fit us as Japanese, and has not necessarily been Westernized.

I believe that the relationship between Western modernization and the modernization of Japanese civilization subsequent to the Meiji Restoration (1868) has been one of parallel evolution. In the initial stages of this evolution, Japan lagged behind. We had no choice but to import many elements from the West and to draw up a rough design for progress based on the Western model. The next step was to make the whole system function. Here it was not simply a matter of importing things from the West. Each time a new element was introduced, the entire system had to be readjusted to ensure continuous growth. Sometimes new elements were brought in from the West, but at other times they were invented in Japan. A parallel narrative describes the West. Automobiles and televisions did not exist at the dawn of modernization. When new elements appeared on the scene, old systems in the West, too, had to be readjusted in order to ensure continuous growth. These new elements sometimes originated in a Western European country, or were brought from the New World. Or, as in the case of television antennae, they appeared first in Japan, the distant Far Eastern outpost of advanced civilization.

As Japan modernized, it was not necessarily aiming for Westernization, and this remains the case today. Japan has always had its own agenda. Since many similar conditions existed in Western European countries as well as in Japan, both regions progressed along parallel paths. In this light, I feel that it is not very pertinent to engage in a genealogical debate over which number of cultural elements came from which source.

Japan, an advanced civilization

As I have said, it is not a meaningful exercise to separate out the disparate elements of modern Japanese culture and sort them into categories based on lineage. It would not enhance our understanding of the core characteristics of Japanese culture. Let us therefore leave aside analyzing the materials that make up a culture, and instead examine the design of modern Japanese culture as a whole, as well as the characteristics of the Japanese way of life. When we do so, one conclusion is simple and clear: the Japanese way of life is that of an advanced civilization. If we wish to avoid Toynbee's labeling system, we can simply call it modern civilization instead. To reiterate, the issue here is not where the constituent parts of a civilization came from, but how they operate together. We can leave aside the question of whether modern Japanese culture is 'pure' or 'hybrid,' and state with confidence that Japan is one of the most advanced of modern civilizations.

The term 'civilization' (*bunmei*) was commonly used in Japanese public discourse prior to World War II. It seems puzzling that in the postwar period the term has been largely replaced by 'culture' (*bunka*), as for example in the phrase 'country of culture' (*bunkakoku*). Perhaps because of Japan's loss of pride after defeat, it has given up its claim to being a 'civilized' country. But even after defeat in the war, Japan is still a country with a sophisticated civilization. Some aspects are even more advanced than they were in the prewar period. Without going into too much detail, let us note that Japan has enormous industrial power, highly developed transportation and communications networks, and comprehensive systems of administration and education. Schooling is widespread and goods are abundant. The standard of living is high, as is average life expectancy, and the death rate is low. Art and scholarship are advanced.

I do not mean to claim that Japan's condition is ideal. On the contrary, I am often discontent and critical of our shortcomings. We are installing microwave networks, yet local telephone lines are inadequate. We have railways, but roads for cars are impassible. The chemical industry, shipbuilding, and optical instruments are impressive, but machine tools are substandard. We have several hundred universities, but they lack funds for research. But despite these disparities, there is no doubt that the Japanese way of life is that of an advanced civilization.

Any theory of Japanese culture that denies Japan's identity as an advanced civilization makes no sense at all. This identity must be the basis of our thinking about Japan's present and future. We must view changes or upheavals, whatever they may be, as moving our civilization in a forward direction. Civilization itself is what holds us together, and it offers us traditions that deserve our protection.

'Zone One' and 'Zone Two'

Japan's status as an advanced civilization is a separate matter from its status as a capitalist economy. It is not inevitable that all capitalist economies will give birth to advanced civilizations, nor is it true that a country with an advanced civilization, like Japan, will never become a socialist country.

Within the 'Old World' (defined above as Eurasia and North Africa), only a few countries have managed to become advanced civilizations. The only countries that have completely attained a state of advanced civilization are Japan and a few Western European countries on the other side of the world, although there are some other countries that are close to achieving this state in certain respects. There is a marked difference between these few most advanced countries and countries such as China, India, Russia, the Southeast Asian region, the Islamic world, and Eastern Europe.

To introduce my analysis of this phenomenon, I propose dividing the Old World into two regions and labeling them 'Zone One' and 'Zone Two.' If we think of the Old World as an ellipse, the smaller Zone One exists only around the eastern and western edges of the oval, the eastern portion being particularly small. Zone Two occupies the entire remaining area of the ellipse.

Comparisons among the Zone One countries

It is very interesting to compare the paths taken by the eastern and western portions of Zone One during this century. Naturally there are differences among the various trajectories of Zone One countries such as Great Britain, France, Germany, and Japan. But I feel that we have been putting too much emphasis on these differences: the paths are actually quite similar. This becomes clear when we compare the trajectories of Zone One countries to Zone Two countries such as India or Russia.

Consider, too, that although Germany and Japan are geographically distant from one another, their paths have been particularly similar. Such differences as do exist can be explained as the result of separate cultural lineages. We need not go into great detail as to the similarities, which are well known: both countries rose from the ashes of defeat in World War II to make spectacular recoveries; during the war, both were under fascist governments; even further back, both were late to join the other world powers in the colonization process but eventually became empires. Italy presents a rather similar case.

Britain and France are somewhat different of course, but on the whole both have many similarities with Germany and Japan, particularly in that all of them engaged in imperialistic aggression and built capitalist economies. During the war they were on opposite sides, but interestingly, in the postwar present, both winners and losers have suffered a decline in their fortunes. Not a single one of them retains anything like its prewar influence. And yet, in activities such as mountaineering, we find that all of the climbers who have succeeded in scaling the 8,000 meter high peaks of the Himalayas are from Zone One countries.

Characteristics of Zone Two

Zone Two is characterized by some very interesting phenomena, in particular the sudden rise of many of its countries after World War II. From the Soviet Union to China, India, Pakistan, and Yugoslavia on to Morocco, there are dozens of countries increasing in power, despite the wide variety of their circumstances. The fact that Zone Two encompasses all of these newly-risen countries shows the usefulness of the concept. The area of Zone Two is similar to that defined by the term 'developing regions,' but it is a far less ambiguous and relativistic idea.

Zone Two includes a great number of countries that became independent after the war. This is a marked difference from Zone One, where not a single country newly achieved independence in the postwar period. The countries of Zone Two were colonies or semi-colonies before the war, or else were suffering various hardships. In the past, there had been several large empires in Zone Two. Some, like czarist Russia, carried out modern imperialist-type invasions, but because these countries lacked the underpinnings of capitalism, their situations were different from those of the Zone One imperialist powers. World War I wiped out the vestiges of the old Zone Two empires. Three of its great empires – Russian, Austro-Hungarian, and Ottoman – collapsed.

The great number of revolutions that have occurred in Zone Two countries over the last thirty years is also striking. If we add to that count the number of successful independence movements, the total is quite amazing. One could think of these events as occurring in several waves, or again one could distinguish among them several different types. One strain begins with the Chinese Nationalist revolution and extends all the way to the Egyptian revolution of a few years ago. Key figures in this movement include Sun Yat-Sen, Kemal Ataturk, Nehru, Sukarno, and Nasser. Another type of movement is the proletarian revolution, beginning with the Russian Revolution, and later the birth of new regimes in China and Yugoslavia. And again, there are the different cases of North Korea and the Eastern European countries.

In contrast, not a single Zone One country has undergone a revolution in those same thirty years. If we had to search for similar events, we could only come up with the abdication of the German emperor after the defeat in World War I, or that of the Italian emperor after World War II, which were hardly as momentous. Naturally, Zone One countries have experienced revolutions, but these occurred further back in history. Britain was the first, followed by France. The last in the series were the mid-nineteenth century revolutions of unification in Japan, Germany, and Italy.

I realize here that some may object to my simplifications. However, I believe that I have stripped away minor differences to reveal major similarities.

Capitalism and revolution

I have distinguished between the countries of Zone One and Zone Two and indicated some of the characteristic developments of each during the modern period. But I am less interested in the commonalities of historical development within zones than I am in the underlying cause: the way of life in the communities of each zone. We could also call this the functionalist design of culture, or the general structure of society.

My theory is that the structure of society in Zone One and Zone Two regions differed from the beginning. Zone One societies have commonalities and exhibit similar responses under similar conditions; the same can be said for Zone Two societies. But between Zone One and Zone Two societies there are great differences, which developed as the result of various conditions.

Advanced capitalism is of course the characteristic economic system of Zone One countries. The bourgeoisie has effective control of power, which was achieved through revolution. The fact that this achievement of power was historically possible indicates that the bourgeoisie already had substantial influence before their respective revolutions. The Zone One countries have in common a strong early-developing bourgeoisie. The bourgeoisie was fostered by the system that preceded the bourgeois revolutions, which was of course feudalism. Here again is a striking commonality among Zone One countries: they all passed through a period of feudalism.

Zone Two presents an opposite scenario. Capitalist systems were undeveloped in the regions of Zone Two. Historically – that is, up until the rapidly-changing present – there was not a single example of an advanced capitalist economy in this area. Revolutions usually gave rise to dictatorships, rather than transferring power to the bourgeoisie. The characteristic system of Zone Two countries prior to revolution was not feudalism, but either despotic or colonial rule. Under such conditions it was difficult for a bourgeoisie to flourish.

I find it very interesting that one of the key distinctions between Zone One and Zone Two is the existence of feudalism prior to revolution. It suggests that the Zone One countries have had parallel evolutions, not only during the recent decades of modern development, but as far back as the feudal past. One could argue therefore that the development of modern Japanese culture since the Meiji era was in keeping with the laws of history. The rapid advancement of Japan was inevitable, and not simply the result of Westernization or the 'conversion' of its civilization. To reiterate, if one analyzes Japan's modern history as a process of Westernization or conversion, one is limited to viewing cultural elements in terms of their geographic origins. One should not forget to consider how the structures built from those elements actually function.

Comparative studies of feudalism

There are a number of very detailed comparative studies of the history of feudalism.[19] Happily for the purpose of my argument, historians commonly accept that feudalism in Japan and feudalism in Western Europe followed similar paths. Naturally one could point out differences between the feudal systems of, say, Japan and Germany, but this is another instance in which minor differences can be stripped away to reveal major similarities. Here again, the contrast with Zone Two is useful in emphasizing the commonalities within Zone One. The term feudalism is sometimes used to describe various historical periods in places such as China, India, Iraq, and the Mongolian steppes. But in these cases I see only a superficial resemblance. We can call these cases feudalism only by enlarging the definition of the term itself. It is clear that these feudal systems are essentially different from the type of feudalism that fostered the bourgeoisie and led to capitalism in the Zone One countries.

With the concept of parallel feudalism as our starting point, we can identify further parallel phenomena in the social evolutions of the Zone One countries during or near the time of the feudal age. One example is religious change. During the middle ages, popular religious movements flourished, and something we can call a citizenry emerged. Guilds were established, autonomous cities developed, overseas trade began, and peasant rebellions occurred. All these events took place in both Japan and Western Europe. I will not go into further detail here, but I hope that one day I can study these features of world history in greater depth.

In the latter half of the feudal age, however, the paths of historical development in the eastern and western portions of Zone One diverged somewhat. This was due to Japan's adoption of the singular policy of national isolation (*sakoku*). As a result of this policy, Japan's scattered colonial footholds in Southeast Asia faded away instead of developing into a proper colonial empire. They did not follow the pattern of early European colonies such as Goa, Pondicherry, or Calcutta. Japan's efforts to invade and colonize Asia were delayed by more than two hundred years, as was the dismantling of Japan's feudal system. The growth of a bourgeoisie was hampered by the absence of capital accumulation from colonial trade and administration.

In the natural course of historical development in Zone One, Japan should have taken on the role of colonial administrator in the East similar to that of Britain and France in the West. With the profits derived from colonies, Japan could then have gone through an industrial revolution of its own before the Meiji era, were it not for the policy of national isolation. If so, Japan might have engaged in a battle with Britain much earlier on, perhaps somewhere in India. As it was, this battle between the eastern and western nations of Zone One was deferred until World War II, with the result that both sides suffered great damage, and ended up losing their respective colonial empires.

Comparative studies of despotic empires

Among the countries of Zone Two, there must also be examples of parallel evolution. Unfortunately I am not aware of any research on this topic – perhaps it has not attracted as much attention as the parallel evolution of feudalism in Zone One. I think a comparative sociological study of the Zone Two despotic empires such as czarist Russia, Qing dynasty China, and the Mogul and Ottoman empires would be fascinating. Even with just a cursory glance, one can see various examples of parallel phenomena: a resplendent court, vast territorial holdings, a complex ethnic composition, the existence of borderlands, the possession of tributaries rather than colonies, the unchanging ignorance and poverty of the peasantry, powerful provincial officials, landlords with vast estates, and of course corruption and decline. We can also note other parallel phenomena that resulted from colonization by Zone One nations. For example a comparison of the Yi dynasty in Korea and the Bao Dai in Vietnam would be fruitful. One could study assimilation policies and the formation and attitudes of the local intelligentsia under colonial rule. My knowledge of these topics is sketchy, but here I wish to point out directions for future research.

An ecological view of history

Once upon a time I thought that I would like to major in world history. I was told that one could major in Japanese, Asian, or Western history, but there was no such field as world history. Inevitably some may find my approach amateurish. Some have said of even Toynbee himself that he does not deserve to be called a historian. Others have criticized that there is no fundamental difference between the theories of history of Toynbee and those of Shirayanagi Shūko. I felt relieved when I heard these criticisms – I realized one does not necessarily have to be a historian to study history.

The reason for my interest in world history is that I would like to know the broad general laws of human history. My method in this article involves the use of comparisons to find parallel evolutions in the course of history. My theory of history is based upon the study of ecology.[20]

With that in mind, I would like to take a moment to clarify my terms. As I have said, I want to examine the changes that occur in the ways of life of certain communities. For this purpose the word 'evolution' is not appropriate because it is too tied to blood lineage and genealogy. In the field of ecology, the term 'succession' is used to describe the development of natural communities of plants and animals. To a certain extent, succession theory has succeeded in identifying the laws that govern such changes. If we apply the succession model to the history of human communities, we may be able to identify the historical laws at work. At the very least, the succession model is more concrete and less metaphorical than evolution.

Earlier I criticized as insufficient the genealogical analysis of cultural elements. If this approach were used to study a forest, it would describe the lineage of the various species of trees. In contrast, my 'way-of-life' or functionalist approach would ask first whether it was indeed a forest, and if so, what type or form of forest could it be. The species of the trees would not matter. Although we use such terms as deciduous broadleaf or evergreen, in reality very rarely do we find a forest consisting entirely of a single species of tree. Indeed, the methodology of plant ecology was developed precisely in response to the fact that most biological communities consist of a variety of species. If this were not so, one could make do with just a geographical study of flora.

The theory of succession postulates that under a given set of conditions, a community's way of life will progress through a sequence of changes in accordance with certain laws. Human beings are not plants, thus may not follow the same path. Still, my working hypothesis is that the succession model can be tested on human communities. I am tempted to name this approach 'human ecology,' but unfortunately that calls to mind a certain rather facile theory put forth by sociologists of the Chicago school.[21] Still, as human ecology has a wide meaning, it may be possible to come up with something more philosophically refined. If I succeed, we would have a powerful new way of looking at history. I will call this the 'ecological view of history,' or to be more succinct, 'history as ecology.'

Evolutionary and ecological views of history

I explained above that my analysis divides the Old World into Zone One and Zone Two, and that each zone has its own characteristic form of succession. The old evolutionary view of history posits that there is only one path, and that everything will, sooner or later, follow it to the same destination. Any seeming divergences are explained as some other developmental stage that will eventually lead to the same place. In reality, biological change certainly does not work this way. From the ecological viewpoint, there are naturally many paths of change. In this view it is not surprising that the societies of Zone One and Zone Two developed different ways of life.

I shall not go into great detail here about the precepts of ecology. Simply put, the phenomenon of succession occurs when, as a result of the accumulation of interactions between the subject organisms and their environment, the existing way of life becomes difficult to sustain and gives way to a subsequent way of life. Or to put it in slightly more technical terms, succession refers to the self-movement within a subject-environment system. Naturally, in places where conditions are different, the laws of change are different.

I realize that even if we use an ecological theory as a model, several issues remain to be addressed: the 'climax' that comes at the end of succession; competition; and cooperation. But let us leave these to be considered on another occasion, and now cast our gaze back into history.

Ancient empires

When I drew the distinction between Zone One and Zone Two, I focused on the developments dating from the emergence of feudalism in Zone One. In fact, however, the histories of the communities in each Zone differed even before that. I would like to extend this idea of Zone One and Zone Two back to ancient history.

At the beginning of ancient history, Zone One was not in the picture at all. It was merely a hinterland where the brilliant light of the ancient civilizations of Zone Two barely penetrated. The primitive way of life of the early Japanese and Germanic peoples, for example, is well known. Zone Two regions had already built grand empires when Zone One peoples slowly followed along, establishing minor imitations. In the eastern portion of Zone One, the Japanese created a state based on the legal and administrative codes of the Sui and Tang dynasties in China; while in the west the Frankish kingdom was modeled on the Roman Empire. Today's Western European civilization is usually viewed as the direct descendent of the Mediterranean civilization of the ancient Greeks and Romans, but I disagree. I see ancient Mediterranean civilization as the western counterpart of ancient China – both typical Zone Two civilizations. Modern Italy occupies the same geographical space as ancient Rome, but is not its direct successor: the former is a typical Zone One modern nation, while the latter was a Zone Two type empire.

After the ancient period, the paths of the two Zones diverged dramatically. In Zone One the turmoil of the Dark Ages was succeeded by the feudal system. In Zone Two, however, an orderly social system did not develop. Vast empires were built which then fell into decline, and were built up once again.

Arid terrain: the seed of destruction

We must ask ourselves why the regions of Zone Two did not follow the same orderly development as Zone One. Then we must ask why the eastern and western portions of Zone One, despite their great geographical separation, went through such a similar developmental process, almost as if by common consent. These questions are examples that test this ecological theory.

Let us therefore consider the ecological structure of nature in the expanses of the Old World, namely Eurasia and North Africa. A prominent feature is the presence of a massive stretch of arid terrain which cuts diagonally across the entire continent, from northeast to southwest, extending into North Africa. This area consists of deserts and oases, or semi-arid steppes. Adjacent to this diagonal swath we find wooded steppes or savannas.

Most ancient civilizations existed right in the middle of this arid region, or in the adjacent savannas, again almost as if by common consent. The civilizations of the Nile, Mesopotamia, and the Indus valley were of this type, and even those of the Yellow River and the ancient Mediterranean were similar in essence. This was most likely due to the demands of cultivation and irrigation. Out of these early civilizations emerged the Zone Two empires, such as Byzantium, Russia, and India, none of which shed this characteristic quality. Meanwhile, forested regions such as Southeast Asia and Siberia have only recently stepped onto the stage of civilized history. Even China did not develop its wetter southern regions until a later period.

These arid regions of Central and Western Asia and North Africa were the source of great evil and destruction. Although my research career began with a study of the ecology of nomadic peoples, I still cannot explain why the peoples who emerged from the arid regions exhibited such awesome destructive power. I can only say that, on numerous occasions since ancient times, unruly masses have come forth from these arid regions and raged through the civilized world like a storm. The civilizations of the ancient world often had difficulty recovering from the assaults of nomadic violence.

Although the nomadic peoples were the main source of destruction and set the example, they were not the only destructive force. Later on, intense violence emerged from the civilized societies on the outskirts of the arid region. These sources of violence included the Huns, Mongols, and Tungus in the north, and Islamic societies in the south.

Indeed the history of Zone Two civilizations is largely one of conquest and destruction. Dynasties thrived only when they could effectively eliminate violence. Even then, they had to remain on guard, prepared for attacks from new sources of violence. This was a tremendous waste of productivity.

It may be an oversimplification, but I believe that this never-ending cycle of construction and destruction was the defining nature of Zone Two. It was possible to build these grand societies, but only temporarily, because they could not mature sufficiently to allow mounting internal contradictions to work themselves out through revolutionary change. The conditions of the region dictated this outcome from the start.

With the arrival of the early modern age, nomadic forces were subdued for the first time, allowing the four great Zone Two empires to flourish: the Chinese, Russian, Indian, and Ottoman empires. Ironically, in this later historical period, it was the Zone

One powers scattered along the periphery of Zone Two that became the source of intense violence and threat to the great empires. In the long run, revolutionary developments in Zone Two areas were postponed until this century, when they took place under pressure from Zone One. When they did finally occur, they were different in nature from Zone One revolutions.

Autogenic succession

It must now be clear that Zone One was fortunate in its environment. Located in the temperate zone, it received adequate amounts of rainfall, and consisted of highly productive land. Originally, it was mostly forested; hence when the standard of technology was low, it was less likely to become the fountainhead of civilization than the arid region. However, once a certain level of technological development was reached, the temperate forest posed no obstacles such as a tropical rainforest might present. Above all, this region was at the 'edge' of the world. The violence characteristic of Central Asia rarely extended there. With further good fortune, the societies of Zone One were able to build up their defensive capabilities sufficiently for those occasions when invasions did threaten. The German knights successfully fought in East Prussia against Genghis Khan and Hulegu Khan. The Japanese samurai triumphed against Kubelai Khan's forces in northern Kyūshū. Both of these outer margins managed to escape being trampled by the cruel Mongols. Later the Ottoman Empire's attempt to invade Western Europe was foiled at the siege of Vienna. The division between 'eastern' and 'western' Europe had a functional equivalent in Asia in the Korean Strait.

Zone One was like a greenhouse, insulated from the attacks and destruction perpetrated by Zone Two. Societies within Zone One, sheltered and blessed with a favorable environment, were able to develop smoothly and pass through several developmental stages to reach the present day. If we apply ecological terminology, we can say that succession progressed in an orderly fashion. In Zone One societies, the motive force of historical development came from within the community: this is called 'autogenic' succession. In contrast, in Zone Two, history was often changed by forces external to the community: this is known as 'allogenic' succession.

A better life

After having journeyed back and forth through history, I will
devote the remainder of this section to the problem of modern
civilization, and to a consideration of the tasks currently
confronting the nations of Zone One and Zone Two. Before that,
however, I would like to digress slightly in order to bring up two
points relevant to my final arguments.

The first point is the role of the foremost desire common to all
modern human beings. If there is such a thing, I believe it must be
the wish for a better life. It seems that the search for a better life
can persuade and motivate virtually every human being. In some
countries, religion is still a potent force, but as a whole the desire
for spiritual peace no longer competes with the desire for a better
life. Everyone wishes for an improved standard of living, both in
Zone One where the standards are relatively high, and in Zone Two
where standards are relatively low.

The second point is the transplantable nature of the elements
of civilization. I touched upon this earlier in my discussion of
the modernization of Japan's civilization. It is this nature that
allows people in the countries of Zone Two reason to hope that
life tomorrow will be better than today. As I mentioned, the
origin of the various elements of modern civilization is
irrelevant. One need only introduce the essential elements into
a community and assemble them to suit the particular needs of
the community, just as the Japanese have done. The crucial thing
is the technology itself, not the wholesale adoption of a foreign
spirit.

However, it should also be clear by now that Japan's history of
modernization does not provide a fitting model for the newly
awakened societies of Zone Two: their circumstances differ too
greatly. At the time when Japan imported many elements of foreign
civilization – mostly from Western Europe – it already had the
human resources to implement them. Japan had an energetic
bourgeoisie, fostered during the feudal period and liberated by
revolution. The Japanese had already developed a modern citizenry
when foreign technology was introduced. Perhaps some Western
Europeans at the time worried about the potential for disaster when
handing over modern civilization to the Japanese, but in the end
nothing aberrant emerged. Developments in Western Europe and
in Japan took a similar course.

Socialism in Zone Two countries

Zone Two differed from Zone One in that its societies did not pass through a feudal stage and did not develop an influential bourgeoisie. However, these countries did, and still do, have masses yearning for a better life tomorrow. Therefore, governments with powerful leaders have taken on the role, equivalent to that of the Zone One bourgeoisie, of pushing forward revolutions and pursuing a higher standard of living in the most effective way possible. This explains the establishment of communism and socialism in many of the Zone Two countries. It may seem paradoxical, but one could say that communist and socialist governments are trying to play the role that capitalism plays in Zone One. In any case, it seems certain that the standard of living in the Zone Two regions will rise.

However, despite the present commonality of rising standards of living, it is possible that civilizations in Zone Two will operate differently from those in Zone One, just as in the past. Recent phenomena such as China's 'human wave' lead me to suspect that something unique will develop in Zone Two, beyond the imagination of Zone One. I sense that there may be enduring differences between the consciousness and behavior of people in societies which have passed through a feudal stage and those which have not. One possible difference is that individuals in a society that has experienced feudalism have, overall, a relatively strong sense of self. In contrast, the individuals of a society which has not experienced feudalism are more collective in their orientation. I am not familiar with any data from personality surveys so I cannot substantiate this hypothesis with hard evidence, but I offer it as a topic for future research by cultural or social anthropologists.

The ghosts of the four great empires

Finally, let us bring to a close our discussion of the present and future of the two Zones. The nations of Zone Two, as I have mentioned, have been on the rise during the modern period. Waves of revolutions will probably continue, as will the energetic drive to modernize and civilize these societies. The lives of the people will become easier, approaching the standards of the Zone One populations.

What might be the result of the rising standard of living? I do not believe that it will cause particular Zone Two countries to disappear or disintegrate – each community will continue to develop. Zone Two was originally composed of great empires surrounded by satellite regions. Although the empires have since disintegrated, the communities that supported these empires remain in good health. If these communities continue to flourish internally, who can say that some among them will not become expansionist again, on the model of the old empires? Indeed, signs of such a trend can be detected in various areas of Zone Two today.

It seems likely that Zone Two will come to consist of four coexisting expansionist blocs: the Chinese bloc, the Soviet bloc, the Indian bloc, and the Islamic bloc. These are not empires per se, but here I must admit – although for pride's sake I had hoped not to borrow from Toynbee – that they may be the 'ghosts' of the old empires. The Qing, Russian, Mogul, and Ottoman empires were destroyed by revolution, but they have left their ghosts behind. What then will be the fate of the people in the numerous small countries of Zone Two, and what of the many ethnic minorities tucked away in various corners of the giant ghosts? Those of us who live in Zone One communities consisting of a single ethnic group are not faced with this problem. But it is a major issue confronting the peoples of Zone Two.

Commerce

What then are the issues now facing the nations of Zone One? The era of colonialism is drawing to an end. It is unseemly that countries such as Britain and France still hang on to their colonies – the time is coming when they must let them go. As colonial empires pass away, a different set of rules of international behavior has come to be accepted as the norm. Now it seems that commerce is the best way to maintain the high standard of living in Zone One and to achieve a better life tomorrow. In this sense, Japan and Germany can be proud of themselves compared to Britain and France, because they are employing fair commercial methods.

The topic of commerce leads immediately to the problem of rivalries among Zone One countries, and to the issue of the relationship between Zone One and Zone Two. Now that Japan has been admitted to the United Nations, it must address its ties with the Asian and African regions and with the industrialized nations of the free world. I mention this as an important issue, but alas it must be left for a future discussion. Other Zone One issues that should be highlighted for future analysis include the problems of bureaucratic systems, centralization versus decentralization in community structures, and the question of socialism in Zone One countries. Each of these unresolved tasks is faced by Zone One countries in general, and Japan in particular.

In conclusion, I would like to acknowledge with appreciation the influences which helped shape my ideas in this paper. The ideas set out above were formulated gradually during my trip last year (1955) as a member of a research expedition from Kyoto University. We journeyed to the Hindu Kush region, returning by way of Afghanistan, Pakistan, and India. I had the opportunity to travel with Herbert F. Schurmann, a Western European-born American historian at Harvard University, who engaged me in stimulating discussions and offered me many valuable ideas. After returning to Japan, I presented an outline of my ideas to the research group on the French Revolution at the Institute for Humanistic Studies at Kyoto University who, while not supporting my theories, did provide useful criticism. The philosopher Ueyama Shunpei and the human geographer Kawakita Jirō critiqued my work and provided useful insights. I sense strongly that my major weakness in this work is that I have not actually been to Europe, which I sincerely hope to remedy in the near future.

(February 1957)

4 A New World Map of Civilization: A Search for a Comparative Theory of Civilization

Commentary on Chapter 4

I wrote 'A New World Map of Civilization' (Shin bunmei sekai chizu) at the end of 1956, at about the same time as 'An Ecological View of History: Japanese Civilization in the World Context,' included as Chapter 3 in this volume. 'An Ecological View of History' was actually written first, but its publication in the journal *ChūōKōron* was delayed until February of 1957. Thus the first half of 'A New World Map of Civilization,' through 'The geography of aristocracy and commoners,' appeared earlier, in the January 1, 1957 issue of *Nihon Dokusho Shinbun*.[1] The latter half of 'A New World Map of Civilization,' from the section 'The geography of family and supra-family,' came out in the February 4 issue.[2]

The two articles are complementary in terms of their content. In 'An Ecological View of History' I sketched the framework for a theory, which I then attempted to develop more concretely in 'A New World Map of Civilization.' Even though I wrote 'An Ecological View of History' first, in retrospect it simply laid the groundwork for a larger plan. My choice of subtitle for 'A New World Map of Civilization' – 'A Search for a Comparative Theory of Civilization' – indicated my greater ambition to establish a systematic comparison of civilizations.

This ambition has continued to the present. Chapter 11 'Methodological Notes on Comparative Religion' is one extension of that effort. Ever since I wrote 'A New World Map of Civilization' I had planned to set out comparative theories on education, commerce, agriculture, revolution, and family as well, despite my embarrassment at proposing so many theories without concrete specifics. 'A New World Map of Civilization' was the initial, rough proposal for charting a vast expanse of unexplored fields.

Archetypes of daily life as a typology of civilizations

Why is it that, with all the scholarship on the practices of human life, there is no field of the study of civilization? Until now, what has passed for research on civilization has simply been critiques or theories of civilization rather than a proper discipline. The task of such a discipline would be to discern guiding principles for the improvement of human life by considering the trends of modern civilization and the behavior of humans therein. It is not that we lack for materials to study: our daily experiences are in themselves the raw data. In fact, there is an overabundance of source material, perhaps rendering the task of analysis more difficult. We must use synthesis and insight as our chief instruments, since conventional methods of scientific analysis are unworkable.

One of the most brilliant critics of modern civilization is the French historian André Siegfried. His work *Aspects du XX Siècle* is fascinating for its accurate portrayal of the direction of twentieth century civilization.[3] Siegfried's methodology rests on insights into and syntheses of the daily experiences of human life. Speaking from his position as one human being in the midst of modern civilization, he sensed that recent developments had brought about a certain crisis in civilization.

However, one cannot simply extend from the syntheses and insights of the individual researcher to a picture of the modern face of human civilization as a whole. For example, the 'streamlining of housework' is sometimes considered the defining sobriquet of our contemporary era. While that may be the situation for some, for the great mass of others their concern is that they cannot rationalize their housework even if they wished to. In other words, although we speak of 'modern civilization,' conditions throughout the world differ so greatly that we really cannot define it so simply.

What Siegfried described as civilization was in fact a local phenomenon that could be applied to the United States, Western Europe, and Japan; but it cannot pass as a theory of civilization that encompasses the entire contemporary world. Indeed, when we examine his *Voyages aux Indes* as an example of his critique of the civilization of a less familiar region, we see that his handling of the issue is entirely different.[4] In my consideration, the fatal weakness of Siegfried's theory of civilization is his lack of consistent methodology in making regional comparisons.

When I formed my initial impression that we were surrounded by the raw materials upon which to base a theory of civilization, I was thinking primarily of individual local civilizations. But when we try to expand to a global-scale comparative theory of civilization, we are confounded by a lack of data. A given civilization consists of the myriad details and overall design of the life of local residents. It is not sufficient to garner knowledge about various civilizations from books, nor have I been able to walk through the entire world to accumulate enough material.

Although I do not feel competent to address the very complex issue of comparative civilization, I would like to take some preliminary steps by discussing a few topics in the modern world. My thought is that perhaps we could begin by setting up a simple typology of modern civilizations, based on the establishment of their relative positions within the various regions of the world. Since we lack equivalent information for each country on social conditions in the early modern period, this method may be imprecise. But I propose the typology below as a working hypothesis on the connection between history and present day civilizations.

The geography of tradition and revolution

It goes without saying that the need to consider the issues of 'modern civilization' in terms of the reaction of existing communities to a new mode of life only arose in the wake of the Industrial Revolution. As every community to greater or lesser degree began to encounter conflicts with old traditions, I think that two distinct patterns of confrontation occurred. Each type brought about a restructuring of the social order thorough enough to be reasonably termed a revolution, and yet there were important differences between the two models in terms of the links between pre- and post-revolutionary periods. The first pattern I will describe includes the Western European countries, such as Britain, France, and Germany, as well as Japan. The four major empires of Russia, China, India, and the Ottomans, and the many smaller countries surrounding them, belong to the second model.

In the first model, the degree of social restructuring due to revolutions was not extreme. It was not unlike the shedding of skin that accompanies the growth of an organism. Specifically, the countries that followed the first pattern formed capitalist systems under the newly attained control of a bourgeoisie, which had gradually developed during the feudal stage. In appearance, major reform was achieved through revolution, but under the surface there was significant retention of past traditions. For example, the four nations listed as members of the first model all remained monarchies, at least on the surface. Although the French went as far as regicide during the latter stages of their revolution, Napoleon appeared as emperor soon thereafter, reinstating the peerage, familism, and classical education. A place for traditionalists remained.

In the second pattern of change, the revolutions occurred later chronologically, and were more drastic. In these countries, the emperors and the ruling classes were banished, and leadership was assumed by a new type of strong nationalistic dictator. The revolutions were often accompanied by devastating civil wars or territorial fragmentation, in some cases more than once. These repeated fractures eliminated the past and cleared the way for the future. The metaphor of shedding the skin as a consequence of internal growth does not apply here. This model was one of desperate adaptation and violent rebirth of an organism in response to urgent external pressures from modern civilization. The forced modernization ensuing from these revolutions often went at such a furious pace that in some cases it overtook the development of advanced capitalist nations.

The geography of settlers and virgin forests

As long as we are speaking of conflict with tradition, we should consider the development of modern civilization in a locale with an entirely different precondition, namely the absence of traditions in the New World. Here, the settlers encountered resistance to change only in the form of traditions, learning, or habits of mind brought over from the Old World. In order for communities of immigrants to enter into a new mode of civilized life, it was necessary only to break with the traditions of the Old World. I say 'only,' although certainly there was considerable friction in this process of breaking away. Nevertheless, within a short time, new communities developed into some twenty or so nations of the New World. It is interesting to note that these communities were established at about the same time that the Old World was struggling with the shedding of its skin. It may be said that the attitude of New World settlers toward civilization was defined by the combination of their unbounded hope and trust in the possibilities of a new mode of life together with a certain complex they retained regarding Old World traditions. Despite their ignorance of old traditions, they seemed to place a surprisingly high value on preserving them.

Turning to the actual physical conditions of civilization in the New World, we find regional variations. In North America the settlers set out to build from scratch a civilization where nothing existed. Their chief opponent was nature, not tradition, and moreover the nature they encountered was not harsh and unyielding, but rather abundant and conducive to success. Hence the development of the United States into an extraordinary civilized country.

The civilizing of Central and South America was not the same, owing either to the different temperament of the settlers or the different nature of the environment. In this region, even to the present day, civilization exists in juxtaposition to untamed virgin forests. The only region of the world where such a primitive form of nature remains on such a large scale is Central and South America. The nature of Asia and Africa, by contrast, has borne the footsteps of human history since long before the rise of modern civilization. Central and South America form the world's virgin territory for civilization.

The geography of industries and engineers

Modern civilization might be defined as the mode of human life that was reformulated around the new, larger scale lifestyle which grew gradually as a result of the Industrial Revolution. The successful realization of modern civilization has been achieved in three regions of the world: Western Europe, Japan, and the United States. These are the world's factory zones and industrial areas. We cannot understand the mechanism of modern civilization without considering the industry at its core. The structure of modern civilization is in many ways similar to that of a factory. Indeed, Japan is sometimes called Asia's factory.

Factories need engineers. From the factory head on down, the engineers who operate the modern civilized nations – equivalent to massive factories – are members of the bourgeoisie, which became the ruling class after the revolution. The system driving the factories is so-called advanced capitalism, with ongoing nutritional supplements provided by colonial territories.

In the huge decrepit empires and their satellite countries, which followed the second pattern of change, drastic revolutions were intended to repel the pressure of the advanced capitalist nations and to create factory zones of their own. At the present moment their urgent efforts appear to be headed for a degree of success. This effort will no doubt proceed for a while longer.

The countries following this second model lacked a bourgeoisie who could become the engineers operating the factories because the massive despotic empires that were their precursors failed to nurture one. By default, the operation of the newly built factories required powerful dictatorial leaders as a sort of emergency engineer squad. This kind of leadership was a proxy who could perform the functions of the bourgeoisie in advanced capitalist nations. Those who had been the poor and the downtrodden serfs under the old despotic empires began to take their place in the factories as the laboring masses under these strong 'emergency' leaders. Their modernization will proceed as they lead a parallel existence to the modern proletariat of the capitalist nations.

The geography of poverty and starvation

As capitalism has advanced, civilization has raised the overall standard of living in the world, even for those at the lowest stratum of society. Nevertheless, there remain many people living in wretched conditions even in the prosperous capitalist nations.

We Japanese are ourselves very poor, or at any rate we think that our share of prosperity is too small relative to our great effort and performance. But in truth we cannot apply the term poverty to an advanced capitalist country like ours. The massive, decaying despotic empires left tremendous poverty in their wake. Presumably a major goal of the revolutions in that area was to improve living conditions, but in actuality this has not been much realized. In Japan we often use the term 'Asiatic level of low wages,' but anyone familiar with the true conditions in the bulk of Asia would never casually use this phrase in reference to Japan.

Starvation is the gravest and most tangible evidence of poverty. In Japan we complain of not having enough to eat, but our talk of 'starvation' is really symbolic. There are tens or perhaps hundreds of millions of people in this world who are vulnerable to actual starvation. Chronic malnutrition, laborers about to topple from hunger, the vast masses left behind by the general advance of civilization – these are major issues confronting our modern world.

The geography of railroads and airplanes

A widespread transportation network is essential to the rescue of victims of disasters such as floods and famines. An effective communications network that can relay current information on conditions in affected areas is also necessary. In many regions of the present world, this type of infrastructure is sorely lacking. There has been impressive progress in recent years, but measured in terms of kilometers of railroad per capita or per unit of area, it is still woefully insufficient. The construction of paved roads for automobiles is the best way to tide over this crisis for now.

The use of the airplane has brought a new phase of civilization to undeveloped areas. The sudden jump to a new phase differs from the gradual evolution of transportation in capitalist nations, where airplanes were simply the latest stage in the progression from horse carriages, to steam trains, to electric trains, to automobiles. In undeveloped areas the airplane sometimes makes a debut as the first stage of a new transportation network. The airplane has played a striking role in the development of inner Asia and South America.

However, the role played by airplanes in development raises concerns as to who has the power to use this mode of transportation. Naturally the same problem occurs with communications technology as well. With the advance of radio technology, for example, localities deep within undeveloped regions are for the first time coming into the sphere of world communication. But who has the wherewithal to use this capability?

The geography of aristocracy and commoners

Even within the capitalist nations, where airplanes or tele-communications do not represent a sudden leap in civilization, not all people have equal access to advanced technologies. It is the wealthy few who can freely use these facilities. I myself have yet to take a domestic flight within Japan, due to the expense. In the same way, or perhaps in a different way, the masses of people in the newly developing countries are not able to use the conveniences of modern civilization. For the time being access there is likely to be limited to the new leadership class – the equivalent of the bourgeoisie in capitalist nations – or to operators of their factories, or to those approved by them.

Traditional aristocratic systems have been abolished almost everywhere, in both capitalist and underdeveloped nations. Japan abolished its aristocracy after the Second World War. In both types of nations, however, a new type of aristocracy has grown out of the processes of their respective establishments.

As for 'commoners,' finding their proper place in society is one of the greatest questions faced by modern civilizations of all types. I think that the direction followed by Japan in recent years offers a positive example for the future of the rest of the world. The advanced capitalist nations as a whole are ahead of others in fostering a large middle class and placing it at the core of society; but in Japan this trend is especially apparent. As evidence consider the unparalleled development of large department stores patronized by ordinary people, and the absence of the custom of tipping. In Japan it is almost impossible to make overt class distinctions based on observable externals such as clothing or behavior.

The geography of family and supra-family

The progress of a civilization is not measured solely by improvements in the material standard of living. It also entails the freeing of individuals from the chains of various binding social strictures. But how are modern individuals liberated from the heavy burdens of old social systems?

In Japan, it appears that the end of the Second World War brought about a fundamental revolution the social system. One aspect of this revolution has been the decline of the '*ie*,' or household, system. The revised Civil Code abolished the succession of family headship, and removed the right of the eldest son to sole inheritance of property. Inheritance rights were guaranteed to all children. The extended family system that had endured for generations disappeared, replaced by a modern family structure consisting of a married couple and their children.

That is the case in theory, at least, although in practice the *ie* still exists in Japan. An *ie* is more than just a household or an extended family. The construct of the *ie* includes the enduring vertical connection between generations of ancestors and generations of descendants, the family crest, and the honor of the family name. Needless to say the attendant pressures on the individual member are considerable.

In Western Europe as well, primogeniture and the 'family system' existed until recently. It was only twenty or thirty years ago that Britain legally abolished its own family system. The existence of similar practices in Japan and Western Europe derives from the fact that both passed through a feudal stage of historical development.

In the areas which I have described above as following the second pattern of delayed, radical revolution, there was not an equivalent pressure exerted by a 'family system' lingering on as a relic of the feudal period. In China and the Islamic countries, for example, the common practice was to divide succession or equalize inheritance. In these regions, a modern-looking family system was in place long ago, whereas the countries that did pass through a feudal stage have only recently arrived at a 'modern' family system.

With regard to the liberation of individuals, the key obstacle in countries of the second pattern seems to lie outside the immediate family. The enduring feudal family systems typical of countries of the first pattern sustained family pressure for a long time, but they did dissolve most other types of blood relationship groupings. In the second region, however, we often find supra-familial groups unknown in the societies of the first zone. Across the straits, just one step away from Japan, we find a society where the clan-exogamic surname system functions. In other regions, deeply rooted caste or tribal systems restrict the behavior of individuals. These are such ingrained practices that they cannot be quickly abolished by a piece of legislation. But without doubt radical reforms of recent years will gradually displace these supra-familial constraints on the people of this region. It looks, however, to be a long and treacherous road.

The geography of working women

One of the major social transformations of this century is the remarkable rise in the status of women. Half of the human race consists of women, and yet this massive population has, almost without exception and throughout the world, occupied a lower status than the male half of the population. Now women are gradually gaining the same status as men in legal, economic, and social terms. All countries aspiring to modernize must surely include as part of their program a promise of improved status for women.

Progress towards equal status for women will be steady, but the realities of the situation will make for a long and difficult road. There are still vast numbers of women in the world who lack freedom of marriage or divorce. Many countries do not allow widows to remarry. If one were to color on a map the regions where polygamy is legal, one would be shocked at how widespread this practice is. But now the direction of change seems to be fixed. Doubts may linger as to whether the monogamous system common to civilized nations is indeed the best system for the human race. But at least it appears that all regions of the world have now begun to consider monogamy as the only acceptable practice for a civilized nation.

In Japan, it may have seemed to us that the liberation of women from their long dark history of oppression occurred in one fell swoop after the Second World War. But in terms of sudden liberation, the change in women's status in Russia and China was far more explosive and radical. In capitalist areas such as Western Europe, women's rights have gradually expanded since the feudal period as the result of a long series of reforms. Japan in fact followed this pattern.

The modern concept of women's liberation itself is a product of the advanced capitalist region. The feudal system applied strict, specialized regulations to the status of women within families. Yet at the same time a new type of family relationship, not unlike the relationship among modern citizens, was evolving within the commoner class formed under feudalism. When Commodore Perry arrived in Japan – the only Asian nation to pass through a true feudal period – he found that the status of married women in the mid-nineteenth century was unparalleled in other Eastern countries.

The early stages of capitalism relied heavily upon women in the labor force, namely, the female factory workers in the textile mills. The tragic histories of factory girls are inscribed upon the capitalist development of Japan, Western Europe, and the United States. As if in response to this hardship, movements for the expansion of women's rights advanced in parallel in each of these areas. However, the achievement of concrete political results in the form of women's suffrage took place at different times, depending upon the respective circumstances of each nation. Japan and Germany granted the vote to women some twenty years later than the United States.

Even in the advanced capitalist nations, there remain many unresolved issues regarding the social status of women. Despite dismal labor conditions, women have come forward to work within the capitalistic framework, thereby gradually raising their social status. The number of female factory workers in Japan and Western Europe is very high. There is also a spectacular advance in the number of women in civil service and in the entrepreneurial sector. It appears that the number of working women will continue to increase, and that the social status of women will rise further.

In Russia and China too, where communist revolutions have succeeded, the number of women laborers has dramatically increased, and their status has risen remarkably. Yet it seems that the problem of balancing family and work has not been completely solved.

The geography of schools and newspapers

One of the distinguishing features of Japanese and Western European societies is the wide distribution of education. In these areas, illiteracy is almost nil. The remarkable success of compulsory education has begun a veritable new chapter in the history of the human race, as the ambitions and abilities of the vast masses have been aroused. The spread of education was both a result of and one of the conditions for the advance of capitalism.

One result of widespread education is a high level of unity within a community or nation. Once the precondition of mass education has been met, mass communication can exercise its influence. There have been significant developments in journalism in Japan, Western Europe, and the United States which demonstrate that public opinion has begun to flex its might. Newspapers now play a major role as agents in the formulation and transmission of public opinion.

The role of mass communication is entirely different in Russia, China, India, and the Islamic nations. Radio is the major channel of mass communication, while print journalism is quite undeveloped. Radio is employed as an effective tool to convey the will of the rulers to the ruled, and for foreign propaganda. Public opinion is either very weak or does not exist at all. Yet somehow the leaders of these nations must listen to the voices of the voiceless people. I am not saying that democracy cannot be fostered in these areas. The methods and results, however, will inevitably be very different from nations with widespread education. This is reflected, for example, in how votes are cast and the meaning of these votes.

What is essential at this juncture is the rapid eradication of illiteracy. At the very least the huge population of illiterates must be taught how to read and write. This is a massive task requiring intensive effort and much time. It will be interesting to see what changes will occur in this world once education is actually extended to these people.

The geography of individuation and atrocities

I sometimes wonder if Japan and Western Europe tended to produce more individuated human beings even before the spread of modern education. Or perhaps one could say that in these countries, forces fostering the development of individuals, even amongst the further reaches of the commoners, were already at work before the modern period.

Some people believe that the Japanese have poor self-awareness as individuals. But when compared to the world as a whole it would be more accurate to say that, on the contrary, Japanese are a people with a marked streak of individualism. This is because the feudal system in Japan was initially built upon the self-conscious actions of individuals, and allowed for a certain degree of freedom of action by individuals.

In the region of the old despotic empires, still under the shadow of their legacy, individuals are much more lacking in individualism. Individuals exist within a collective mentality; or one could say that the value of each individual is low. As in the ancient Inca Empire, individuals are readily sacrificed to achieve a given goal. People's labor is conscripted for enormous constructions reminiscent of ancient Egypt. Time and again one sees phenomena that would be unthinkable in Western Europe or Japan, such as large scale bloody purges, long term internment of prisoners of war, or the tactics of the human wave.

I do not mean to suggest that crimes against humanity are the monopoly of the region of former despotic empires. Certainly there have been repeated atrocities in Japan and in Western Europe. But it must be noted that in the latter areas, most atrocities have been directed at other, or outside, peoples. Further study may show that the ethnically uniform nations that grew out of feudalism have a strong tendency to discriminate against other ethnic groups, alongside the value they place upon their own individuals.

It is important to conduct further research into the nature of atrocities. Merely depicting and deploring such harrowing events is not enough. An objective study of the nature, circumstances, and participating parties to such acts will guide us towards an analytic framework.

The geography of jealous gods

Much as human beings vary by region, the temperament of deities seems to differ significantly from place to place throughout the world.

In an earlier, less globally connected era, the deity of a given locality existed in a self-contained system, whether monotheistic or polytheistic. In such self-contained systems, fundamentally, deities do not tolerate deities of other systems. But nowadays, as we look around the world, it appears that there are significant variations in the degree of tolerance shown by local deities towards other deities. The usual approach to comparative religion is to consider the major faiths of the world, such as Buddhism, Christianity, or Islam, in their separateness. However, in order to incorporate the meaning of religion into a theory of civilization, it is necessary to move away from this kind of genealogical classification. I believe that a functional analysis of the present day roles played by the deities of various locations will be much more useful.

To take one example, consider the great variations in social function within the single religion of Buddhism. The degree to which Buddhism dominates Burmese or Thai society bears no comparison to its much lighter role in Japan. This is due to more than just the sectarian differences between the Theravada Buddhism of the former and the Mahayana Buddhism of the latter. In Mongolia people also follow Mahayana Buddhism, but in practice it is far more exclusionary than in Japan. These kinds of differences can be seen within Christianity as well. Has not the God of Britain, Germany, France, and America shed much of the jealousy still shown by the God of Poland and Hungary?

Unfortunately, jealous gods can produce lamentable tragedies, as we saw during the vicious sectarian violence between Hindus and Moslems at the time of the partition of India and Pakistan.

It is difficult to explain this variation in the temperament of the gods, but I think it is related to the fact that in Zone One, that is, Japan and Western Europe, the division between sacred and secular powers occurred early on. In Zone Two, that of the old despotic empires, the leaders of the spiritual world were for many centuries also the leaders of the secular world. The Czar of the Russian Empire acted as the head of the Russian Orthodox Church, while the Sultan of the Turkish Empire was also the head of the Islamic faith.

Perhaps it is not too much to say that even after the collapse of the despotic empires, the characteristic temperament of their local gods remained. Consider the speed and strength with which new 'spiritual' principles, such as communism, have unified the various countries of Zone Two. Consider too the new high priests of these countries, with their insistence on melding the secular and sacred worlds into one.

The geography of bureaucrats and bureaucratism

The current era might be called the 'age of bureaucrats' throughout the world, be it in Western Europe, Japan, the United States, the Soviet Union, China, or the newly developing Asian nations. Some of these nations already have a strong bureaucratic system, while others are rapidly putting one into place.

In all regions the origins of bureaucracy extend far back in history. In Japan and Western Europe, complex bureaucratic systems existed prior to the revolutions. In these areas the development of a modern bureaucratic system dates back to the end of the early feudal period and the expansion of the monarchy. This led to the formation of a bureaucratic class within absolutist governments such as the Bourbon monarchy in France and the Tokugawa shogunate in Japan. However, in these examples the provincial regions remained under the control of feudal lords. Once revolution brought about national unification through the elimination of these feudal vestiges, the bureaucrats of the central government could directly govern the entire nation. This condition was absolutely essential for the modern nation-state to secure its place among the great powers of the world. This process occurred in synchrony with the monopolistic concentration of capital.

Bureaucracies are often plagued by bureaucratism, an evil that inevitably accompanies the excessive concentration of power. When officialism runs rampant, the creative abilities of the individual are stifled the instant he is admitted into the administrative establishment.

The concentration of power and wealth has gone too far in Japan and Western Europe. This is a time when efficiency must be attained by a new decentralization.

The situation is different in Russia, China, India, and the Islamic nations. There, the historical purpose of the bureaucratic system was to serve the ancient despotic empires, as for example the mandarins of Imperial China. The corruption and collapse of these empires brought about a decentralization of power. The successful establishment of new governments is contingent upon the re-concentration of power. Meanwhile the rising tide of nationalism also drives the trend towards strengthening national bureaucracies. We can expect that powerful bureaucratic systems will continue to grow in this region.

It would seem that neither First nor Second Zone countries have discovered an effective way to prevent their bureaucracies from becoming mired in bureaucratism. The human race is capable of producing talented individuals, but less skilled in the area of fully harnessing such talent.

An undistorted picture of the world

Despite the vast variety and diversity of human life on this planet, I do not think of it as a chaotic or disorderly place. Day by day occurrences may seem random or surprising to us, but I believe that closer consideration may actually reveal the laws that govern the evolution of human civilization.

There is a trend toward the unification of the world, but this has not actually been achieved. We are each attached to one particular fragment of land among the many around the globe. We cannot escape from this land, but we should at least be able to overcome the bonds of our local attachment to ponder the issues confronting the entire earth. Only by placing our own problems within the context of global history can we picture the earth without distortion.

As I continue my attempt to formulate a comparative theory of civilizations, there are many important issues still to discuss, such as the distribution of resources and populations, of races and tribes, and of health and disease. Regrettably, I must leave these for another occasion.

(February 1957)

5 Japan in Ecological History

Commentary on Chapter 5

The Institute for the Science of Thought (Shisō no Kagaku Kenkyūkai) customarily holds a symposium on a designated topic at its annual meeting. In the summer of 1957 I was invited to speak at the symposium on the topic of 'Japan in Ecological History' (Seitaishikan kara mita Nihon). [1]

Afterwards, I was sent a transcript of my talk so that I could review it for publication in the *Shisō no Kagaku Kenkyūkai kaihō* (Bulletin of the Institute for the Science of Thought). Unfortunately, that autumn I was pressed with preparations for my research trip to Southeast Asia and had no time to edit the text. I took the transcript with me to Thailand, and the text of my talk was not published.

Fortunately, the transcript remained, and I am including it in this volume with permission from the Institute for the Science of Thought.

1

I understand that the overall topic of this symposium is 'Perceptions of Contemporary Japan.' I have been asked to speak on 'Japan in Ecological History.' It has been difficult to organize the many ideas I have about what to say today. Although I sought the advice of several colleagues in Kyoto, and continued to discuss this on the train to Tokyo, my thoughts have remained unsettled. Even now I feel apprehensive.

There are several reasons for my apprehension, beginning with the title of the talk. 'Japan in Ecological History' seemed a reasonable topic at first, so I readily agreed to speak about it. Upon further reflection, however, I felt uneasy, because the nature of my own conceptual method is rather difficult to adapt to this title.

Thus I have decided to digress somewhat from the given topic in order to focus on and analyze the uneasiness that this title has given me. My talk today may not be a straightforward discussion of the ecological approach to history. Instead, I would like to use the time to reflect upon what has happened since I began presenting my theories on ecological history last year.

When I speak here of 'an ecological view of history,' I am of course referring directly to 'An Introduction to an Ecological View of History: Japanese Civilization in the World Context,' the essay I published in *Chūō Kōron* about six months ago. That was an overall exposition of my theory. A more specific development of this theory was presented in 'A New World Map of Civilization,' which was published in two installments in *Nihon Dokusho Shinbun*. As many of you have already read these essays, I will merely offer a summary here, rather than a detailed account.

My contention is that we can divide the Old World – that is, Asia, Europe, and North Africa – into two clearly distinct models, based on their present condition as well as on the historical processes leading up to the present. I have called these two areas 'Zone One' and 'Zone Two.'

Zone One comprises Japan and the Western European nations. Although these areas are distant from one another, I classified them together based on the similarities of their present civilizations and the dynamics of their historical development until now.

Zone Two consists of all the remaining areas of the Old World. There are four major blocs within Zone Two: the Chinese world, the Indian world, the Islamic world, and the Russian world. These four worlds have many aspects in common.

In the two essays I mentioned, I tried to impose some conceptual order upon the global history of the Old World, in the form of the mutual give and take between Zone One and Zone Two. Moreover, I explained from an ecological viewpoint why the differences between the two zones arose. For further details, please refer to those essays.

2

To be sure, I expected a certain amount of reaction when I introduced my theories. It is natural that criticism will ensue whenever new ideas are presented.

There has indeed been quite a lot of repercussion. My theories were featured as new ideas in many newspapers and magazines, and I received various criticisms. I was invited to lecture and to participate in discussions as well. Indeed, my presence here today is the result of yet another reaction radiating from the presentation of my theories.

However, when I look back at the substance of the responses to my work, it was quite different from what I had initially expected. I had anticipated two types of criticisms, as to my theories and as to my facts. First I imagined people would question the suitability of my proposed theory for understanding the geography and history of the world. These would be critiques of my scholarly methodology and of the formulation of theory. Secondly, I expected questions about my facts and specifics, for example, whether India and the Islamic region were really as I had described. I feared the discovery of factual mistakes or biases. I even prepared replies to the anticipated criticisms.

However, when the lid was opened, the kinds of reactions that came flowing out were quite different from what I had anticipated. There were some along the lines mentioned above, but most were quite unexpected. Many readers somehow saw my ecological history approach as an attempt at a 'theory of Japan' and responded in those terms. Apparently for these people Japan's position in the world is the paramount issue, and they found one answer in my ecological history theory. To put it bluntly, their mindset consists of ranking the world's nations as if in a military organization, and their interest was in fixing Japan's place in this ranking. In my ecological history approach, Japan 'ranked' very highly, so it was of interest to these people, or perhaps not of interest. Many of the responses I received were of this nature. Typically the discussion would then proceed to whether Japan was a less developed country or a developed country.

However, my intention was not to propose a 'theory of Japan.' As I expounded my ideas on ecological history, I did of course give some prominence to Japan, but that was merely to use Japan as a readily available source of material. My theory was intended to cover the world, or at least the Old World, in its entirety. Thus, if the ecological view of history is a 'theory of Japan,' then it must also be a theory of India, a theory of the Islamic world, and a theory of Western Europe. I was not theorizing only about Japan, and I was frankly disappointed to see that the reactions focused so heavily on Japan. It was perhaps natural that I felt discouraged at the lack of serious criticism of my overall structural theory in which I took the most pride.

Up until this point I had not had much contact with Japanese intellectuals and was not familiar with their typical problematics. I was amazed by their depth of concern and intensity of feeling for Japan. These Japanese intellectuals were utterly caught up in their thoughts of Japan, or perhaps to be more straightforward, they had an utter lack of interest in the rest of the world. Whenever the subject was another country they did not display much curiosity. They became excited only when some other country was compared to Japan, or when Japan was the direct subject. This tendency to place oneself at the center, no matter what the topic, seemed incredibly narcissistic to me.

Actually, this is deeply related to my disquiet with today's topic. The title given to me was 'Japan in Ecological History,' but I have not placed my focus solely on Japan. Yet I must respond to the demands of these intellectuals; and the dejection I feel at having to do so makes my spirit uneasy.

3

Let me make clear that I do not disapprove of interest in Japan. On the contrary, I myself have a deep interest in Japan, but the scope of my interests is not limited to my country.

Since I first presented my ecological view of history, many people have asked how I came to develop my ideas. One of the reasons of course is that my initial field of specialization was ecology. Also, my first work as a researcher was in the arid regions, and in ecological history the arid regions are of great theoretical importance. But perhaps the major factor leading me to my ideas was that I am a Japanese.

The fact is that Europeans and Americans are shockingly ignorant about Japan. As a result, they believe the myth that European civilization is the paramount civilization of the human race. They have developed a linear theory of developmental stages, with European civilization at the pinnacle of progress, and have placed the other countries of the world along this line of development. Meanwhile, the majority of Asian and African scholars reject this scheme as a rationale for European dominance, and yet they do not differ much from Europeans in their belief in the myth of a superior European civilization. It is typical that they too know hardly anything about Japan or Japanese civilization. In such circumstances it was hardly likely that anyone would have proposed something like my ecological view of history, with its emphasis on the parallel evolution of civilizations. It is necessary to have a thorough familiarity with Japan's particular characteristics in order to conceive of such a theory.

This does not mean that all Japanese think about history from an ecological viewpoint. Indeed, there are many intellectuals who are doubtful or critical of ecological history. Perhaps in the past this was only natural. During the Meiji (1868–1912) and Taishō (1912–1926) periods, the gap between Japan and Europe or America seemed obvious. Drawing from this experience it was inevitable that the paradigm of linear progression from undeveloped to developed nations would be accepted as the most fitting, rather than a model of parallel evolution. But now a generational shift in perspective seems to be at work. The parallel evolution model, which is implicit in my ecological approach to history, may be more popular among the generation who came of age during the Pacific War, who do not see Japan as undeveloped relative to Europe.

This new generation of intellectuals differs from their Meiji and Taishō predecessors even more greatly as regards the regions discussed in their theories. Traditionally, Japanese intellectuals developed their ideas by comparing Japan to Europe. The great expanse of the Asian continent was not in their field of vision. In contrast, the ecological view of history takes as its starting point the observation of Asian countries. This is the result of the various opportunities I have had, dating back to the prewar period, to travel to Asian countries. It is also evidence of the rapid deepening of relationships between Japan and Asian nations both during the Pacific War and afterwards.

As I have said, Japan is mentioned quite a bit in my ecological history, but this is simply a way to provide a well known point of comparison for us when discussing Asia; not unlike the function of a control group in scientific experiments. From the beginning, the purpose of the ecological approach to history was to understand not Japan, but various Asian areas other than Japan. To put it another way, my ecological approach to history was born as I began to detach my concerns from Japan, or perhaps as I freed myself from Japanese nationalism. The crucial factor that allowed this intellectual separation to occur was of course the changes in the postwar world that brought me the opportunity, ten years after the war, to visit and directly observe these Asian countries.

4

After discussing today's topic on the train to Tokyo with my colleagues, there remains one point on which I feel unresolved. All of my close colleagues urged me to try putting theory into practice at today's session. The ecological history of the Old World describes the present structure of the world and posits the processes which led to it. But it does not deal with how we ought to proceed in the here-and-now, under Japan's present circumstances. These are the issues my colleagues thought I should address.

If you have read 'An Ecological View of History' you already know that it is not a discussion of what we 'ought' to do. It is a statement about global structure and my theory of the formulation of that structure; it is not a judgement of the current situation or a prescription for reform. I have discussed the *Sein*, or what is, not the *Sollen*, or what ought to be. No matter how hard one tries one cannot transform my essay into a prescriptive statement of what ought to be done.

Indeed, I think that I was able to come up with the idea of ecological history precisely because I did not concern myself with what ought to be done. It is not that I lack an interest in putting theory into practice or discussing what ought to be. But I do think that it is important to keep the issues of 'is' and 'ought' distinct. Therefore, despite my colleagues' recommendation, I have no intention of speaking prescriptively today.

And yet, since I introduced 'An Ecological View of History,' many of the reactions to it have been about what ought to be. Many people read my work as if it were a prescriptive proposal. Then they either asked what ought to be done, or else drew their own conclusions about what I meant, and criticized my work accordingly. But I have not put any statements about what ought to be done in my ecological approach to history.

This stress on the *Sollen* over the *Sein* was the second aspect of the reactions to my work that caused me great surprise. I was nonplussed by this inclination of Japanese intellectuals, having had no idea until then that they felt so strongly about putting theory into practice. My belief had been that a sound theory can be established only when the self lets go of the attachment to practice. Upon closer consideration, I realized that the arguments in the Japanese press are nearly all assertions as to what should be, based on a belief in the importance of practice. I had been mistaken in my understanding of the role of discourse and theory in Japanese life: in fact they usually give guidance as to what ought to be done.

I consider concepts such as the ecological view of history to be a product of intellectual curiosity more than anything else. I had not predicted that my idea would be taken as a guide to putting theory into practice. It was quite unexpected that the theory of ecological history was immediately engulfed in the wave of the theory of practice.

5

Once I realized that Japanese intellectuals have a greater interest in practice than in theory, it was that phenomenon itself which most intrigued me. I would like today's talk to be an inquiry into the reasons for the primacy of practice over theory among intellectuals in Japan.

What I mean by the term intellectuals is the cultured intelligentsia of Japan: that class of people who are loyal readers of the monthly review magazines, and who have a strong interest in politics. They have a particular interest in Japan's politics, without exhibiting much enthusiasm for international affairs. Here, let me reiterate the intense and exclusive attachment to Japan that I noticed among many of the respondents to my theory of ecological history. It occurs to me now that this devotion to Japan is actually a fixation on Japanese politics. Even when the subject seems to be about Japan in general, the discussion is somehow always linked, either explicitly or implicitly, to how Japanese politics ought to be carried out rather than to Japan's actual situation. Often the individual intellectual speaks as if he himself shoulders responsibility for the politics of all Japan.

I think that Japanese intellectuals, as a class, occupy a position very close to that of Japanese politicians. It may even be that politicians and intellectuals are branches from the same tree. At the very least, the standards by which they measure life and society are the same. Simply put, they all believe that engaging in politics is the most valued activity in life, and that governance of the people is the most important issue in society. They insist on judging all things from the standpoint of political practice.

Taking this perspective a step further, I think that the mainstream of the Japanese intelligentsia consists of people who would have been politicians if they had had the chance. Their innate personalities had strong political tendencies from the start, but circumstances did not allow them to gain political office. That is, they are politicians *manqués*.

Thus there are many people who could or would move laterally to become politicians if circumstances allowed. One finds them not only within the civil service, but also in the press and in education. Eminent persons who are prepared to take political power exist everywhere. No doubt you are well aware of several recent cases of successful lateral moves of this type. Japan has an abundance of potential cabinet ministers. Setting aside the question of whether most of these people truly want to take office, at the very least the aspiration to political power forms the basic theoretical construct for their statements.

The great majority of intellectuals, however, will never be able to make the lateral move into politics, and they lack the opportunity to exercise political power. Nevertheless they maintain the mindset of a politician. Although they are not actually involved in the work of governing the populace, their thinking is always as if they were. Since they never get a chance to govern, they become filled with frustration. It seems to me that the political lectures of the present day intelligentsia – if I may be excused for expressing it in such a contentious manner – are expressions of frustration. The intellectuals who lecture us on political topics are not unlike those less-than-great baseball players who retire to become baseball commentators, or else perhaps those retired *sumō* wrestlers who once upon a time aspired to become grand champion, only to end up as commentators.

6

The tendency among Japanese intellectuals to think and talk like would-be politicians is no doubt a heritage from pre-modern times. The prototype for this group was the samurai warrior class of the Edo period (1600–1868).

The warrior class, at least towards the later part of the pre-modern period, was made up of career military men in the standing army who in actual practice served as bureaucrats. Their awareness of their importance as statesmen was the foundation of their consciousness. They were always in a position of administering political power from above – even if only in a small way – hence their focus on practical implementation. In addition, they were clearly a highly cultivated class of intellectuals. Thus the work of the intellectual and the work of the political practitioner were consolidated in the warrior class.

The education received by members of the warrior class, which supported their position as intellectuals and rulers, was very practically oriented. Everything they learned was understood to relate to the political ideal of statecraft. Nowadays we speak of 'politically connected businessmen' (*seishō*) to describe those who operate on the boundary of politics and business. Similarly, scholars in the Edo period might be called 'politically connected scholars' (*seigaku*) in the sense that their concern was always about how to combine politics with learning. I think that most present day Japanese intellectuals have inherited this tradition of deeply intertwined scholarship and politics. Areas of scholarship that lack practical applications elicit very slight interest or understanding.

The various perspectives of scholar, statesman, and warrior that had been consolidated in the person of the pre-modern samurai, have in modern times been fragmented. First the role of the warrior class as professional military men was eliminated; then there were the difficulties of maintaining a dual status as politician and man of culture. It is clear enough that the social function of 'men of culture' has been inherited by present day intellectuals. The consciousness of modern intellectuals retains the residue of the self-importance of the warrior-scholar-statesmen of an earlier era. And yet modern intellectuals lack any political or military role. Herein lies the source of perpetual frustration, the curse of the modern Japanese intellectual.

7

I do not think that it is only Japanese intellectuals who exhibit this trait of frustration. Drawing upon my admittedly fragmentary knowledge of other countries, it seems that France is very much like Japan. There are many highly educated people who form a cultured intelligentsia, and their consciousness tends strongly towards the practical and political. Jean Paul Sartre could be seen as a representative example of this tendency. He and his peers are constantly thinking of political activity as regards how politics and society 'ought' to be. They treat as their own the same issues with which statesmen are concerned. Yet, the probability of them having a turn at governing the country is nil. Under these circumstances, their major energy goes into political debate. It seems to me that there are many such characteristics common to Japanese and French intellectuals, allowing for wide areas of mutual sympathy. I imagine that the case in Germany is also similar.

I gather that the situation is quite different in nations such as China, India, the Soviet Union, and the Arab and Southeast Asian regions. In those countries the intellectuals are also the political leaders. My impression is that there are hardly any intellectuals who are not directly involved in the political power structure. In these figures, the roles of political practitioner and intellectual are consolidated. Indeed, it is because they are well educated that they are political beings. Accordingly, in these places one does not see the phenomenon of politically aware persons knocking about like loose cannon, feeling frustrated at being cut off from political power. Yet neither does free political discussion typically occur in these countries. One reason is of course the strong control of expression practiced by many of the governments. But I think that another reason may stem from the role of intellectuals.

This difference in the position of intellectuals, and the effect on free expression, appears to me to correspond to the difference between the Zone One and Zone Two regions as described in 'An Ecological View of History.' In Zone One, to which Japan and the Western European nations belong, there is a split between political consciousness and political practice. That is, there are many intellectuals who are not political practitioners but whose political consciousness is well developed. In contrast, in the countries of Zone Two, political consciousness and practice are unified in the figure of the intellectual. Those intellectuals with the consciousness of a politician are in fact practicing politicians.

8

The difference in the situation of intellectuals between the first and second Zones is apparent in the current world, but it seems to me that it was not always so. For example, in the early Meiji period in Japan, I think that the split between statesmen and intellectuals was not so definitive. The intellectuals of the period were not frustrated and cut off. The circumstances then were similar to those of the newly developing Zone Two countries nowadays.

What has changed since then to cause the appearance of so many intellectuals inflamed with political awareness, yet alienated from political practice? I believe one change was the widespread dissemination of education, which was a cornerstone of modern Japanese civilization from the Meiji period onward. As I have mentioned above, politics and learning had been unified during the Edo period. Higher education was offered to a set class within the general population – those eligible to perform as statesmen. Thus there was no chance for a split between statesmen and intellectuals to occur. However, the spread of universal education starting in the Meiji period meant the mass production of intellectuals well beyond the numbers required to fill the ranks of statesmen. This inevitably resulted in a gap between practicing statesmen and those who were imbued with a statesman's consciousness but devoid of political power. The latter evolved into frustrated intellectuals whose chief role is the pursuit of political debate.

Another origin of the split between politicians and intellectuals was the fact that, as Japan industrialized and modernized, the traditional study of statecraft became less and less a practical field of training for politicians. The formerly central link between politics and the academy lost its importance in favor of the link between politics and business or industry. Later still, the link between politics and technology also became extremely important. Unfortunately, business and technology were areas of ignorance for intellectuals educated in the tradition of culture and statecraft. The leadership of modern society shifted to those whom we might call 'business intellectuals' and 'technological intellectuals' – in short, the beginnings of a technocracy. As a result, alienation and frustration increased among those intellectuals who were the bearers of culture and statecraft.

In this sense it could be said that the appearance of this kind of disenfranchised intellectual – bearing the consciousness of a statesman, yet separate from, and sometimes in opposition to, the state – is a corollary to the development of industrial society. This characteristic of industrial development appears in most of the Zone One region, including Japan, France, and Germany. The circumstances in Britain may have been somewhat different, perhaps because of the greater requirement for educated personnel to rule its vast colonial empire. It seems that the alienation of the class of non-statesman intellectuals did not progress very far there; but perhaps a separate consideration of this point is necessary.

To summarize the position of modern intellectuals in the context of the history of civilization, they can be viewed as a type of non-adaptive group created by the development of highly industrialized modern societies. They constitute a kind of backward region within modern society: while their statements usually take a progressive or radical form, their actual function is more often like a braking mechanism on the progress of civilization. This group actually performs a conservative, or in some cases a reactionary, role. This is not necessarily a negative force. Their role is to apply appropriate brakes to the potential for reckless speeding contained within modern civilized society. An automobile without brakes is the very embodiment of danger.

Is it too optimistic to say that we who live in the Zone One region can feel secure because our nations have created a stratum of intellectuals that can function effectively as a braking mechanism? In any case, I feel safe in forecasting that a similar intellectual class will be fostered in the countries of Zone Two, as higher education spreads and industrialization progresses.

This discussion was the result of my reflections on the characteristics of Japanese intellectuals, based on reactions to my ecological view of history, and my attempts to understand them in the context of the history of civilization. Perhaps an expansion of these thoughts could lead to a comparative theory of intellectuals, as part of a general development of applied ecological history; or perhaps to a comparative theory of education. I will leave that discussion for another occasion.

Although the content of my talk has strayed from the given topic, 'Japan in Ecological History,' I would hope that I have discharged my responsibility for today.

(July 1957)

6 Travels in Southeast Asia: An Ecological View of History, Continued

Commentary on Chapter 6

From November of 1957 through April of 1958 I traveled in Southeast Asia as the leader of a six-member scientific study team sponsored by my employer, Osaka City University. We took three jeeps with us from Japan to our starting point in Thailand and were able to see quite a lot of continental Southeast Asia, visiting Thailand, Cambodia, Vietnam, Laos, and part of Malaya.

My travelogue about Vietnam and Laos was published by Chūō Kōron Publishers as Volume 8 of their 'World travels' series (*Sekai no tabi*). [1] Later, I wrote about the entire trip in 'Southeast Asia travelogue' (*Tōnan Ajia kikō*). [2] Iwanami Shashin Bunko, a photographic series, put out two compilations of photographs under the titles 'Thailand' (*Tai*) [3] and 'Travels in Indochina' (*Indoshina no tabi*). [4] The investigations of our study team, which focused on the biology and anthropology of the region, were described in three volumes published in English. [5]

My particular eagerness to study this region grew from a desire to expand my concept of a comparative theory of civilization. I wanted to establish the position of Southeast Asia within the scheme that I had begun to formulate during my previous trip to the Asian continent in 1955.

The following essay, 'Travels in Southeast Asia' (Tōnan Ajia no tabi kara), [6] was written upon my return from Southeast Asia, and was published in the August 1958 issue of *ChūōKōron*. For inclusion in this collection, I have added the subtitle 'An Ecological View of History, Continued' (Bunmei no seitaishikan: tsuzuki) to better reflect its significance. My observations in Southeast Asia prompted me to modify the view of world structure that I had presented in my earlier article 'An Ecological View of History: Japanese Civilization in the World Context' (Chapter 3 in this volume).

What do we know about Southeast Asia?

In the past few years there has been a marked increase in the appearance of the term 'Southeast Asia' in the Japanese press. One gets the sense of an emerging public awareness of the importance of this region. But how exactly is Southeast Asia significant, and indeed, what kind of place is it? What is the particular significance of the region for us as Japanese, and what are our perceptions?

It is well to ask whether we Japanese in fact have any perception of Southeast Asia at all. Actually, we hardly know anything about this region. I am ashamed to admit that my own knowledge prior to my trip was quite scanty, and I know that I am not the only one with such a shockingly low level of awareness. Several highly educated intellectuals asked me whether Thailand was the same as Siam.

I do not necessarily believe in the usefulness of accumulating trivia about every topic under the sun, but it seems to me that we should at the very least be familiar with the names of the countries of Southeast Asia. Not many of us would be able to list them correctly, and naming the capitals would be more difficult yet. As for recognizing national flags – even those of countries involved in recent upheavals – we would fail abysmally. Sadly, the flags of Thailand and Cambodia were hardly ever flown at the recent Asian Games; and Laos did not even send a team. How many Japanese could recognize the Laotian flag?

Unfortunately this ignorance does not seem to stop us from holding plenty of opinions. We blithely discuss the topic regardless of whether the ideas we express are our own or secondhand wisdom. Of course, everyone has pretty much the same opinion, favoring friendly and amicable relations. No one is spoiling for a fight. It is all well and good to have this consensus in favor of friendship and amity with Southeast Asia, but we are vague on the specifics of how to be friendly, and with which nations. Since the discussion is not based on knowledge, it is no more than a gut feeling. There is no theoretical or analytical foundation to support the promotion of friendship and amity.

Southeast Asia is not truly terra incognita for the Japanese. Hundreds of thousands of us had direct personal experiences in the area during the Second World War. This only makes the prevailing state of ignorance nowadays all the more disappointing. It serves as an acute reminder that soldiers lack an aptitude for gathering knowledge.

Inadequate sources of information

In recent years several major political events have occurred in Southeast Asia, including a coup d'état in Thailand, civil war in Indonesia, and reparations negotiations with Vietnam. The press coverage of these events was minimal and the commentary was rudimentary. These Southeast Asian events never became a hot topic of discourse among Japanese intellectuals, nor did they rouse lively interest among the public. Contrast this to the vivid coverage of similar events in places farther away from Japan, such as Hungary and Algeria.

This disparity could be explained in many ways, but whatever the reason, I believe that it is wrong for Japanese to view the problems of Hungary or Algeria as central to the flow of world history, while regarding events in Thailand or Indonesia as local phenomena. The upheavals in Hungary and Algeria are of course world issues, with particular import for Europe. In just the same way, the incidents in Thailand and Indonesia are world events, with particular import for Asia. My objection is that when we Japanese view world events, we tend to be pulled into a Euro-centric viewpoint.

As I have mentioned, our ignorance of Southeast Asia means that our opinions and vague feelings of goodwill lack grounding. Our inability to go beyond abstract, general discussion is quite disturbing. Our lack of knowledge about Southeast Asia stems from, among other things, the absence of information sources. For example, although Bangkok is considered the most important city in the region, no Japanese newspaper has a correspondent there. To me this defies comprehension: how serious can we possibly be in our contention that Southeast Asia is important? Even when events there are reported, it is difficult for us to grasp their significance. A regular daily flow of information is necessary to understand the context of the region. It seems to me that the flow of information from Europe and the Middle East meets this standard much better.

Furthermore, it has been my experience that there are almost no books available in the Japanese language for anyone hoping to do research on Southeast Asia. There are plenty of books by foreigners, and it is possible to find some volumes on economics in Japanese; but there is almost nothing on general topics. One must resort to scouring the used bookstores for works written during the Second World War. This is a striking contrast to the many volumes on the Middle East and Eastern Europe, not to mention the legion of works on Western Europe and the United States.

And yet, as I have mentioned, many Japanese intellectuals feel free to discourse at length on the problems of Southeast Asia, despite our woeful ignorance of the region. What does this signify? Most of the so-called cultured people who travel abroad choose to go to the United States or Europe. Their knowledge of Southeast Asia is limited to an impression of unbearable heat at the Bangkok airport. If Southeast Asia is indeed important to Japan, why is it that more of us do not go there, or why are we not encouraged to go?

I heard that the Ministry of Foreign Affairs was planning to create a post for a 'cultural diplomat' to represent Japanese culture abroad. I thought this was a positive step, and was pleased that Southeast Asia was initially proposed as the destination. Unfortunately this plan was rejected in favor of sending the diplomat to Paris. Is our treatment of Southeast Asia no more than empty fanfare?

Despite the ignorance of Southeast Asia that I shared with my fellow Japanese, I eagerly set out on my journey to the region.

Travels in Southeast Asia

My travels in Southeast Asia lasted for five months, from November 1957 to April 1958. Southeast Asia includes many countries: Burma, Thailand, Malaya, Indonesia, Laos, Cambodia, Vietnam, and the Philippines, just to list the independent nations. There are also the territories of Singapore, Sarawak, and North Borneo, among others.

It would have been impossible to see all of these countries during one trip. Once we arrived there we traveled overland in jeeps, without using air transport. I visited the four countries of Thailand, Cambodia, Vietnam, and Laos. On the ship voyage home, I stopped over in Singapore and Penang.

It may be presumptuous to make statements based on the limited experiences of my trip, but even so, I was pleased to gain a great deal of new information which led me to consider the various issues described below. My quest for knowledge also led me to many interesting experiences, but I will save the description of those for a later opportunity. Here I will present the ideas that occurred as I made my observations. I was especially concerned to analyze, firstly, the particular position of Southeast Asia within the broader history of Asian civilization; secondly, the difference between the position of Southeast Asia and that of Japan; and finally, the relationship between Southeast Asia and Japan.

The concept of Asia

I would like to begin by discussing the concept of Asia as a whole. I often encounter Europeans whose lack of knowledge about Asia astounds me. They confuse things from Japan, Korea, and China; and that is often the least of their mistakes. Perhaps the term 'Orient' is conducive to confusion, as it includes the entire region from Turkey to India to Mongolia to Japan. It is true that from the vantage point of Europe, all this territory lies to the east, but the concept of 'the Orient' is a passive one, simply meaning 'not the Occident.' Furthermore, the term Orient has given rise to misconceptions as the meaning has evolved over time. Initially, it referred to the eastern part of the Mediterranean: the region including Turkey, Syria, and Mesopotamia. From a Japanese viewpoint this is certainly not the East, but rather the far western area. I find it impossible to think of Japan and Lebanon as belonging to the same 'Oriental' region. There are some people, such as the Association for Oriental Studies ('Oriento Gakkai' in Japanese, also known in English as the Association for Middle Eastern Studies) led by Prince Mikasa, who use the term Orient correctly: as a proper noun denoting a specific, limited area. They do not use it to refer to the East or the Eastern region in general.

As Japanese, however, we should not be too quick to disparage the Europeans, as most of us are also guilty of indiscriminate use of the concept of the Orient. In our case as well, this is a mistake born of ignorance. Historically, of course we did not think of the entire expanse from the Islamic countries to Japan as one region sharing similar features. Once upon a time, our idea of faraway lands was defined by the word '*karatenjiku,*' that is, Cathay and India. But at some point our perspective shifted and we began to use terms like 'Orient' and 'Oriental.' I cannot offer historical evidence, but I suspect that we adopted this meaning of the Orient from the European concept. If so, then we are in the ironic position of looking at our own part of the world, the so-called Orient, with a borrowed European mindset.

Even if we use the word 'Asia' instead of 'Orient,' similar issues arise. After all, who created the idea of the Asian continent? 'Asia' is inadequate even as a simple geographical designation, since it merely names the portion of the Eurasian continent that excludes Europe. Were we to blindly follow suit, letting our use of the term lead us to a sincere belief that 'Asia is one,' either historically or culturally, it would be evidence of sloppy reasoning and startling ignorance.

Zone One and Zone Two

It should be clear by now that we cannot think of Asia as a single entity or a homogeneous space. I would like to reconsider, in a more analytic fashion, what actually constitutes that place we call 'Asia.' The outline of an answer can be found in my earlier essay 'An Introduction to an Ecological View of History: Japanese Civilization in the World Context.' The basic thesis that I presented there was as follows.

First, I posited that categories such as Orient and Occident are meaningless. These categories were a form of genealogical classification, based upon the historical paths of cultural propagation in various regions. I chose instead to consider the question from the standpoint of functionalism, based on the design and mode of daily life of communities or regions. Seen in this way, all of the Old World (that is, Asia, Europe, and North Africa) could be divided into two categories: Zone One, comprising Japan and Western Europe, and Zone Two, the entire mass that lies between these two peripheral areas of Zone One.

The peoples of Zone One originated historically as groups of 'barbarians,' or those outside the sphere of civilization. After absorbing civilization from Zone Two centers, these populations passed through stages of feudalism, absolutism, and bourgeois revolution. In the contemporary world, the nations of Zone One have achieved a high level of modern civilization, built upon a capitalist foundation. As for Zone Two, it was host to all of the major civilizations of antiquity. However, instead of a feudal period, the regions of Zone Two saw the development of vast despotic empires, which were

Figure 6.1: Diagram of Zone One and Zone Two Regions

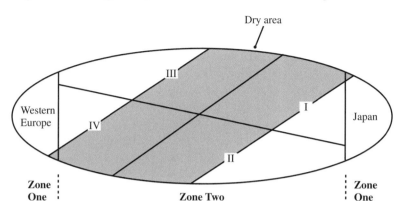

riven by internal contradictions. Many areas of Zone Two eventually became colonies or quasi-colonies of Zone One countries. In recent years, the nations of Zone Two have experienced a series of revolutions, and are at last attempting to follow a path toward a new kind of modernization.

A schematic representation of my theory (not presented in my earlier essay) can be seen in Figure 6.1. The Old World as a whole is encompassed by a horizontal ellipse. If one draws vertical lines just to the inside of each edge, the areas at the outside extremes make up Zone One, while the bulk of the oval between the two verticals is Zone Two. The peripheral areas of Zone One, namely Japan and Western Europe, happen to have followed very similar courses of historical evolution. To understand the wealth of parallel phenomena in their histories, despite their geographical separation, we must scrutinize the vast expanse of Zone Two that lies between them.

The structure of the Old World

The ecological makeup of the Old World is defined by the dominating presence of a vast swathe of aridity at its heart, cutting diagonally across the Eurasian continent from northeast to southwest. This area has played a significant role in the historical evolution of the Old World. Since ancient times, the dry center of the continent has been a veritable nest of evil, the source of violence and destruction. Waves of violence, perpetrated by nomadic tribes and others, have repeatedly swept from the dry center to wreak destruction upon the surrounding civilized societies. The civilizations unlucky enough to border upon the arid center often suffered so severely from these attacks that they were unable to recover. This was the historical nature of Zone Two.

The regions of Zone One were sheltered by their distance from the sources of violence in the dry center. They were also favored by their position in the relatively gentle environment of the mid-latitude temperate zone. Japan and the nations of Western Europe are typical of Zone One in that they benefited from a veritable greenhouse of protective circumstances. They have arrived at their present state through a process of internal development, pushed along by several episodes of self-renewal.

Just as there were parallels between Japan and Western Europe in Zone One, I have noticed that there were parallel developments among several areas in Zone Two. Zone Two was historically divided into four sections – call them communities, or worlds, or spheres of civilization – the Chinese world, the Indian world, the Russian world, and the Mediterranean-Islamic world. These are indicated, respectively, as I, II, III, and IV in Figure 6.1. Each civilization took the form of a vast imperial power surrounded by satellite countries. Despite the collapse of these old empires, a sense of unity within each cultural sphere has endured into the modern age. There is still a strong possibility that these four major blocs could re-emerge in some new form.

Above is a summary of what I have called the ecological view of history. If we follow this approach, Asia as a region loses all coherence. If we tried to describe the Old World using the term Asia, we would say that only the western part (or in other words the western section of Zone One) is not part of Asia; while the rest of it lies either wholly or partially within Asia. My point is that for purposes of understanding this region, it does not matter whether it lies inside or outside of so-called Asia. From the perspective of cultural influences, there are Zone Two areas such as the Russian world which seem more European, while one part of Zone One – Japan – has a culture derived from Asian sources.

As I have mentioned, there are significant differences between Zone One and Zone Two in the dynamic of their historical evolution. This has resulted in a great divergence in social system, religion, and culture. This can be seen in the particular case of Japan, a Zone One country despite its proximity to the Zone Two countries of the Chinese world and the Indian world. Although it is geographically situated in Asia, Japan is dissimilar to the other Asian countries. It is actually in the same functional category as Western Europe.

An analysis of Southeast Asia

I went to Southeast Asia bearing in mind this preliminary theory of ecological history. I was curious to see whether I would be able to use the theory to analyze Southeast Asia.

My first question was whether Southeast Asia was part of Zone One or Zone Two. This was readily answered: all of the great variety of civilizations that make up Southeast Asia belonged to Zone Two. There were no characteristics indicating inclusion in Zone One.

Over the course of history, the Southeast Asian region has seen the rise and fall of many dynasties, but none of the countries developed a feudal system like that in Japan and Western Europe. In more recent times, most of the countries were colonized by the nations of Zone One. Thailand maintained its independence, but it suffered a long period as a quasi-colonial state, hemmed in by the great powers.

Currently, none of the nations of Southeast Asia has achieved the stage of advanced capitalism, and none could reasonably be termed a highly advanced modern civilization. However, I wish to correct a widely held misconception, by stating that these Southeast Asian countries are not undeveloped. During the prewar period, we customarily referred to this area as the South Seas, or sometimes the Outer South Seas. Due to our use of terms such as 'aboriginals' or 'natives,' many Japanese imagined the countries of this region to be backward and barbaric. In fact Southeast Asia is not like that at all. It was home to grand civilizations from early times, and even now the countries of the area are endowed with impressive cultures and institutions.

Of course, the differences in level of development among the Southeast Asian countries preclude generalizations. In the mountain areas live minority tribes who could certainly be characterized as primitive or undeveloped. But overall these are respectably functioning countries. Thailand and Vietnam have a transportation and communications infrastructure; Thailand even offers television broadcasts. Education is quite widespread, and the governments are reasonably well administered.

However, even the more developed Southeast Asian nations are clearly at a different stage than Japan. The definitive difference is in industrial power: during our travels we saw hardly any factory chimneys. In addition, their transportation and communications networks are thinly spread. Although the outward look of the major cities may appear similar to Japan's, the inner physiology is quite dissimilar.

Particularities of Southeast Asia

It is clear that Southeast Asia is part of Zone Two, but where should it be positioned in the Figure 6.1 diagram? Based on actual geographical location, it should be placed just to the lower right of the Indian bloc (II). However, this position would not be an accurate representation of the actual relationship between India and Southeast Asia. Although India has had a deep influence on Southeast Asia, it would not be accurate to say that Southeast Asia is truly part of the Indian world. There has been considerable divergence between the two, both in the past and in the present.

Perhaps it is too forced to shove such an extensive area as Southeast Asia into any single one of the four blocs of Zone Two. To position this region in a way that will enhance our understanding of its place in the history of civilization, it may be necessary to create a special area apart from the four blocs. When I was considering the same question for the case of Japan, I was able to situate it as seen in Figure 6.1, but I came to realize that modifications to my theory might be necessary to accommodate Southeast Asia.

I would like to examine the particularities of Southeast Asia in terms of its place in the history of civilization. One thing that struck me during my travels there was the great diversity among the countries. The region is composed of many different nations, each with its own government, currency, border, and customs control. Visas are necessary to pass from one country to another.

The demographic makeup of each country is also different. Even within each nation there are a variety of peoples. I do not mean that the list of ethnic groups is any longer than in other regions. India and China have a large number of ethnic minorities, but in each of those places there is one overwhelmingly dominant majority group that has spread its culture over a large area of the country. This is not the case in Southeast Asia. There is no one incontestably dominant ethnic group that can represent the entire region. Peoples of different lineages exist side by side. Each nation is made up of various peoples who are quite different linguistically, religiously, and in terms of manners and customs.

In Japan, we often think of India as a part of Southeast Asia. There may be some rationale for this idea in the field of economics, but we should avoid this tendency when discussing the culture of the region. India is a major nation and civilization unto itself. It is certainly not a part of Southeast Asia. In contrast, a key feature of Southeast Asia is that it is a collection of diverse small countries.

As a footnote, I would like to point out that the term 'Southeast Asia' is often abused by others. Japan was once included as a participant in the Southeast Asian Film Festival, although I understand that this oversight has been corrected by renaming it the 'Asian Film Festival.'

A mosaic configuration

Let us turn now to the specific cultural characteristics of the various Southeast Asian nations.

A consideration of the linguistic makeup of the region immediately confirms our impression of great diversity. As I have mentioned, within each country there are many ethnic minorities using a variety of languages. Moreover, even the core national languages of each country differ greatly. The Burmese spoken in Burma, on the western edge of Southeast Asia, belongs to the Tibeto-Burmese language group. Thai and Laotian both belong to the Sino-Tai language group. Cambodia uses the Khmer language, which derives from the entirely different lineage of the Mon-Khmer language group. The affiliation of the Vietnamese language is unclear, although there are many theories. The languages spoken in the Malayan states and Indonesia are similar, but unrelated to any of the other languages of Southeast Asia. The Philippines also uses still different languages.

The writing systems vary as well. Burmese, Thai, Laotian, and Khmer each have their own characters. They share a common origin in old Indian letters, but now they have become entirely different. The Thai and Laotian writing systems are the only two that can be mutually read with reasonable ease. Vietnamese is written in Roman alphabet and Chinese characters. In Malaya and Indonesia both Roman alphabet and Arabic writing are used, while the Philippines uses the Roman alphabet alone.

In the area of religion as well, the profusion of differences makes for a complicated situation. Theravada Buddhism is the dominant practice in Burma, Thailand, Laos, and Cambodia. In Vietnam one finds Mahayana Buddhism, Confucianism, and Taoism. Malaya and Indonesia are mainly Islamic, while the Philippines is primarily Catholic.

The great diversity of the region extends to other areas of life as well: clothing, accessories, architecture, and tools. Even if one were to spend a long time in a Southeast Asian country, becoming accustomed to its way of life, this familiarity would not carry over to a neighboring country. A so-called 'Southeast Asian mode of life,' or a 'Southeast Asian culture,' does not exist.

Neither can one make much of a generalization about the historical evolution of the area. With the exception of independent Thailand, most of the region was colonized by Western European nations. But even among those colonized, the histories are different. Laos, Cambodia, and Vietnam were colonies of France; Burma and Malaya were under British rule; and Indonesia was a Dutch colony. The Philippines was first a Spanish territory and then became a U.S. territory. The occupation of these countries by Japan during the Second World War is almost their only common political experience.

Migration of peoples

I think that Southeast Asia must be considered one of the more unusual regions in today's world. It is true that Western Europe is similar in that it is also a haphazard collection of many small countries. But the countries of Western Europe are not as different from one another as those of Southeast Asia. The peoples of Western Europe are either Latin or Germanic ethnically; religiously their difference is merely between two strains of Christianity, Catholicism and Protestantism. Overall, Western Europe is clearly a single consolidated sphere of civilization. In contrast, it is hard to regard Southeast Asia a consolidated region.

Let us examine the history of Southeast Asia in order to understand how it arrived at its present condition. One of the most striking differences from Japanese history is that the course of Southeast Asian history is full of great ethnic migrations and exchanges of peoples.

The Mon and Khmer peoples who formed countries in ancient Burma, Thailand, and Cambodia are believed to have originated in India. They were forced to migrate eastwards when the Aryans arrived in India from the west. The distribution of ethnic groups resulting from this migration some thousand years ago was entirely different from what it is today. The territory of the Mon tribe was located in the Irrawaddy River plain in Burma, and the Mae Nam plain of present day Thailand. A large Khmer nation extended from northeast Thailand to Cambodia, Laos, and Cochin China. The ruins of its capital have survived as the famous Angkor Wat. The Cham state was located in southern Vietnam. Other culturally related states existed in the Malaya and Java areas. All of the above derived from Indian culture, with similar forms of architecture, sculpture, and religion – Brahmanism or Malayan Buddhism, later Theravada Buddhism.

The present day placement of ethnic groupings in Southeast Asia did not come about until significantly after the ancient migration of peoples from India. The Burmese and Thai ethnic groups, originating in southwest China, gradually migrated southward. In Yunnan there had been an impressive Thai civilization since the seventh century A.D., but in the thirteenth century it was invaded and destroyed by Kublai Khan's Mongol forces, precipitating a large-scale migration. The Mongols also invaded Burma. The Thai people founded the nation of Thailand, settling in current day Laos, Thailand, and the Shan region of Burma, while the Burmese populated Burma.

The Vietnamese are also known as the Yuenan people, signifying their origins in Yue. In the pre-Christian era, they had already migrated to the Tongking Delta. As they gradually moved southward along the coast, they clashed with the Cham state, finally conquering it in the seventeenth century. They pressed further southward into Cochin China, establishing the Annam empire. Meanwhile, the once large and powerful Khmer empire was squeezed between the Thais and the Vietnamese, and shrank to the size of present day Cambodia. Subsequently, the history of the area was characterized by successive invasions by the Western Europeans and the Japanese.

The humid region

A summary of the history of Southeast Asia leads us to the following conclusions. First, the ecological conditions of the region were not conducive to the development of human civilization. The dense tropical forests covering much of the area hindered the development of great civilizations. In ancient times, this was a relatively backward, barbaric land, not unlike Japan. At a later historical stage, empires were formed in imitation of the great civilization of a neighboring region – China – again a process similar to that in Japan. However, while Japanese civilization remained relatively sheltered, in Southeast Asia the invasions of neighboring civilizations, or the side effects thereof, created a historical pattern of decline and destruction. The end result was a region that contained an intricate mosaic of old and new elements. It would be fascinating at this point to delve into the complex ecological issues that bear upon the region's potential for settlement and productivity. Despite the relevance and interest of these questions, I feel I must omit them here in order to move on to the next issue, the refinement of my schematic representation of the ecology of Old World civilization.

The historical circumstances of Southeast Asia suggest certain modifications to the diagram displayed earlier in this essay. Figure 6.1 was meant to depict the geographical distribution of the environmental factors that shaped the historical progress of each region of the Old World. Of particular significance was the vast belt of arid land extending from southwest to northeast. As I noted previously, human history initially developed either in this dry area or in the semi-arid lands bordering it. Thus the existence of this arid belt was of great historical import.

Suppose we were working out a schematic diagram for a distribution of ecosystems. If we saw an arid belt of deserts and steppes in the middle, and bordering this some regions of semi-arid savanna, then we would naturally expect to find the forests of the humid region at the outermost edge. Indeed, this is the actual distribution of ecosystems in the Old World. If we then wanted to add to the diagram another border area, inserted between the arid

Figure 6.2: Revised Diagram of Zone One and Zone Two Regions

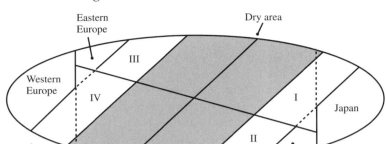

belt and the humid area, it should be drawn diagonally, parallel to the arid belt. This is in fact the modification I have included in Figure 6.2.

Once this new line is drawn, the position of Southeast Asia within the ecology and civilization of the Old World becomes clear. It lies in the humid eastern part of the Old World, bordering upon the civilizations of India, China, and Japan. This is the triangle jutting southeastwards from the landmass of China.

The meaning of the revised diagram

The revision of my diagram of the Old World clarifies many issues in addition to that of the position of Southeast Asia. A comparison of Figures 6.1 and 6.2 shows that the latter gives us much more information.

First, we see that the shape of Zone One has altered. In the original, Figure 6.1 depicts the two sections of Zone One as near semi-circles at either end of the Old World ellipse. In the new, Figure 6.2 shows that the two pieces of Zone One are shaped somewhat like an open fan. Also, the eastern and western portions of Zone One are no longer symmetrical. This more accurately represents the subtle points of climatic difference between Western Europe and Japan – although of course overall they are quite similar. Figure 6.2 clearly suggests that Western Europe has slightly lower temperatures than Japan. Western Europe is exposed to the northwest, while Japan faces southeast. It reflects the fact that a greater proportion of Western Europe is at higher latitudes than Japan.

The shape of Zone Two has also changed. In Figure 6.1, the areas of the four great civilizations (China, India, Russia, and the Islamic world) appeared more or less as triangles, with all four meeting at their apexes. In Figure 6.2, the area of each civilization looks more like a parallelogram, angled from southwest to northeast. The territory of each civilization includes two different ecosystems, an arid belt and a semi-arid borderland.

A further advantage of Figure 6.2 is that it suggests the historical dynamic wherein the major ancient civilizations influenced the development of later, secondary civilizations. The model of civilization for ancient Japan was provided by the Chinese Empire from the time of the Han dynasty. The 'barbarians' of ancient Europe looked to the Roman Empire, situated on the Mediterranean Sea, for the foundations of their civilization. In Figure 6.2, the portion of Zone Two at the northeastern extreme of the oval, looming just to the north of Japan, can be read as northern China. This is perfectly mirrored by the protruding southwestern corner of Zone Two, which can be understood as southern Europe, lying just to the south of Western Europe.

The geometry of history

Naturally, I do not pretend that the full scope of human civilization can be explained through such a simple diagram. If we scrutinized it we would find all sorts of exceptions and defects. I have no argument with those who find intolerable the idea of depicting the extreme complexity of human history with such a simple model. Nevertheless, in order to depict complex phenomena in a comprehensible form we must always resort to some sort of idealization. Theory is our tool in this process. We should be able to fashion an appropriate model for any theory derived from the idealization of phenomena. This is the way scientific theories are developed.

Thus, despite its crude simplicity, I believe my diagram is useful in understanding the overall picture. In this case, the process of idealization can be seen in the depiction of the Old World as a smooth horizontal ellipse. In reality, of course, the contours of the Old World are quite irregular due to its many peninsulas and seas. In my idealized world, all of those features have been abstracted.

I am convinced that the use of a geometric diagram to explain history, far from being a foolish exercise in abstraction, is based on sound principle. From an ecological viewpoint, history could be defined as the phenomena that occur as a result of the ongoing interaction between human beings and the land. Or to put it another way, history is the evidence left to us of the self-movement of the ecosystem. Of the various factors that determine the course of this self-movement, the conditions of nature are the most important. The distribution of natural conditions is not random; it is in fact geometrical.

While space does not allow for a detailed discussion, I would like to mention the distribution of climatic type as one example of geometrical distribution of natural conditions. In fact, the inspiration for my ecological approach to history was deeply entwined with the groundwork on classification of climatic types, and distribution of particular modes of life within each climatic area, which have been issues since the time of W.P. Köppen. The global distribution of climatic types is so dauntingly complex that it cannot be expressed in a geometric diagram. However, if one eliminates local influences, and highlights the basic underlying phenomena, it becomes possible to create a kind of idealized distribution diagram. This is what I mean by a climatic distribution diagram of an idealized continent.

This distribution diagram is geometric in the extreme. All local phenomena have been erased from the idealized continent. The factors determining climatic type, such as the range of temperature according to latitude, the effect of the prevailing westerly winds that accompany the earth's rotation, and the resultant distribution of rainfall, are reduced to what might be called mathematical geography. The diagram is simply an exercise in calculations and geometric plotting.

The representation of Old World civilizations by somewhat similar geometric forms, as I have attempted here, is thus perhaps not so strange. It is based on a consideration of the distribution of climatic types. This type of graphic method has rather more theoretical weight than a loose analogy or a clever trick. My figure is in effect the distribution diagram of civilizations on an idealized continent.

Southeast Asia and Eastern Europe

Figure 6.2 is a peculiar combination of symmetry and asymmetry, As a result of its elliptical shape and the diagonal lines, we can find various sets of two corresponding geographical points situated at opposite ends of the diagram and facing different geographical directions. These points exhibit different characteristics due to their different orientations, while at the same time, sharing similarities. The pairing of Japan and Western Europe is perhaps the most familiar example. When we search for other corresponding pairs, we notice that the region opposite Southeast Asia in the diagram is that area lying along the western edge of the Russian world, to the east of Western Europe and the north of the Mediterranean-Islamic world. In other words, according to the diagram, the 'match' for Southeast Asia should be Eastern Europe. Are there in fact any similarities between them?

Defining the boundaries of Eastern Europe poses a problem, but in the same way that we excluded India from the definition of Southeast Asia, I will exclude Russia from Eastern Europe. Thus the countries included are Poland, Czechoslovakia, Hungary, Yugoslavia, Rumania, Bulgaria, and Albania. One could argue for the inclusion of Greece as well.

Comparing Southeast Asia and Eastern Europe may seem odd at first, but closer scrutiny reveals many apparent correspondences in terms of their place in a theory of comparative civilizations. First of all, each region is an aggregation of many small nations. In addition, each area is a sort of intermediate or border zone, surrounded by three major world civilizations.

As in Southeast Asia, the wide variety of peoples in Eastern Europe, and the degree of dissimilarity among them, is striking. The main ethnic and linguistic groups are Slavs, Latins, and Greeks. But Albania is different, and Hungarian is not even an Indo-European language. It is also difficult to find any unity in terms of religion. Statistically, Catholics form the majority in Poland and Hungary, while followers of the Greek Orthodox faith predominate in Rumania, Bulgaria, and Yugoslavia. Moslems form over ten per cent of the population of Yugoslavia, not to mention the Jews and other minority groups also dwelling in the region.

The historical experiences of the two regions are also similar. Much like Southeast Asia, Eastern Europe was repeatedly invaded by the greater powers surrounding it: the Russian, Mediterranean-Islamic, and Western European worlds. In more recent history, the countries of the regions were territories of other powers: Hungary was part of the Austro-Hungarian Empire, while Yugoslavia was a territory.

My sparse knowledge of Eastern European history prevents me from extending these comparisons any further. I hope to have the opportunity to visit Eastern Europe someday; in the meantime I intend to study its history. At this point in time, the best I can manage is a working hypothesis on the comparisons between Southeast Asia and Eastern Europe.

The two World Wars

In my previous essay, I referred to the collapse of the remaining Zone Two empires as a consequence of the First World War. The great empires of the Russians, the Austro-Hungarians, and the Ottomans were swept away. However, from the point of view of the former territories of these empires, it meant that a vast region had been liberated from imperial rule. Out of the First World War emerged most of the nations of Eastern Europe: Poland, Czechoslovakia, Yugoslavia, Rumania, and Bulgaria.

In Southeast Asia, most of the countries have only recently achieved independence. They were liberated from their colonial status as a result of World War II. In other words, the Second World War formed the nations of Southeast Asia.

It might seem that these events in Eastern Europe and Southeast Asia were entirely unrelated. But if we think in terms of the status of each of these regions within the history of civilization, we can see they are in fact related phenomena, indeed part of the same series of events. In other words, the two World Wars had corresponding effects in the liberation of Eastern Europe and Southeast Asia, the two intermediate regions of the Old World.

Most of the Eastern European nations are currently 'people's republics,' which would seem in contrast to the many kingdoms in Southeast Asian. Yet, at the time of their independence, many of the Eastern European nations were kingdoms as well. Moreover, some of the Southeast Asian nations have recently been transformed from empires to republics.

Currently, it seems clear that the dominant influence on Eastern Europe is the overwhelming political power to its east. However, not every Eastern European country has become a satellite of the Soviet Union, nor can we predict what may happen in the future. There have been periods in the past, such as during the Napoleonic Age, when Eastern Europe was under Western European control. Similarly, Southeast Asia was for a time under the domination of the Japanese Empire, which is different from the current regional power structure. Both of these areas have a persistent vulnerability to domination by one of the major spheres of world civilization, even if this may take the form of peaceful influence.

In any case, both Eastern Europe and Southeast Asia are intermediate regions wedged in amongst several major civilizations. Their place within the history of civilization seems to me to be one of instability.

Japan and Southeast Asia

I would like to return to our discussion of the relationship between Japan and the Southeast Asian nations. As I consider the history of this relationship, I will refer to Figure 6.2.

As the only nation of the Zone One type in East Asia, Japan was the sole actor in a role which in Western Europe was taken on by many nations.

We are not concerned here with Japan's actions toward the northeastern area of the Asian continent. When we look at the seas extending to the south of Japan, we find that at around the same time that the Spaniards set sail to plunder abroad, the Japanese were also boarding their ships in search of plunder overseas. While the Spanish brought with them a statue of the Virgin Mary, the Japanese took along a banner depicting Hachiman Daibosatsu, the god who protects warriors. Under the guise of divine guidance, the Spaniards and the Japanese killed followers of other faiths and seized their wealth. The Japanese in their Hachiman ships plundered the coastal regions from South China to Southeast Asia. This was the first chapter in the relationship between Japan and Southeast Asia.

The next phase took place during the late sixteenth to early seventeenth centuries, when ships licensed by their respective governments plied the waters of Southeast Asia in search of trade. The Portuguese came first from the west, establishing footholds throughout the region, beginning with Malacca. Dutch, British and French traders followed. At about the same time, trading ships from

Japan arrived, bearing the official vermilion seal of the government. The Japanese established a number of communities with significant populations in various Southeast Asian locations. Among the more well known were Tourane (now Da Nang) and Faifo (now Hoi An) in Vietnam, and Ayuthia (now Ayutthaya) in Thailand. There were also communities in Luzon, Java, and Cambodia. Vestiges of this era remain today: in Hoi An can be found old Japanese graves, as well as buildings reportedly built by Japanese. I have also heard that quite a few people there claim Japanese ancestry.

The third stage in the relationship between Japan and Southeast Asia took place during the colonial period. Britain, France, and the Netherlands used the footholds they had gained during the trading stage to gradually expand their territories under a variety of pretexts. Japan, however, was left out of this process, as it coincided with the government's implementation of a singular policy of national seclusion. The power of Japan as a nation had been growing rapidly until this time, but with the implementation of national seclusion, this growth ceased. The Japanese communities in Southeast Asia faded away for lack of support.

The seclusion policy delayed Japan's momentum towards colonization of Southeast Asia by over two hundred years. Perhaps it is meaningless to engage in speculation on the 'what ifs' of history, but I cannot help but think that if not for the seclusion policy, a significant portion of Southeast Asia might have become Japanese territory. Or again, Japan might have fought a war with the European powers over claims to territory much sooner than it actually did.

I am not saying that the seclusion policy was unfortunate. I simply wish to point out that up until its advent, Japan's role in international power politics was similar to that of Britain, France, and the Netherlands. Japan's later behavior as a regional power was not solely the result of a surge of militarism after the Meiji Restoration (1868). It grew from the gap between Japan and Southeast Asia in terms of their situation in the history of civilization, and from the similarity of circumstances between Japan and Western Europe.

Modernization

Let us examine in greater detail the above-mentioned gap between Japan and Southeast Asia, in terms of their situation in the history of civilization. In the mid-nineteenth century, Japan ended its policy of national seclusion, and went through a process of thorough and revolutionary self-renewal as a result of the Meiji Restoration. Within a short time, the Japanese began exploring the world abroad with great vigor. Meanwhile, most of the Southeast Asian region had already become colonies of the Western European nations. Siam (Thailand) was virtually the only independent country. King Chulalongkorn, the extraordinary and illustrious ruler of Siam, assumed the throne the same year as Emperor Meiji in Japan (1868). His enormous efforts to modernize Siam are often compared to those of the Emperor Meiji. In this respect, it might appear that Japan and Siam were beginning from the same starting line in the mid-nineteenth century. Actual conditions, however, differed significantly between the two nations. Even though Siam maintained its independence, its territorial integrity was under constant threat from the great powers surrounding it. It was forced to accept unequal treaties as well as unsolicited advice from foreign advisors on a range of issues. Japan was one of these great powers pressuring Siam. Japan did not seize any territory in the region (until the Second World War), but it did send advisors, and shared the same extraterritorial rights as the other powers. It was not until 1937 that a completely equal treaty between Japan and Siam was signed.

The events during and after the Second World War are well known. Japan chased out the western colonial powers under the guise of 'liberating' the Southeast Asian colonies. From the perspective of the peoples of Southeast Asia, however, one ruler was merely supplanted by another.

On the basis of its colonial possessions, Japan modernized vigorously, evolving into a bloated industrialized monster such as one can see nowadays. The Southeast Asian countries, meanwhile, followed quite the opposite course. Colonization rendered them thin and weak, and modernization did not progress. It is only since the end of the Second World War that these nations have been able to attempt development and modernization. The Zone One nations are now assisting in this effort in various ways.

Heterogeneity and homogeneity

A comprehensive theory of civilization for Southeast Asia should by rights cover many more topics than those treated above. These would include the potential for industrialization, the distribution of resources and population, the features of local social structures, and the issue of overseas Chinese and other ethnic minorities. Unfortunately I must leave these to another occasion.

In the preceding discussion, I may have placed too much stress on the dissimilarities between Southeast Asia and Japan. Therefore, in my conclusion I would like to include a balanced accounting of both similarity and difference.

In terms of subjective feeling, Southeast Asia is in fact very much like Japan. To Japanese eyes, neither the urban areas nor the countryside seem exotic. The faces of the people are indistinguishable from Japanese faces, and the shapes of the houses are similar. There are rice paddies and mountains full of greenery. The people are polite and seem favorably disposed towards the Japanese. It almost seems strange to encounter a language barrier. These were my impressions based on my experiences there; in short, it was a very comfortable place for a Japanese visitor.

I became very fond of the people and the land of Southeast Asia. In all of Asia, this was the one region for which I felt the strongest emotional affinity. My emotional bond with Southeast Asia was stronger than that with Korea, northern China, or Mongolia. It was certainly much stronger than my feelings for India, not to mention Afghanistan where I had felt almost no affinity at all.

And yet even in distant Afghanistan, I once had an intellectual say to me, 'After all, we are both Asians.' I concealed my surprise at the time, but I interpreted it to be an abstract conceptual statement devoid of any true emotional underpinning. It was clear that the man speaking did not personally believe that we were alike. But as long as the geographic denotation of 'Asia' existed, we would both be considered 'Asians.'

However, I harbor great doubts about the validity of this idea that 'we are all Asians.' The idea of pan-Asian homogeneity has meaning only in terms of the abstract or of sensibilities. In terms of logic or material reality one could never argue that Asia is homogeneous. Japan is a particular case in point. Both the course of its history and its present material conditions are different from the rest of Asia. How could one possibly see Japan and Southeast Asia as the same? Japan could not become more like Southeast Asia by giving up its industrial base, no more than Southeast Asia could industrialize overnight. The differences remain.

A new relationship

These questions of similarity or difference, however, are entirely beside the point of whether relations between nations are amicable or hostile. Indeed, one could cite many examples of terrible things that have occurred under the rubric of similarity or homogeneity. Ideas stressing the homogeneity of Asia have been circulating in Japan ever since Okakura Tenshin pronounced 'Asia is one.' The slogan 'same writing, same race' (*dōbun dōshu*), referring to the Japanese and the Chinese, is part of the same rhetorical stance. Despite such slogans, the relationship between China and Japan worsened dramatically during the modern period. Such ideas of racial unity became the basis for Japan's promotion of the Greater East Asia Co-Prosperity Sphere during the Second World War.

It should be possible to build good relations between nations on a foundation of mutually recognized differences. Saying that 'we are all Asians' is no more than a diplomatic fiction. I understand that this sort of diplomatic fiction can be effective, and in its place it is not entirely meaningless. But fiction is fiction, after all, and we must not resort to it when we consider the reality of future relations between Japan and the Southeast Asian nations. I have come to think that we must positively acknowledge our heterogeneity, and on that basis learn how to unite our diverse facets in a mutually beneficial way.

(August 1958)

7 The Fate of the Arab People

Commentary on Chapter 7

The year 1958 was one of great turmoil in the Middle East. Egypt and Syria joined to form the United Arab Republic. Soon thereafter, Jordan and Iraq formed a federal union. There was an uprising in Lebanon, and a revolution in Iraq. As the crisis developed, the United States and the United Kingdom sent troops to the region.

In the wake of these events, *Shūkan Asahi* (Asahi Weekly) published a special emergency issue called 'Crisis in the Middle and Near East.' I was invited to contribute the following essay, 'The Fate of the Arab People,' as a commentary on the upheaval from the perspective of the history of civilization.[1]

Never having been to the Arab nations, I had some trepidation that I might make unintended errors. Nevertheless I decided to accept the assignment as an exercise in applying my theory of civilization in ecological history.

Chūkintō – The 'Middle and Near East'

In a recent 'Yūrakuchō' column in the evening edition of the daily *Mainichi Shinbun*, Mr. Ukai Nobushige opined, 'It seems strange in this day and age to be using such a British-centric place name as the "Middle and Near East".'[2] I agreed with the alternative proposed by Mr. Ukai, the more neutral term 'West Asia.' Indeed, the Kyoto University group conducting research on this region is called the 'Southwest Asia Research Group' (Seinan Ajia Kenkyūkai).

In that same column, Mr. Ukai chided me personally, saying 'Even in Mr. Umesao's ecological view of history, the so-called "Middle and Near East" seems to remain the Middle and Near East.' This prompted me to review the categorizations I had used in my work on the theory of civilization until now, but I was unable to find anywhere that I had used the designation 'Middle and Near East' to describe a region. To be accurate, I had merely stated that there were many books and articles that dealt with the Middle and Near East. The Middle and Near East, as a term and as a concept, may be convenient for international journalism, but I agree that it does not have much meaning in the context of the theory of civilization.

Are Arabs Asian?

Some people think of the current series of incidents in the Middle East as part of a more general Asian problem. I disagree with this, and indeed with the very idea that Asia is a single region. What we call 'Asia' is composed of several heterogeneous parts. Linking the stretch of territory from Japan to Morocco as one large Asian-Arab region has no substantive meaning. When we voice our support for the anti-colonial struggles of the Arab countries, it is not because we are relatives, but for entirely different reasons.

Is there any point to calling Arabs 'Asians' or 'Orientals' like ourselves? Professor Izutsu Toshihiko, who recently completed a colloquial translation of the Koran, claimed that to do so was no more than a 'trick of words.' He states that the Koran embodies an ethos completely remote from our own. Izutsu quotes Taha Hussein, a leading intellectual of present day Egypt, who proclaims that Egyptians are not Orientals but European heirs to the Greek cultural tradition.

Of course, this assertion breeds its own misunderstandings. To begin with, the concepts of Asia and Europe are too crudely defined to be of much analytical use. The course of history has not necessarily proceeded with a clear demarcation between Asia and Europe. To understand the position of the Middle and Near East in the context of the history of civilization, we must consider the historical and geographical structure of the entire Old World including Asia, Europe, and North Africa.

The Mediterranean-Islamic world

Observers tend to link the stunning recent events in the Middle and Near East to the U.S.-Soviet conflict. Of course the Cold War is a factor, but it would be more accurate to view these incidents as the unfolding of a basic historical issue particular to this region. This issue is the reconstruction of the Mediterranean-Islamic world.

From the perspective of the history of civilization, it is impossible to understand the so-called Middle and Near East without also considering the Mediterranean Sea. Many ancient empires developed by linking together the Mediterranean coastal regions with areas to the east, extending toward Persia. The empire of Alexander the Great, its successor the Saracen Empire, and more recently the Ottoman Empire are but a few examples.

Just as there is an enduring sphere of Chinese civilization despite the historical change of dynasties, the Mediterranean-Islamic region formed a single cohesive 'world,' through the many divisions and changes of empire since ancient times. In fact, I believe that the Old World (excluding Japan and Western Europe) comprised four such enduring and self-contained units: the Chinese world, the Indian world, the Russian world, and the Mediterranean-Islamic world. Each of these worlds has maintained its basic integrity in the face of a history of divisions and collapses. The enduring structure of each area consists of an enormous central empire surrounded by satellites. Each of these imperial structures has had an incarnation in the modern period, respectively, the Qing dynasty, the Mogul Empire, the Russian Empire, and the Ottoman Empire.

Reestablishing the 'empire'

The upheavals now occurring in the Middle and Near East are undeniably struggles between Arab nationalism and imperialism or colonialism. But also, in their other aspect as the replay of an old historical dynamic, these struggles will ultimately lead to the reestablishment of a large new Mediterranean-Islamic 'empire.' This time, it is not the Turkish people who will become the core of the empire, but rather the Arabs who constitute the vast majority of the area's population.

While the typical ethnic nationalist movement is divisive and secessionist, the current expression of Arab nationalism also includes unifying tendencies in its urge toward the reestablishment of an 'empire.' Although it is no small matter to forge a nation out of the combination of several countries, it appears that this process will continue in the Middle and Near East. Ideas such as the United Arab Republic, an Arab federal union, or a Maghreb federation of North African nations are being raised repeatedly. Perhaps the outcome will be the initial establishment of a major Arab state, followed by the coalescence of the Mediterranean-Islamic world around that center. Issues such as the politics of oil and the presence of the Jewish state may act as catalysts for this centripetal response.

The direction of regeneration

The current borders of the Middle and Near East were decreed at the convenience of the colonialists. This arbitrary carving of boundaries was similar to the territories of Chinese warlords or the regional principalities of India. The ethnic nationalism here is rooted in different conditions from that in Southeast Asia.

In the modern era, the four major imperial worlds, beset by profound corruption and contradictions, ended up as colonies or quasi-colonies. In the late nineteenth century, China, once considered a 'sleeping tiger,' was likened to a 'dying old pig'; while the Ottoman empire was dubbed 'the sick man of Europe.' All of these empires collapsed. But despite their fall, the cohesiveness of each region did not vanish. The strenuous reform efforts that followed the collapse of each empire can be interpreted as attempts to reestablish order and unity in each 'world' under a new system.

The Russian bloc was the first to succeed in regeneration through revolution. Subsequently, China and India appear to be on their way to reestablishing their worlds. Of the four areas, the Mediterranean-Islamic world is the farthest behind in the process, but the current events there are following the same course.

I cannot predict the precise method of regeneration in the Mediterranean-Islamic world. It is conceivable that the modernization of this area will take place under the aegis of communism, following the examples of the Soviet Union and China. Islam will not be an effective breakwater against communism; it will only be able to adapt and transform under new circumstances.

Even if a cohesive Mediterranean-Islamic world is reestablished, new problems will doubtless arise. What will be the relationship between the Arabs and the non-Arab Islamic countries such as Turkey and Iran? What kind of adjustments will occur in relations with the neighboring Russian and Indian worlds? I believe that all of the four major blocs I have described will have to confront these commonly held issues some day.

(August 1958)

8 Traces of India in Southeast Asia

Commentary on Chapter 8

When I returned to Japan in the spring of 1958 from my travels in Southeast Asia, I received requests to write articles about the region for various publications. I suppose the fact that I had been there must have seemed quite exotic. At the time, the extent of Japanese interest in Southeast Asia was no more than a few encouraging slogans, and hardly anyone had spent time in direct observation. The following is one of my essays from 1958, which was published in *Nichi-In Bunka* (Indo-Japanese Culture), the journal of the Kansai Nichi-In Bunka Kyōkai (Kansai Japan-India Cultural Association).[1] I wrote it in a lighthearted vein, but I have chosen to include it with the more serious essays in this volume, as it treats related topics.

Southeast Asia and India are often treated as one unit, and at times India may even be counted as one of the Southeast Asian countries. However, I argue here that the two areas should not be grouped together, as they have entirely different characteristics in terms of their geography and the history of their civilizations. That being said, it is true that Indian customs and civilization have historically exerted a strong influence on the Southeast Asian countries. Even in the present day, one can discover traces of this influence: it is these residual Indian influences that I have described in this essay. Thus the title 'Traces of India in Southeast Asia.'

The meaning of Indochina

Earlier this year, I made a research trip to Southeast Asia, visiting Thailand, Cambodia, Vietnam, and Laos, and also the cities of Singapore and Penang. In this essay, I would like to share some of my observations from this trip.

All of the places I visited are located on what is commonly called the Indochinese peninsula. Strictly defined, Indochina refers to the three countries formerly under French rule: Vietnam, Cambodia, and Laos. However there is a broader definition that encompasses the entire peninsula jutting out from the Asian continent into the South Seas; this includes Thailand and Malaya. Although I was initially unfamiliar with the origin of the name Indochina, once I arrived there I was struck by how fitting it was. My honest impression upon seeing these countries was that the region was indeed a composite of India and China.

Faces

The faces of the people of Indochina looked entirely Chinese to me. The Thais, Laotians, and Vietnamese all migrated long ago from China, and it is clear that they are racially close to the Chinese. Indeed, although the Southeast Asian populations include many 'overseas Chinese' of more recent vintage, it is hard to distinguish their faces from those of the true locals. In Thailand there are many people of mixed ancestry, so it is even more difficult to tell them apart. Our inability to distinguish amongst the faces in Thailand was not due to our role as outsiders: even the Thais themselves could not see the difference. However, the distinction between overseas Chinese and Thais became clear once people spoke. The first generation overseas Chinese spoke with a particular accent, no matter how fluent their Thai.

Japanese also look very much like Southeast Asians, except for their generally lighter skin. Once tanned, it would be hard to tell most Japanese apart from Southeast Asians. This similarity points to the fact that racially we are all members of the Mongoloids of East Asia. In this regard, the Southeast Asians are definitely different from Indians, who are of the Caucasoid race, even though they are usually called Asians.

Forms of writing

Upon arrival in Thailand one is faced with lines and lines of Thai writing. To my eyes, the letters looked somewhat like the notations used in the ancient ritual of incense burning in Japan. The faces of the Thai people may look the same as the Japanese, but when I saw this exotic lettering, I realized anew that Thailand is indeed a foreign country. In towns one sees signs using Chinese characters, due to the presence of many overseas Chinese, but they are far outnumbered by the signs in Thai. The use of Thai script apparently is mandated by law.

In Cambodia, the lettering seemed even more unfamiliar and difficult than Thai writing. I managed to learn a few Thai and Cambodian letters, but it was impossible to make much progress in the short time that I was there.

The development of Thai writing derived from Cambodian writing. Cambodian lettering is in turn clearly related to Indian writing – not the Devanagari script currently in use in India, but the writing used in South India in the sixth to eighth centuries.

Architecture

It appears that the Southeast Asians are not producing much in the way of good design at the current time, with the exception of some modern architecture in Thailand.

These buildings are modern reinforced concrete structures, which incorporate traditional Thai architectural motifs. The roofs are rendered in complex layers, with decorative plates along the edges. This is a melding of Thai and Western styles. Government buildings as well as those of the Economic Commission for Asia and the Far East (ECAFE) and other international agencies are all designed in this manner. They are assertively Oriental, and quite beautiful.

The salient feature of Thai architecture is the complex layering of its roofs. I wondered about the origin of this style. It did not seem to be from India, as it looked nothing like the many Indian-style buildings in Thailand. Le May's history of civilization[2] traces the origin of this kind of roof to Yunnan, but I would still like to ask the opinion of an architectural historian.

The *naga*

Chulalongkorn University, Thailand's premier institution of higher education, is located on a beautiful campus in Bangkok. Its buildings are adorned with lovely modern Thai style roofing in green and orange. It is hard to believe that these are school structures.

Soon after my arrival in Bangkok, I had my first view of a carving of a *naga*, or multi-headed cobra, in one of the university buildings. The banister of a stairway formed the body of the creature, and at the bottom were the reared neck and heads of the snake, with its eyes glaring fiercely. It looked not unlike the Japanese eight-headed dragon monster, or *orochi*, but the *naga* had an odd number of heads, either seven or nine. It seemed to be bearing large spoons upon its back.

I do not understand the symbolism of the *naga*, but its origin is unmistakably Indian. Old Thai Buddhist statues bear *nagas* on their backs, where we would expect to see a nimbus in Chinese or Japanese statuary. *Nagas* can be found all over Thailand, especially in temples, and are prevalent in Cambodia and Laos as well. These are all areas that were influenced by ancient Indian culture.

The *garuda*

The g*aruda* is another strange symbol that appears as a rooster-like monster. Its face and body are human, but it has wings.

In Thailand, the *garuda* is the monarchic crest. This symbol is used in the same way as is the chrysanthemum crest by the Japanese imperial family. Just as the Japanese Imperial Navy placed the chrysanthemum crest on the prows of its battleships, the various governmental agencies of Thailand's monarchy display the *garuda* in their lobbies. In Bangkok I attended a garden party at the invitation of the King of Thailand. The invitation card was printed in Thai, and was embossed with a large *garuda*.

The *garuda* came from India. It appears in the *Ramayana*, the ancient story of Prince Rama. I was amazed at the splendid *garuda* in the drawings of the research report of the Chu-yung-kuan by Kyoto University.[3] What is more, the statues on either side of *garuda* were backed by *naga*. It seems that this symbol spread from India to Southeast Asia and, in another direction, crossed the deserts of Central Asia all the way to the Great Wall of China.

The *Ramakian*

While in Bangkok I had a chance to see a performance of the classical drama the *Ramakian*. It was a highly ritualized performance, in glittering costumes with pointed, upward-curving shoulder pieces.

The *Ramakian* is clearly a derivation of the classical Indian myth, the *Ramayana*. I cannot analyze the differences myself, as I am unable to read the text of either one. According to a specialist I consulted, the two plays are quite different. Nevertheless, the overall structure of the story and the major characters are the same: the journeys of Prince Rama; the wistful Princess Sita; and the heroic exploits of the monkey Hanuman as he rescues Prince Rama.

In the town of Luang Prabang in northeastern Laos, I saw a group of elementary school boys learning a curious dance in the schoolyard. Their odd movements made me wonder what kind of dance it was. I was told it was Hanuman's dance. I was quite impressed with the depth of penetration of this Indian myth into the cultures of the Southeast Asian peoples. Almost everyone knew the story, which caused me to wonder why it had become so thoroughly ingrained in these societies.

Present day India in Southeast Asia

Many aspects of Southeast Asian civilization – Cambodian writing, *nagas*, *garudas*, and the *Ramakian* – were transmitted from ancient India. Once upon a time, the glory of Indian civilization permeated this region. In contrast to that past glory, the profile of modern India in Southeast Asia is quite humble.

When I was in Singapore, I noticed more Indians than elsewhere in the region, and one could see Tamil writing in the shop windows. But in Bangkok and towns further east, the only Indians one comes across are gatekeepers or a few tailors.

In Phnom Penh, the capital of Cambodia, I discovered an Indian restaurant and went in to order some curry. It was a sore disappointment. When I was in India, I had eaten curry every day, but this curry was unpalatable, especially compared to the delicious Chinese food available everywhere. In present day Southeast Asia, at least, the influence of India is no match for that of the Chinese.

(September 1958)

9 The Countries of the 'Mediant'

Commentary on Chapter 9

In 1961, restrictions on overseas travel by Japanese nationals, which had been closely regulated since the Second World War, were finally eased. Public interest in foreign countries began to rise rapidly. ChūōKōron Company published a ten volume series entitled *Travels around the world* (*Sekai no tabi*). This was a compilation of travelogues, organized according to world region, with an introduction to each regional volume. I was asked to take charge of Volume 2, *From India to the countries of the burning sands* (*Indo kara nessa no kuni e*). The following is the introduction that I wrote for the volume.[1]

Although I wrote this piece as a general commentary on the region, in simple layman's language, I have decided to include it in the present collection since it touches on several important issues related to the history of civilization. For example, my musings on the relationship between overseas Indians and overseas Chinese include ideas on a comparative theory of commerce that I wish to develop in the future. I also make use here of the concept of the 'Mediant,' introduced in my 1956 essay 'Between East and West,' the first chapter of this volume.

The Mediant

Here in Japan, making comparisons between the Kantō region, centered on Tokyo, and the Kansai region around Osaka is a popular conversational gambit. This is more than an idle discussion, since it speaks to the distinct historical differences between the two areas. In some ways, Kantō and Kansai can be seen as representing two major currents of Japanese culture.

However, the more we consider the specifics of Japanese culture, the more we see that there are many aspects that cannot be explained by the division of the country into the broad categories of Kantō and Kansai. Not only does this schema exclude Kyūshū and

Hokkaidō, but the boundary between Kansai and Kantō is itself not clear. For Tokyo dwellers, the region as far as Izu and Atami seems familiar – part of their own sphere as it were. Beyond the Hakone mountain range, Kantō ends and another region begins. In a similar vein, residents of Osaka and Kyoto know the territory up to Lake Biwa very well, but feel that anything beyond Sekigahara is no longer part of Kansai. Thus, although we refer to the division between the Kantō and the Kansai regions, they do not share a common boundary. In between these two regions lies a large intermediary area belonging to neither.

I would like to suggest that an analogous situation exists on a global scale. We often theorize about the comparison between the Orient and the Occident, and in most cases these theories are meaningful to some degree. However, we encounter difficulties when we attempt to determine the specific extent of the Orient or the Occident.

Suppose a 'typical' Japanese were journeying westward from Japan through Asia. As far as Singapore or Rangoon, the territory would seem intuitively familiar, and definitely 'Oriental.' From Bengal onward, however, he would encounter many unfamiliar things that did not seem Oriental. The overall impression would be of a very different region. Conversely, as Europeans head eastward, their overall impression of being in the 'Occident' lasts about as far as Greece. It seems that when they reach Turkey or Egypt, their sense of difference increases and they no longer consider the area part of the Occident.

Thus, although our discourse is framed in terms of Orient and Occident, in reality there is an enormous intermediate region, which belongs to neither category. If this region is neither Orient nor Occident, how then should we think of it? My proposal is to call it the 'Mediant,' in order to emphasize its intermediary location between the Orient and the Occident. In fact, the present volume, *From India to the countries of the burning sands* of *Travels around the world*, covers precisely the area that I am suggesting we call the Mediant: the Indian subcontinent and the Middle East.

A region for 'just passing through'

I fear that we Japanese are especially ignorant about the Mediant region. There are only a few accounts of travel in this area. I imagine that assembling one of these 'world travels' series must involve a hard choice among a plethora of European and American travelogues. But those who have traveled in the Mediant with serious intent are so few that source material is far from abundant. If passage through the Mediant qualified as a visit, we would count a much greater number of visitors. Travel to Europe has recently become more convenient with the increase in air routes, and every day many people are carried through the air over these countries in both directions. But travelers just passing through do not learn much beyond a vague acquaintance with place names such as Calcutta, Karachi, or Beirut.

This phenomenon of a region that is largely 'passed through' has a parallel in the domestic situation in Japan. With the advent of many express trains along the Tōkaidō Line, it has become quite easy to travel between Tokyo and Osaka. This has not led to more awareness of the localities along the Tōkaidō Line amongst Tokyo or Osaka businessmen. They pass the time en route either sleeping or reading magazines. The places along the way seem to exist in order to be ignored. At most, travelers learn the names of the major stops.

To the passengers on the 'Europe Express' flights, the long stretch of the Mediant countries is like the region of Tōkai farm villages: they exist only as part of a boring distance. Passengers prefer to sleep or read magazines to pass the time. It would be preferable if the countries did not exist at all, if such a thing were possible. That is why direct air service to Europe via the polar route became so popular when it was inaugurated.

There are many travelogues and guidebooks on Tokyo, Kyūshū, Hokkaidō, and the Kansai region. But there are fewer accounts of places along the well-traveled Tōkaidō Line, such as Mikawa or Suruga. If one got off the train in these areas, one could take an enjoyable side trip. This is all the more true of India and the Islamic nations, where the wealth of sights is not boring in the least. In order to see these areas, however, one must get off the train, or disembark from the airplane, and travel on land. To those who make this commitment, this vast region sheds its guise of a distance-that-must-be-passed-through, revealing instead its rich essence.

The difficulty of traveling

I commented on the need for commitment, because, frankly, commitment and effort are necessary to travel in the countries of the Mediant nowadays. It is in no sense an easy area in which to travel. This is one substantive reason for the scarcity of visitors to this region; it is not necessarily that people have simply ignored the Mediant to concentrate on the Occident. Of the Mediant countries, India and Pakistan are among the most open to travelers. Even so, when I commented upon returning from India that 'It was very enjoyable,' a person who had lived in India for many years asked me, 'How on earth did you travel, if you can say your trip through India was enjoyable?'

While I did not think of myself as a particularly savvy traveler, I certainly understood his point. If one attempts to travel in India as one might elsewhere, one will no doubt encounter many privations.

As a whole, the countries of the Mediant do not show much eagerness to receive foreign travelers. Although there are some posters in airport lobbies promoting tourism, I am not sure how genuine this effort to solicit visitors really is. Obtaining visas can be difficult, or even if visas are granted, some countries may not allow visitors to travel freely within their borders. Many European countries do not require Japanese nationals to obtain visas, but in the Mediant, Pakistan alone follows this policy of free access.

Furthermore, transportation systems and accommodations for travelers are generally inadequate. This is not a problem for those who hop as lightly as a skipping stone across the region, staying in first class hotels and traveling by air. Overland travel, however, requires careful planning. One often sees travelers in India carrying along their own bedrolls. On trips to outlying regions, it may certainly be more convenient to take one's own sleeping gear. As for transportation, the railway network in India and Pakistan is developed enough to allow at least third class train travel anywhere. Bus routes cover the entire Mediant region. But neither of these is very comfortable. The best way to travel is perhaps by jeep or automobile, but here too there are many obstacles. Roads are often rutted, and gasoline may be difficult to find, especially in Afghanistan.

Another particular trial for Japanese travelers might be the cuisine of the region. Curry is the main dish in India and Pakistan. No matter what one orders, what shows up on the table is curry in some shape or form. A full course meal consists of dish after dish of curries, with only slight variations in flavor. The main meat available throughout the Mediant is lamb. Those who are repelled by the odor of lamb may not be able to tolerate the food. I had a friend who especially disliked this cuisine. During his travels in Pakistan and Afghanistan, he subsisted on cucumbers, like a cricket. He slimmed down considerably.

The presence of overseas Indians

I wrote partly in jest about the food problem, but it is actually an important topic. The cuisine of the region is deeply connected to the history of Mediant civilizations.

Earlier I stated that the Mediant stretched from Bengal westward, but in fact it would be more accurate to think of it as beginning in East Pakistan, since Burma is clearly one of the Southeast Asian countries. For air travelers on the 'Europe Express' the distinction between Southeast Asia and the Mediant is of course irrelevant. However, the land traveler will find distinct differences between these two regions, both culinary and otherwise. The distress that Japanese may feel at the cuisine of the Mediant is unlikely to occur in the countries of Southeast Asia. Even deep in the Southeast Asian countryside, one will not encounter much trouble with unfamiliar food. A major reason is that there are Chinese restaurants everywhere in Southeast Asia. The Chinese know how to enjoy their meals as much as, or perhaps even more than, Japanese. Of course there is bad Chinese food, but even that is tolerable for the Japanese palate. In any case it is better than being inundated by curry. In areas where there are overseas Chinese, we Japanese can be assured of a palatable meal at the very least.

The reason we Japanese encounter difficulties with unfamiliar food in the Mediant is due to the absence of overseas Chinese. Whereas the Southeast Asian cities of Singapore and Penang are virtually 'Chinese' cities, Calcutta is a different matter. There are a few Chinese residents and restaurants, but they are scarce in comparison to Southeast Asia. As one travels further westward through the Mediant, they become still more rare.

In Southeast Asia, not only the culinary world, but the entire economic realm seems to be dominated by overseas Chinese. But if the overseas Chinese are so influential in the Orient, why are there so few of them in the Mediant? One of the reasons must be that even the famously adaptable overseas Chinese are no match for the Indians. In places such as Thailand or Malaya, the economic dominance of overseas Chinese is generally ascribed to the low business aptitude of the local people. The brilliant economic success of overseas Chinese in these areas is presumably due to the lack of competition. India, however, is a different matter. From ancient times the Indians, too, have been an innately commercial people. In their own land they naturally held the advantage, and quelled any competition from other ethnic groups. Indian businessmen have succeeded abroad as well. There are many Indians doing business in Singapore, and their presence becomes stronger in more western areas. In eastern Africa, overseas Indians dominate the commercial sector, just as the Chinese do in Southeast Asia.

At present, border issues are causing considerable tension between China and India. Their parallel status as major power players in Asia tends to lead to rivalry. On the smaller scale of ethnic interactions as well, there have been rivalries between overseas Chinese and overseas Indians for a long time.

Anthropological distribution

I suspect that while it may be easy for most people to accept that India and southwest Asia are not part of the Occident, there will be resistance to the thesis that they are not part of the Orient either. In case the 'overseas Chinese index' is not sufficient, I would like to elucidate a few more measures of distinction between the clearly 'Oriental' countries of Southeast Asia and India and her westward neighbors.

First of all, when one crosses from Orient to Mediant, it is immediately obvious that the faces of the people are different. Proceeding from the east, one sees completely Oriental faces as far as Burma. Indeed, it is hard to tell Burmese apart from Japanese. When the Japanese Army occupied Southeast Asian areas during the Second World War, this similarity in facial type amazed the local people and gladdened the Japanese soldiers. Since the war was fought in a region populated by Mongoloid peoples (to use the anthropological term) they should hardly have been surprised.

From the Bengal region westward, there is a drastic change in the look of the people. The vast majority of people have sharp features and high noses. To our Japanese eyes they look Occidental, apart from their dark coloring. Of course there are many mixtures of faces and features, but they seem clearly Caucasoid. These facial features stretch from Bengal and India all the way to Iran and the Arab world.

The peoples of Mongoloid lineage reach their furthest western extent in the northern part of Asia, rather than in the south and southwest. For example, Tibetans are often indistinguishable from Japanese. Mongoloid peoples have passed over the Himalayas and the Hindu Kush, and their faces can be spotted along the edges of the Indian and southwest Asian world. The populations of Assam, Bhutan, Sikkim, and Nepal are examples of this, as are the Hazara and Moghol tribes of Afghanistan.

Southeast Asia and the Mediant region are also divided by a linguistic border, in addition to the racial divide between Mongoloid and Caucasoid peoples. The linguistic makeup of Southeast Asia is quite complex, but its major language groups, the Sino-Tai family and the Tibeto-Burman family, are clearly of Oriental origin. From Bengal westward, the situation is different. Of the many languages spoken in India, for example, the major ones belong to the Indo-Aryan language family. This makes them related to German, English, Russian, French, and Greek. Bengali, Hindi, Punjabi, Urdu, Ceylon's Sinhara, Afghanistan's Pashto, and Iran's Persian are all related as well. The only significant languages of the Mediant that do not belong to the Indo-Aryan language family appear along the western edge of the region: Arabic and Turkish. These two have separate lineages: Arabic is a Semitic language, and Turkish is Altaic.

A difficult place to understand

There seem to be further dissimilarities between Southeast Asia and the Mediant in the area of demeanor, body language, and mindset. It is difficult to map out in a precise anthropological way differences that are a matter of subjective feeling, but I do know that most Japanese feel they share the same basic temperament as Southeast Asians. In contrast, we seldom feel we share a disposition with people from India and farther west. It is an interesting phenomenon that many of the Japanese students who have gone to study in India return to Japan with a dislike for Indians. Even if one could measure the degree of natural affinity between peoples of different nationalities, it would be hard to detect one between Japanese and Indians.

The author Hotta Yoshie wrote, 'As far as Burma, the virtue of humility is the foundation of spiritual life; but from India to the west the virtue of self-assertion is dominant.'[2] This may very well be true, implying that the basic human temperament in India and westward is different from that in Japan.

Mutual understanding between Japan and the nations of the Mediant tends to be extremely difficult, due to these differences in basic temperament. Japan has considerable cultural commonality with China and Southeast Asia. As for the nations of Europe, our cultural backgrounds are different, but our parallel stages of development, and our similar social circumstances, are again conducive to mutual understanding. In contrast, the countries of the Mediant have an entirely different cultural lineage from Japan, and none of these nations is highly industrialized. Of all the regions of the world, the Mediant may be the most difficult for the Japanese to understand, because the problems we face are so different.

Countries connected by land

The great variety of countries that make up the Mediant renders generalizations difficult. Furthermore, in the Mediant as in Asia as a whole, the nations are so fragmented and separated from one another, that nowadays it is more difficult than ever to speak of the idea that 'Asia is one.' However, before plunging into the complex theme of differences below, I would like to indicate the points of unity and commonality among the nations of the Mediant.

First, a major unifying factor is that this region is bound together in one landmass. Ceylon is the only country of the Mediant not connected by land. Some might point out that the Southeast Asian countries of Cambodia, Thailand, and Burma are also joined by land, but the reality on the ground is quite different. The land connection exists topographically, but for the practical purposes of the traveler, these countries are scattered and isolated. The Cambodia-Thailand border is currently closed. There is no overland road from Thailand to Burma, or from Burma to India or East Pakistan. There is an ambitious plan to construct a transcontinental highway through the region, but at the present time, the roadway is broken up in many places. When a team from the daily newspaper *Asahi Shinbun* investigated the course of the Olympic torch on its way to the upcoming Tokyo Olympics, they found this area impassable.

Compared to the situation in Southeast Asia, the Mediant region is mutually much better connected. One could travel overland by automobile all the way from East Pakistan to Turkey. This is no insignificant matter. The fact is that from ancient historical times, there have been numerous cases of peoples originating in the west, advancing gradually through the Mediant all the way to India. Darius of Persia and Alexander the Great of Greece are the best known of the many conquerors who came from the west. Other dynasties that came to rule India originated in the area of Afghanistan. The Mogul leaders Timur and Babur called themselves Mongols, but they were actually from the western part of the Mediant world.

The Indian world

Despite a certain degree of connection and commonality, the Mediant remains a region of dissimilar parts. I would never imitate Okakura Tenshin's proclamation that 'Asia is one' with a similar assertion about the Mediant. The Mediant is not 'one,' but two, three, or many, depending on one's frame of analysis. For example, in terms of the historical cultural structure of the region, it makes the most sense to divide it into two large sections: the Indian world, and the Mediterranean-Islamic world.

Turning first to the Indian world, one should appreciate at the outset the incredible size and diversity of the nation. Thinking of India as a 'typical' nation would only give rise to misconceptions. Not only does India contain many different ethnic groups and cultures, it has also had a strong cultural influence on neighboring countries. In this sense it is helpful to think of India as a 'world' rather than just a nation. One commonly refers to the Indian subcontinent, but its import is so great that it could almost be considered a continent in itself.

At the heart of the Indian subcontinent, or world, is of course the Republic of India. The Republic itself is an enormous state boasting the second largest population in the world after China. Within its borders are territories with different cultures, such as Assam and Sikkim. The Republic of India is flanked on either side by the two sections of Pakistan. Despite their differences in religious makeup (predominantly Hindu versus predominantly Muslim), India and Pakistan are twin nations, born from the same mother entity. Pakistan is also a major nation-state, with a population ranking sixth in the world after Japan. To the north of India, on the southern slopes of the Himalayas, lie Nepal and Bhutan. In the Indian Ocean off the southern coast of India lies the country of Ceylon. We can consider this group of countries as the Indian world.

The Indian world is so complex and diverse that it cannot be explained by means of a few selected basic concepts. The natural environment, for example, varies greatly among its areas. Overall temperatures tend to be hot, but there are large differences between north and south. In the chilly world of the Himalayas and Karakoram, temperatures never soar. The distribution of rainfall is even more uneven. The eastern portion of the Indian world lies within the Bay of Bengal monsoon zone. The rainy season is accompanied by strong seasonal winds, but during the dry winter season, there is hardly any rainfall. The rain forest vegetation that grows there turns green only during the wet season. The southern coastal region is a true tropical rain forest, with year-round rainfall. The central highlands and the northwest are extremely arid. The lower Indus River area is practically a desert, which connects to the 'countries of the burning sands,' that is, the great arid region in the western section of the Mediant.

These environmental differences cannot help but influence the lives of the inhabitants. To cite a simple example, the way of life in the wet paddies of the lower Ganges River is entirely different from that in the dry wheat growing regions to the west. I think many people have a vague image of India as a hot, rice-growing region, but this is hardly accurate. In fact, rice cultivation is more representative of the Southeast Asian mode of life.

Turning to the man-made world, here too the civilization of India defies easy generalizations. In addition to linguistic and ethnic complexities, the religious culture of the region is difficult to grasp. Japanese often expect to find some common ground with the Indian people, based on a shared heritage of Buddhism. Their expectations remain largely unfulfilled, since nowadays Buddhism has a significant presence only in the peripheral locales of Bhutan, Sikkhim, Nepal, and Ceylon. In the more central areas of India and Pakistan, Buddhism has a very low profile compared to the dominant faiths of Hinduism in India and Islam in Pakistan. It is well known that religious tension between Hindus and Muslims was the main rationale for partitioning the Indian Empire into two nations.

The Indian world is large, but fortunately the scope of the present volume is able to cover this diversity to a reasonable degree. In addition to pieces on India and Pakistan, there are essays on the peripheral areas of Assam and Bhutan. Regrettably, treatments of Ceylon and East Pakistan must wait for the future.

The Islamic world

Having introduced the eastern portion of the so-called Mediant, I would like to turn now to the western sector, namely, the Mediterranean-Islamic world. For the purposes of this volume, we will extend our consideration only as far west as Egypt, although normally one would consider North Africa as part of the Mediterranean-Islamic world. Admittedly, it would be more natural to follow the spread of the regional civilization through Libya, Tunisia, Algeria, and Morocco, all the way to Spain. However, in the present series, North Africa is covered in the volume on Africa.

The salient environmental feature of the far-flung Islamic world is of course aridity. Rainfall is exceedingly scarce throughout the region. In the most extreme areas, rain falls only once in several years and even then just a few drops. Thus, despite the great overall size of the Islamic world, the area of usable land is small. Temperatures can be high even in areas that are not in the low latitudes. These are veritable 'countries of burning sands.'

The human species can only survive in areas with water. If there is water, warm regions have the advantage over cold ones in terms of agricultural productivity. In the mostly arid world of the western Mediant, water can be found concentrated in oases and in narrow strips along the course of the great rivers: the Nile, the Tigris, and the Euphrates. These were the only areas in which human civilization could flourish. Thus the development of western Mediant civilization followed the characteristic pattern of 'oasis civilization.' Many of the oldest human civilizations are concentrated in this region.

Current political boundaries divide the western Mediant into many nations. In terms of culture, however, it is helpful to think of the region as consisting of three spheres. The first covers Iran and Afghanistan, populated by an old Aryan lineage speaking closely related variants of Persian. The second is Turkey, whose people are related to the Turkic peoples dwelling far to the east, in Soviet Asia, the Turkistan area of China, and the far north of Afghanistan. Their language is Turkish, an Altaic language. The third sphere consists of the Arab nations: Saudi Arabia, Iraq,

Jordan, Syria, Lebanon, Egypt, and the countries of northern Africa. The inhabitants of all these nations do not share a common history or ethnic background, but through the use of the Arabic language, they have developed a common identity as Arabs.

Needless to say, the Islamic faith serves as the unifying principle for the three cultural areas of the western Mediant. Of all the major religions of the world, Islam is the least familiar to the Japanese. If asked to make a list of the world's major religions, we would probably neglect to include it alongside Buddhism and Christianity. Yet this zealous monotheistic belief rules the hearts of hundreds of millions of people across a vast area of Asia and Africa. The nucleus of Islam lies in the western Mediant.

The tenets of Islam apply not only to the inner spiritual life of the individual, they also govern every aspect of the everyday life of the faithful. Islam prescribes the laws, customs, practices, diet, and manners that should be observed by followers. The omnipresence of Islamic principles in all aspects of life makes Islam more than a religion: it is a civilization. Thus the nations of the western Mediant are not only united by a common religion, they are within the orbit of a single civilization.

The Islamic faith has of course spread to areas beyond the western Mediant. East and West Pakistan, Indonesia, and Central Asia are Islamic in religion. But they are variant from the mainstream Islamic areas because their fundamental cultural characteristics are different. Besides these exceptions, the Mediant includes one completely anomalous nation surrounded by the uniform sea of Islamic civilization. The state of Israel is a newly established nation fulfilling the hopes of Jewish peoples around the world. As is well known, the founding of Israel caused great repercussions in the Arab world. The resultant confrontation between Israel and the Arab nations is ongoing. Another minor exception to the predominance of Islam in the region is the Christian community in Lebanon.

The struggles of the Mediant

I said earlier that the countries of the Mediant were of no concern to passengers on the 'Europe Express.' But political developments since the end of the Second World War do in fact concern us. Before the war, most of the region was under European – mostly British – rule. In the postwar period, many new independent nations have emerged, leaving only a few areas as European colonies or protectorates, such as the Portuguese territory of Goa in India, or the British protectorate of Aden.

With independence, nations such as India and Egypt have become significant players of international politics. Yet most of these nations are poor and undeveloped. Evidence abounds of their impatient yet valiant efforts to create a better future. Earlier I warned that traveling in the Mediant is difficult, but perhaps I should not have criticized these countries. The difficulties of today are probably unavoidable in building a better tomorrow. The people of these countries seem to be ashamed of their poverty and dirt. Especially in Islamic countries, one encounters proud citizens who try to prevent the photographing of scenes they are ashamed of. One could say that the nations of the Mediant are straining mightily to stand tall and proud as new members of the international community.

As one journeys through the Indian and Islamic worlds, one encounters many startling customs and bewildering practices that are based on religion. Both Hinduism and Islam are equally strict about following convention. To us these strictures may seem entirely impractical, indeed to the point of obstructing efforts at modernization. But our criticisms of the ways of other peoples are pointless. The peoples of other countries know full well the effects of their old customs, which are products of their long histories. The civilizations of the Mediant are full of memories of past glory. Even if the people understand that their traditions have become burdens for the present or the future, customs with such a long history cannot be discarded overnight simply for the sake of practicality.

Looking at the world today, it appears that sub-Saharan Africa is also in the midst of the struggles to build a better tomorrow. In this case, the struggle could be attributed to a lack of history. In contrast, the problems of the Mediant nations stem from being overburdened by history, as it were. This is not the problem of the Mediant nations alone, however. Overcoming the obstacles of history is a problem common to all members of the human race.

(January 1962)

10 From Thailand to Nepal: Scholarship, Arts, Religion

Commentary on Chapter 10

For a few years following my 1957–58 research trip to Southeast Asia, I remained sedentary in Japan. Finally, at the end of 1961, I was able to leave on my next journey. This trip covered from Southeast Asia to the Indian subcontinent.

As the second scientific study team of Osaka City University was working in Thailand, I began with a visit to Bangkok and Chiang-mai. This part of my journey is described in *Travels in Southeast Asia* (*Tōnan Ajia kikō*).[1] I continued on to Burma alone; from there I traveled to Chittagon in East Pakistan, through Dacca to India, and from Calcutta to New Delhi. On my return trip, I passed through Nepal and Burma. I spent about a week in each place and made many observations.

Among the writings based on this journey was a five-part travel essay titled 'From my trip to Asia' (Ajia no tabi kara) written for the weekly *Asahi Journal* (*Asahi Jānaru*).[2] I have not included it in this volume as it is irrelevant to our topic. Instead, I have included a three-part essay, originally published in the daily newspaper *Asahi Shinbun*, that deals with my impressions of this trip from a different angle.[3] The subtitle, 'Scholarship, arts, religion' was added later.

Scholarship

On my recent trip to Asia, I was surprised by the stately beauty of the university campuses. The brilliantly colored roofs of Chulalongkorn University and Tammasat University in Thailand impressed me deeply. At the University of Rangoon, the expansive campus and the grandeur of the faculty housing inspired envy in those of us accustomed to the cramped quarters of Japanese universities. Although some may voice criticism of the low quality learning at these places, I believe that one can find many faculty members of admirable character and accomplishment, who are actively engaged in research and training.

And yet, what rather surprised me was the scarcity of research by Southeast Asian scholars on their own countries. For example, there has been very little progress in natural science study by local scholars. An exception is the advanced forestry research conducted in Thailand, thanks to its national resource and timber industry. But in general zoological and botanical research is still in the very early stages. Meanwhile, top level imported scholarship in modern fields such as genetics and biochemistry is avidly pursued.

A similar tendency can be found in the humanities. In Japan, historical research is seen as an essential pillar of our national culture. Thus I was disturbed to find few scholars working in their own national histories in the countries I visited. At Burmese universities, for example, Burmese history is taught with a textbook written by a British scholar. At the University of Rangoon, I met a prominent authority on early Burmese history, Dr. G.H. Luce, who is British. But I did hear that a Burmese professor there, Dr. Kyaw Htay Thu, had recently completed a manuscript on Burmese narrative history.

In the field of folklore studies, one might naturally expect to find indigenous scholars as the most active and productive figures. And yet, the nations of Southeast Asia are weak in this regard as well. One bright spot is the impressive achievement of Dr. Phraya Anuman Rajadhon of Thailand, but even here his work has not launched the same kind of massive tide of folklore studies as did the work of Yanagita Kunio in Japan. In both Thailand and Burma one is more likely to find foreign scholars cultivating this field of study.

I do not wish to imply that scholarly research in these countries is backward overall. Far from it: in Thailand, recent plans to build a nuclear reactor show that in some fields the Thai people have caught up with the advanced industrialized nations. What concerns me in Southeast Asia is the weakness of scholarship in the field of national classics, the equivalent of what we call *kokugaku* (the study of Japanese classics) in Japan. The situation of the field of national classics in Southeast Asia differs greatly from that in Japan. In the latter case, a burgeoning tradition of Japanese studies already existed before the official beginning of modernization with the Meiji Restoration of 1868. In the natural sciences, the traditional study of medicinal herbs formed the basis for research on flora and fauna. In the humanities, research in Japanese history and classical literature already flourished in the pre-Meiji period. Early on, the study of Japanese classics took its place in the cultural canon alongside Chinese classics and Western learning.

In Thailand or Burma, one might consider the study of Pali sutras by Buddhist monks as the parallel to the study of Chinese classics by Japanese. There is also an equivalent practice of Western learning. But the third component of the canon, the study of national classics, is weak. Why is this so? It would not be accurate to ascribe this weakness to the suppression of national culture by colonial powers. Thailand, at least, was never colonized. It would also be wrong to assume that the nations of Southeast Asia do not possess cultures that warrant study. Each country in the region has a substantial, fascinating culture, full of research topics of great value from an outsider's perspective. What we can say by way of explanation is that these countries had comparatively early contacts with the powers of Europe. Their intake of cultural influences was perhaps more rapid than in Japan, and this denied them a similar buffer of time during which the internal development of the study of national classics could mature.

Whatever the cause, the relative weakness of the study of national classics in the South and Southeast Asian region has affected the form of nationalism found there. In Japan, the tradition of Japanese classical studies has supported a widespread consciousness of the uniqueness of Japanese civilization, which has been the core of Japanese nationalism since the Meiji period. Thus the Japanese form of nationalism is internally driven. In contrast, the nationalism of the Southeast Asian nations, although no less genuine or intense, perhaps finds its motive force in a sense of opposition to external pressures.

In a strange way, one could even say that the reason Southeast Asian nationalism, unlike Japanese nationalism, has not aligned with rightist tendencies may actually be due to the underdevelopment of the field of national classics.

Arts

I usually prefer to avoid generalizations that lump together the diverse nations occupying the region from Southeast Asia to the Indian subcontinent. But I must confess that my recent journey through these countries made me aware of the existence of a point in common among them. Or, to put it more precisely, their commonality is marked not by something that exists everywhere, but by something that is absent throughout. They lack works of art, and this to a woeful degree.

Of course I do not mean that there is a complete absence of any artwork. But in comparison to Japan, the dearth of artwork was undeniable. Whether visiting a public building or a private residence, the walls and spaces where we might expect to see something hanging remained empty. In contrast, when I had occasion to visit the home of a resident Japanese or European, the sight of paintings hung in the expected places made me feel reunited with something I had missed.

The countries of this region have splendid artistic histories. I need hardly mention the Khmer culture that grew from ancient Angkor, or the splendid statuary of medieval Southeast Asia. India has given us magnificent ancient sculptures and lively statues of the Hindu gods. I personally do not favor Indian miniature painting, but must admit that their amazing exactitude is the crystallization of a great artistic energy.

However, none of these historical art forms exists any longer. I wondered what had taken their place in the present world. Where is today's Asian art, and where are the artists? Artwork seemed to be found only in museums. In a Calcutta museum, I saw many people who seemed to be art students, copying old deities. In the Rangoon Museum, I saw a collection of modern works by Burmese artists. There were some worthwhile pieces, exhibited alongside decidedly inferior ones. I may sound too cynical, but it seems that in present day South and Southeast Asia both the art and the artists have been shut away inside museums. The region's great historical heritage of artistic production has not continued as a living, vital tradition.

Some people may say that we must be patient: since the nations of this area are still young, their modern artistic practices will in time develop in tandem with their overall development. However, I do not believe that the weakness of present day art can be attributed so simply to general underdevelopment. Rather, it may be that in these Asian nations, aesthetic worth is not very important, at least at the present time. Within the Japanese value system, aesthetic merit holds a very high position. But it seems that in this part of Asia religious merit, or perhaps practical or materialistic values, are ascendant. If this is the case, an alignment of our values will never come about simply through patience.

Leaving aside the question of hopes for the future, the artistic impoverishment of the South and Southeast Asian region is cause for consternation today. In order to bind the world together with garlands of flowers, as it were, it would be best to have as many strands as possible. Sports are an excellent means of transcending borders, and art could be too. But although international cultural exchanges are a laudable goal, I fear that at present we cannot realistically expect artistic exchanges between Japan and the Southeast Asian nations to be very effective. Perhaps this is why our interactions with Asia tend to concentrate in the single strand of political relations.

There is one artistic genre that shows some potential for meaningful international exchange. The art of dance is alive and well in Thailand, Burma, and India. Each locale has its own unique lineage and technique. Of course, the performers may have to come up with special routines and refinements in order to appeal to sophisticated Japanese audiences. But just last year, an Indonesian gamelan dance troupe received great acclaim for its performances in Japan. And when I was in Rangoon recently, the performances of a Chinese ballet troupe were very popular. This shows me that the art of dance can be one of the ties to bind Asia together.

Religion

The peoples of Asia follow a multitude of religious faiths. In Thailand and Burma, Theravada Buddhism is the dominant practice. East Pakistan is Islamic, while the majority of Indians are Hindus. Nepal has both Hindus and Mahayana Buddhists.

The human race as a whole has demonstrated great passion about religious faith, especially for the last thousand years or so. The profusion of religious edifices is a testament to this passion. I tried to visit as many historical sites as possible during my recent trip. Most of these were temples of various faiths, built during the last millennium of religious fervor, although some were even older.

In the Katmandu basin in Nepal, I visited many Hindu temples. One of them was said to date from the fifteenth century, during the Malla dynasty. Strangely enough it looked quite new, with bright clean colors. I was told that the temple had recently been repainted, as it had become old and dirty. But to my eyes, a nearby pagoda that had escaped repainting looked far more sublime. I heard that this one, too, was scheduled for repainting soon. It seemed to me a great shame to remove the patina of age.

This attitude towards historical religious structures was not limited to Nepal. I observed similar instances across the spectrum of religions in the region. In the ancient Burmese capital of Pagan stand several thousand Buddhist stupas, truly great historical relics built before the thirteenth century. Many of them have been completely renovated and painted white, making them look newly erected. Of course the temple was still vital and filled with worshippers.

Also in Burma, in the jungle near Pegu, a strangely shaped hill was discovered during the construction of a railroad in the late nineteenth century. Excavation of the hill revealed the figure of an enormous reclining Buddha, carved in the tenth century. It was fully restored, and nowadays one can view a clean, smooth-faced statue of the Buddha lying under a steel-framed roof. For those of us with a Japanese religious sensibility, this sort of presentation seems too graphic to appreciate.

In Japan, the more a religious edifice becomes weathered and moss-covered, the more deeply it is appreciated. But in these Asian countries, a covering of moss signifies decline and extinction. Moss is scraped away, and the figure or structure is repainted. Although the paint glistens, the glow from the inner depths is obscured.

What accounts for this difference in sensibility? I realized that we should not deride as lowbrow the religious sentiments of these Asian peoples. To the Japanese, religion exists as a part of history. That is why we allow temples to become vacant, molder, and fall to ruin. But for the peoples in these Asian countries, religion is significant above and beyond historical meanings. That is why temples, gods, and the Buddha are never perishable. They must be constantly reproduced and regenerated.

In this sense, religion is truly alive for the peoples of Asia. Perhaps those of us who find beauty in ruined pagodas are the truly lowbrow, as we confuse religious inspiration with aesthetic pleasure.

There is one example of a Japanese custom that can help us understand the Asian religious sensibility. Every twenty years, we rebuild the Ise Shrine. The gods of Ise are alive, and living gods need a new, well-kept abode. Even the Japanese know that Ise should not become overgrown with moss.

Meanwhile, thinking back to the region that stretches from Thailand to Nepal, I remember the disrepair of machinery and public facilities there. It is amazing how lack of maintenance can shorten the lifespan of these objects. Without regular maintenance, machinery quickly rusts and becomes immobile, buildings leak and really do become overgrown with moss. In Japan, by contrast, religious structures may be moss-covered, but machinery is kept shining.

We need to be aware of the great cultural gap in our sense of which things are alive and vital, and which things are part of the dead past.

(February 1962)

11 Methodological Notes on Comparative Religion

Commentary on Chapter 11

As the reader knows, I spent a number of years working out my general theories of civilization, which were presented in essays such as 'An Ecological View of History' and 'A New World Map of Civilization,' included in this volume. Subsequently, I felt it my duty to extend the techniques of comparative analysis to specific areas of civilization, such as religion, communications, commerce, and so on. Towards that end, I collected materials, researched, and wrote many drafts, but various circumstances prevented me from completing the task.

In the summer of 1963, without having finished my comparative religion project, I went to Tanganyika as a member of Kyoto University's African scientific investigation team. I remained there until the following spring, spending most of my time studying the herders of the savanna. I took along my notes on the comparative theory of religion, and during my free time I wrote. The text that I completed in the African savanna was entitled 'Methodological Notes on Comparative Religion' (Hikaku shūkyōron e no hōhōronteki oboegaki). I wrote the first half in a cabin at the Kabogo base on the shores of Lake Tanganyika, and the second half in my tent at Lake Eyasi. Someday I hope to complete a concrete comparative theory based on the methodology presented here.

This essay on methodology was published in the journal of the Institute for Humanistic Studies, *Jinbun Gakuhō*.[1] Because I wrote it as an academic thesis, it differs in tone from the other essays in this volume. I decided to include it in this collection in its original form, as it demonstrates the continuity of my interests since I first presented 'An Ecological View of History.'

I Applying Ecological Studies to Religion

Extending the ecological view of history

It is quite common to employ ecological methodology when theorizing about the origins or early genesis of human civilization. Almost without exception, analyzing the birth of a given civilization involves a careful consideration of the environmental conditions in its place of origin. And yet when it comes to the further development of the civilization, after its earliest origins, it is far less typical to use the methods of ecological analysis. I have often wondered why this should be.

I submit that ecological studies can provide a useful template for the scientific understanding of the entire span of human history. Until now, various scholars have used the methods of ecology to analyze historical phenomena in a piecemeal fashion. I believe that a broad, multi-faceted expansion of these efforts will lead to many new perceptions and problem-solving opportunities.

My previous essay, 'An Ecological View of History,' grew from my supposition that an ecological perspective could be applied to human history. I wanted to discover what new possibilities might be opened by a valid ecological view of history. It was an extremely generalized delineation of my ideas, which evoked many responses, both positive and negative.

In my earlier essay, the 'history' under consideration was restricted in time and place, rather than an overall history of the human race. Nor was my analysis a multi-faceted treatment of the many complex aspects of civilization. The work of expanding the purview, geographically, temporally, and topically, was left to a later date. In this piece I intend to begin my efforts at expansion by taking up the issue of religion in human history, and by considering various analytic methods.

The ecological study of religion

How can the ecological approach to history help us to understand the historical context of religious development? Of course, posing the question in this way assumes that it can be answered through extrapolation from my usual analysis of civilization from the perspective of ecological history. In fact, however, the ecological perspective is not limited to historical analysis, just as religion does not exist only in history. So, to put the question more broadly, how can we understand the phenomenon of religion from an ecological perspective? In this sense, our task could be described as the formulation of a comparative theory of religion from the perspective of ecological studies, or if I may rephrase it thus, the ecological study of religion. The question of the historical context of religion is one part of this more general field.

It would be beyond the reach of this article to set out a complete methodology for the ecological study of religion, or a comprehensive explanation of the development of world religions derived from the ecological view of history. To do so would require the collection of a massive amount of specific data. My modest intention here is to explore some key methodological issues, as a prerequisite to such empirical research efforts.

Until now, the comparative research of religions has dealt mainly with the doctrinal contents of various religions, such as their perspectives on the sacred, the world, and salvation, along with their observances and practices. Let us consider here methods to examine these issues in the wider context of religion as a part of the life phenomena of human beings, including the relationships between religion and the environment, or religion and the land. To put it more specifically, this is an effort to consider the various conditions for religion, such as its origins, establishment, dissemination, and decline, as they correlate to other life phenomena.

The meaning of religion in the context of human evolution

Of all the phenomena of human civilization, religion is perhaps the most difficult to analyze from an ecological perspective. The evolution of human civilization has seen the development of many different patterns of social organization, such as hunter-gatherers, herders, or farmers, each with its particular mode of production and consumption. For such concrete phenomena, understanding the interaction with and restraints imposed by the environment is relatively straightforward. In contrast, it can be quite difficult to draw the connection between external circumstances and the deeply internal phenomenon of religion.

Indeed, there is a great deal about religion that we do not understand. We know that it is a common phenomenon of human society, but what does it mean for human beings? I do not care to launch a philosophical debate about the essence of religious faith, but I would like to investigate the significance of religion in human evolution. In other words, how did religion arise, and what function has it fulfilled since the birth of humankind?

Although it is usually difficult to formulate theories of origin, we must ask why religion came to be. There have been earlier attempts at this task, beginning with E.B. Taylor's well-known theory of animism. Such theories have provided valuable comparative insights into early religious formations, but the absolute origin of religion remains unclear. Thus an apparently ridiculous question such as 'Are apes religious?' is in fact non-trivial. There have been impressive advances in the study of the social behavior of primates in recent years, but nothing has been observed that might indicate the existence of religion among apes. Still, we cannot predict what may come to light with future advances in the field of primatology.

Language is another human phenomenon whose absolute origin is obscure, although somewhat better understood than religion. The use of symbols in the animal world is an accepted fact; and recent primatological research has shed some light on the development of vocal language. Furthermore, there is hard physical evidence, such as the development of the vocal chords and the speech center in the cerebrum, which allows us to place the use of language in the course of evolution. It is clear that a society with language is at a more advanced evolutionary stage than one without. Despite the lack of evidence as to absolute origins, the centrality of language in human evolution is unquestionable.

Unfortunately, we do not have the benefit of similar physical evidence to aide us in our understanding of religion. I do not anticipate that a 'religious center' will be discovered in the cerebrum. Moreover, it is highly debatable whether a society with religion can be considered at a more advanced evolutionary stage than one without it. Certainly we cannot conceive of a society without language, but can we not imagine one without religion?

To understand the function of religion, we should think about whether it is a necessary criterion of human society. Or is it possible that religion only appears at a certain stage in human development, eventually fading away after its set function has been achieved? Or again, does it continue forever as a companion to human life, albeit transmuted into other guises? We know very little about these basic questions. For the time being, let us leave them pending, while we investigate the relationship between religion and the more concrete phenomena of human life.

Shamanism and the belief in heavenly deities

It could be argued that religion is always a 'social' phenomenon, since the various factors affecting the origin and development of religion are, after all, the result of societal conditions. If one follows this assumption, analysis of the interaction between religion and society is the purview of sociology of religion, not ecology. However, the actual facts support the view that the conditions of the origin, spread, and decline of religion are not simply 'social' in nature, just as more generally, the various phenomena of human history do not arise only from 'cultural' causes. There are too many aspects of human civilization that are clearly the result of adaptations to the physical environment to believe otherwise. This holds true for religion as well. For example, there have been attempts to explain the shamanism practiced widely by the peoples of the arctic forest zone as a manifestation of 'arctic hysteria.' Since we do not know how this arctic hysteria is triggered, we might be inclined to embrace the cultural or social explanation of this behavior. But I think it would be more appropriate to view it as a form of neuro-physiological adaptation, or non-adaptation, to a particular environment. It is not enough to simply describe the psychology of arctic hysteria: we must also have a deep understanding of the particular environment of the arctic.

As a further example, take the form of primitive belief typically found in herder societies. After the thesis of Schmidt, this has been widely described as a belief in non-personified heavenly deities. When we speculate on the reasons for the development of this belief, it is not hard to see that a much shorter, more direct line can be drawn from the ecological realities that govern nomadic life than from sociological conditions. At this time we lack concrete evidence proving the correlation between the conditions of a semi-arid pastoral landscape and a belief in non-personified heavenly deities. Nevertheless it seems at the very least that we will find important clues here to answer the question of the conditions influencing the formation of religion.

Once again I would like to suggest that religion can be understood only by keeping firmly in mind a comprehensive knowledge of human life systems, including a full appreciation of the interactions with the environment.

Of course there have been many splendid results in the study of religion through the disciplines of the psychology, the sociology, the ethnology, and the anthropology of religion. Furthermore, the important technique of integrating the physical and cultural attributes of human life does lie within the purview of anthropology. Shamanism and the belief in non-personified heavenly deities have been explored as anthropological issues. One could legitimately ask whether the ecological study of religion, whose necessity I am so avidly asserting, is not in fact the same as the anthropological study of religion. In theory, I agree. I further acknowledge that the technique of integrated, comprehensive description is a particular strength of the anthropological approach. However, the discipline of anthropology has traditionally focused on undeveloped peoples as its main subject of research. The anthropology of religion is typically limited to the study of primitive beliefs such as spirit worship, totemism, or manaism. The so-called higher religions have generally been excluded from research. In my view, however, we must include those higher or more developed religions in order to correctly understand the significance of religion within the overall course of human history. For this reason it is necessary to move beyond the traditional disciplinary boundaries of anthropology.

II An Epidemiological Analogy

The analogy between religion and infectious disease

As we attempt to develop a workable methodology to study religion as a phenomenon of human life systems, we might profit by using an analogy. The analogy that I wish to propose, which I hope will produce valuable clues, is that of disease, particularly infectious disease. Naturally I do not mean to suggest that religion is a disease. Nevertheless, there are a number of similarities between religion and disease. There are several factors that characterize infectious diseases; religion, too, manifests roughly the same factors. I can cite at least five similarities.

First, both religion and disease require the presence of a propagating agent in order to spread. In the case of an infectious disease, the agent is some sort of pathogen, be it a bacteria or a virus.

Religion also spreads through propagation, in this case, of a religious concept or idea. Here the agents may be prophets or founders of religious sects, or the many believers who follow such leaders; or they may be 'propagation specialists' such as priests and monks. These are analogous to carriers of disease.

Second, there is the question of the scale of dissemination. Unless the pathogen of a particular disease is spread through a wide area, an epidemic will not occur. Similarly, it is only when a religious concept or practice is disseminated widely enough that it takes hold as a religion.

Third, when a human body comes in contact with a disease pathogen, it will not necessarily be affected. There are a wide variety of responses depending on the health of the individual. In the same way, particular individuals will respond differently to exposure to a religious concept – some will become 'infected' with the religion, and some will not.

Fourth, the social conditions of a particular place are a major factor affecting the spread of both disease and religion. Social structure, the style of residences, hygienic conditions, and organizations play a decisive role. It is the same in the case of religion.

Finally, the state of the environment is another factor that bears upon both infectious disease and religion. Climate, water supply, and other broad environmental conditions must be considered for their effects upon the spread of religion and disease.

The epidemiology of the spirit

Just as with the study of religion, the study of disease can be approached via several avenues. For example, the study of the nature of pathogens, which are the initial seeds for the spread of disease, lies within the purview of bacteriology, virology, or parasitology. The analogous approach to religion would be the study of specific ideas and practices, which constitute the initial building blocks of religious growth. Pathologists, meanwhile, study the effects of disease upon the body. In that this is a type of objective description of physical experience, its correlate in the field of religious studies must be the method of religious psychology.

We must not forget to mention epidemiology as another essential approach to the study of medicine. This academic field covers the complex of conditions related to the origins, propagation, and demise of disease, especially of infectious and parasitic diseases. Needless to say, social conditions are deeply implicated in the dissemination of infectious and parasitic diseases. But just as important are the broad environmental conditions that are also part of circumstances of a society. Furthermore, the internal conditions of each individual in society must also be taken into account. The epidemiological method synthesizes all of these factors.

Earlier I suggested that the ecological study of religion must comprehensively integrate all of the factors, both external and internal, relating to the origin, propagation, and decline of religion. This correlates exactly with the role of epidemiology in the study of disease. In this sense, what I have until now termed the ecology of religion could also be called the epidemiological study of religion, or better yet the epidemiology of the spirit. Conversely, epidemiology could be seen as the ecological study of disease; and in fact it is sometimes called medical ecology in common parlance. The 'epidemiology of the spirit' is not a direct application of bio-ecological theory, but it does share the conceptual approach and research methodology of ecology.

Epidemic versus endemic

The field of epidemiology originally developed as the study of epidemic diseases, as opposed to endemic diseases. The defining characteristic of the latter is a long-term presence in a strictly limited area, while the former is characterized by a pattern of rapid, widespread propagation over a short period of time. In an epidemic, potentially anyone can become infected, regardless of local climate or ethnic group. Typical examples of epidemic disease are cholera and bubonic plague. Preventing the spread of epidemic diseases requires strict quarantine measures, since the environment offers little or no protection from contagion. Pandemic is the term used for the most severe epidemics, such as the Spanish influenza that swept around the world in 1919.

Endemic disease, in contrast, is deeply connected to a particular locality or environment. Even when it is a continuous presence in one area, it does not rapidly spread elsewhere. Examples of endemic disease are *schistosomiasis japonica* (also known as Katayama's disease) found in the Hiroshima region, or malaria found in the tropics.

However, the distinction between endemic and epidemic is not always clear-cut. Depending upon the circumstances, an epidemic disease can transform into an endemic one, and vice versa. There have been cases in which a disease endemic to a certain locality suddenly becomes widespread, and others where a worldwide epidemic or pandemic settles in one locality to become an endemic disease.

These linked concepts of epidemic and endemic are likely to be useful in the study of religion. Certainly we can call to mind examples both of 'endemic' religions, deeply rooted in the particular environmental conditions of a locality, and of 'epidemic' religions, which have spread across wide areas of the world. What is more, the distinction between so-called endemic and epidemic religions is also porous, with the potential of transformation from one into the other, depending upon the circumstances. Religious history includes examples of locally based faiths suddenly spreading across a wide region; or again of once widespread religions that exist today as relics of the past, limited to a small area.

Now that the fluidity of the concepts of epidemic and endemic is well understood, the field of epidemiology is no longer limited to the study of epidemic disease. It also studies endemic disease, and the conditions for conversion between the two. Traditionally, the study of epidemic and endemic diseases focused on infectious illness spread through bacteria, viruses, and parasites. But the wider scope of today's epidemiology includes non-infectious diseases, or phenomena that are not even diseases in the strict sense. In some instances, epidemiological analysis is applied to certain types of frequently occurring disasters or accidents. It is the task of modern epidemiology to determine the presence of causal factors that might explain the frequency of these occurrences. It is also possible to use today's methods to clarify whether or not a disease is infectious.

We should take note of this progress in epidemiology, and aim for a broader perspective in our ecology of religion as well. This might help us to clarify, for example, whether religion necessarily spreads through 'contagion,' or whether seemingly similar religious practices might arise independently in similar sets of environmental conditions. Earlier I mentioned that the practice of shamanism was common among peoples of the arctic region. It could be that shamanism was propagated among the various arctic peoples. But it could also be that the shamanistic personality, which lies at the core of the practice, is more likely to develop in arctic conditions. Insufficient exposure to ultraviolet light, combined with other conditions, causes a high incidence of rickets in the arctic; perhaps in an analogous way there is something about the arctic environment that increases the occurrence of shamanistic personalities. Here I am speaking only of the origin of the shamanistic personality itself, rather than shamanism as a cultural phenomenon. The cultural practice of shamanism is constructed around the existence of shamanistic personalities, augmented by an interpreter, dancing, and other cultural phenomena. This is very similar to the way in which the various arctic peoples attach different mixtures of cultural additives to the commonly existing disease of rickets, such that the behavior and social position of rickets patients varies from tribe to tribe.

Disease and religion

As I stated when I began this theoretical comparison between religion and disease, I do not mean to suggest that religion is a disease. For one thing, religious believers do not evince any organic abnormalities. And even with our recently expanded concept of disease, it would be too great a stretch to classify religion as a form of contagious mental illness. The question of whether religion is in some way abnormal or pathological in its effect upon the health of humankind cannot be answered until we have a clearer understanding of its function in the context of human history. At the current stage of human history, there does not seem to be a conclusive answer.

Even though we cannot classify religion as a type of disease, the connection between the two goes deeper than merely abstract analogy. Nowadays we tend to think of religion as an exercise of the spirit, whereas disease (including mental illness) is related to the physical body. In the past, however, illness was understood as not simply a physical but also a spiritual disorder. The waves of epidemics in ninth and tenth century Japan were attributed at the time to vengeful ghosts. Even today, many African tribal people believe illness can be caused by someone's curse. Curing such illnesses is believed to require not only physical medicine, but also spiritual healing through magical incantation.

I may be criticized for conflating religion and magic in examples like these. It is true that there are differences. Magic is a utilitarian means to and end, while the nature of religion is less utilitarian and more linked to the sense of purpose of the self. There are theories, such as those of J.G. Frazer, that locate the origins of religion in the inadequacies of magical rituals. Nevertheless, it is often difficult to distinguish between magic and religion in actual practice. It is quite typical for even so-called higher order religions to contain elements of magical rituals. The ancient function of magic as the cause of or cure for illness is yet another aspect of the deep relationship between disease and religion.

History of disease and history of religion

Even if we leave aside the role of magic, there remains a link between religion and disease, in that most religions contain tales of illness within their myths of origin. The major world religions of Buddhism and Christianity are no exception. Prince Gautama Siddhartha of Kapilavastu was motivated by his encounter with sick persons to abandon his palace for an ascetic life in the mountains and forests. Many of the most renowned miracles of Jesus Christ involved healing the sick.

There is no doubt that the existence of disease is one of the inherent conditions of the human race that was conducive to the development of religion. In this sense, disease can be treated as an internal, spiritual experience rather than a physical one, in parallel to the internal, spiritual experience of religion. As such, religion can be seen as the flip side of illness in the formation of our spiritual framework.

I would like to explore this point from another angle by proposing, just as a working hypothesis, that there might exist some relationship between the history of disease and the history of religion. Unfortunately, we have very few facts at hand, since the role of disease in human history is an as yet undeveloped academic field. However, I suspect that once systematic research is conducted, a relationship may be discovered between patterns of infection – particularly the spread of epidemics – and the rapid dissemination of religion. In Japan, we know that the Gion Festival in Kyoto has clear origins as a supplication to banish pestilence. The Buddhist ceremonies known as Gion-e and Imamiya-e are types of services for departed souls. Whatever their origins, the historical background to the rise of such events in medieval Kyoto was the people's fear of the spreading epidemics that accompanied the concentration of population in an urban environment. I am not qualified to give examples from other countries, but it may be possible to discover a relationship between the rise and fall of Christianity, and the ebb and flow of the plague or other infectious diseases.

To summarize my thoughts thus far, I hope that my initial analogy between religion and illness, together with the consideration of parallels between religious ecology and epidemiology in the following section, will be able to take us beyond superficial comparisons. Perhaps it will be possible to position what I call religious ecology as an extension of the field of epidemiology. I hope there will be future opportunities for detailed research in this direction.

III Benares and Jerusalem

The site of Buddha's first sermon

In pursuit of my inquiry into the relationship between locale and religion, I would like to compare the ancient birthplaces of two major religions: Israel, the birthplace of Christianity, and the Ganges river valley, which gave rise to Buddhism.

Turning first to the Ganges, let us examine the town of Sarnath, located on the banks of the river near Benares, in what is now Uttar Pradesh. The prevalence of ancient Buddhist structures, such as the stone pillar of Emperor Ashoka, a large stupa, and monasteries, indicate that Sarnath was once a major center of Buddhism. Sarnath can be thought of as the birthplace of Buddhism, but it is not where the Buddha attained enlightenment. It is told that the Buddha gained enlightenment under a Bo tree in Buddhagaya. This place is now called Bodh Gaya, located to the east of Sarnath, on the outskirts of the town of Gaya in the state of Bihar. There one can find the remains of a temple complex, including a large pagoda and the flourishing successor of the Bo tree under which the Buddha is said to have sat. After achieving enlightenment in Buddhagaya, the Buddha journeyed westward to the Deer Park, where he gave what is known as the first sermon of Benares, also referred to as 'The Sermon on Setting in Motion the Wheel of Truth.' Deer Park is none other than present day Sarnath.

Buddhism has four great holy places: Lumbini, where the Buddha was born; Buddhagaya, where he reached enlightenment; Sarnath, site of his first sermon; and Kusinagara, where he died. Pilgrimages to these sites were popular among the faithful from early on. Sarnath, one of the four holy places, flourished as a major center of ancient Buddhism. In the early seventh century, the Chinese monk Xuan-zhuang visited and wrote on how thriving Sarnath was.

The fate of Buddhism in India

What does one see nowadays in Sarnath? The area was largely excavated in the early twentieth century, leading to the preservation of the remains of monasteries and other sites. The lion shaped capital of the column of Emperor Ashoka was placed in a local museum, along with many other splendid works of art found during the excavations. Sarnath also has more recent Buddhist structures, such as a beautiful temple built by the Mahabodhi Society, an organization of Indian Buddhists. Inside are murals of the Buddha's life by a Japanese painter of Buddhist art. Nearby is a temple built by Chinese Buddhists in a completely Chinese style. Across the way from this, yellow-robed Burmese monks come and go from their lodgings.

This picture of life in current day Sarnath symbolizes the fate of Buddhism in India today. Despite the many artifacts of past glory, there is scant evidence of present day Buddhist activity among Indians. Instead there are Japanese murals, a Chinese temple, and Burmese monks. Why is it that in the very birthplace of Buddhism in India, so much of what one sees is foreign? What has happened to Indian Buddhism?

The fact is that although India is its birthplace, Buddhism has a very low profile in present day India. The status of Indian Buddhism nowadays is not well known in Japan, even among the intellectual class. Certainly very few people can accurately give the percentage of Buddhists in the Indian population: based on my informal surveys, typical answers ranged between a high of thirty percent and a low of five percent. In fact, there are only some one hundred thousand Buddhists in India, which is less than 0.1 percent of the total population. Buddhism hardly exists in India anymore.

Hindu holy sites

As I mentioned above, the ancient Buddhist city of Sarnath is on the outskirts of Benares, a city which traces its history back to the pre-Christian era. Benares is the customary anglicized name of the city, but now that the Indian state is reviving the old Sanskrit place names, the sign at the airport reads Varanasi.

Varanasi is one of the seven holy places of Hinduism. Here Hinduism is alive and well, in contrast to Buddhism. Ardent Hindu pilgrims from all over the country gather at the numerous Hindu temples. Rows of *ghats,* for cremation of the dead, line the banks of the Ganges, while crowds of Hindus bathe in the sacred waters. The bustle of religious activity contrasts sharply with the stillness of Sarnath.

If a present day Buddhist were to visit Sarnath on a pilgrimage to the holy sites, the largest part of his encounter would be with the Hinduism of Varanasi rather than the Buddhism of Sarnath. The scene would likely cause great shock to naive foreign pilgrims who think that India, the birthplace of Buddhism, continues to be a Buddhist country. Once there, it becomes impossible to remain ignorant of the fact that Sarnath just barely clings to existence, surrounded by the swirling flood of Hinduism.

Actually, Buddhism in Sarnath was for some time completely submerged by the wave of Hinduism. After the rout of Indian Buddhism at the end of the twelfth century, Hindus occupied Sarnath and Bodh Gaya. It was only with the excavation of the Buddhist sites in the early twentieth century, and the efforts of the Mahabodhi Society, that Sarnath re-emerged as a Buddhist site.

The occupation of Jerusalem

Let us now turn our discussion to the birthplace of Christianity, in current day Israel. The importance of this region in the minds of Christians can be seen in the phenomenon of the Crusades, which took as their goal the recovery of the so-called Holy Land.

Jerusalem was, and is, a holy site for Christians, as the unforgettable scene of the most dramatic events of the life of Jesus. His last actions, his death, and his resurrection all took place there. The custom of pilgrimage to the Holy Land began early among followers of Christ, and over the years Jerusalem welcomed many believers.

In the early seventh century, Jerusalem was occupied by Moslems. Even so, Christian pilgrimages continued unimpeded. The decisive event that created difficulties for Christian pilgrims was the occupation of Jerusalem by Turks of the Seljuk dynasty in 1071. The new masters of Jerusalem persecuted pilgrims and created a crisis for the Byzantine Empire.

The First Crusade began in 1096, in response to the Pope's call for the recovery of the Holy Land. In 1099 the Crusaders fulfilled their goal by successfully retaking Jerusalem. Subsequently, groups of Crusaders set up several other Christian kingdoms in the Levant. This situation did not last long, however. In 1244, Jerusalem was occupied by the Ayub dynasty of Egypt, and later by other rulers. The land considered holy by the Christians was not returned to their control until the early twentieth century.

Jerusalem, the city of Jews and Moslems

Jerusalem is still a holy site for Christians, but nowadays when pilgrims make their journey there, they find only the remains of the ancient Christian past. Christianity as a living practice does not have much of an existence there any more. The birthplace of Christ is surrounded by other religions.

The Jerusalem of today is divided between two nations, neither of them Christian: the newly created Jewish state of Israel, and the Islamic state of Jordan. Their border runs right through the city, dividing it in two.

Long before the coming of Christ, Jerusalem was the capital of ancient Israel. It was a holy site for Jews, home to the temple of Yahweh. The temple was destroyed after the uprising of the Jews against the Roman Empire in the latter half of the first century A.D., and the Jews were driven out of the city. This situation continued until the ancient Jewish state of Israel was reconstructed in the twentieth century.

For a thousand years, the rulers of the holy city of Jerusalem were not Jews or Christians, but the followers of yet a third religion, Islam. The Moslems also saw Jerusalem as their own 'Holy Land,' based on legend that Mohammed, the founder of Islam, had visited Jerusalem. But even supposing such a visit were historical fact, it still seems a rather tenuous reason to claim Jerusalem as a holy site, compared, say, to death and resurrection. More likely a stronger explanation for the continuity of Jerusalem as a holy site is that Islam was built upon underpinnings of Judaism and Christianity.

IV Method and Hypothesis

The displacement and dissemination of religions

Benares, India and Jerusalem, Israel are geographically distant, yet when we trace a line from their ancient history to their present fate they show a curious similarity. Each place gave birth to what became a major world religion: Buddhism began in Benares, and Christianity in Jerusalem. In the world of today, however, neither faith is practiced in any vital way at the site of origin. They have each been displaced by entirely different religions, which dominate the regions around the respective birthplaces.

I am recapitulating this information because I would like to bring the focus back to the main topic, the relationship between locality and religion. In order to draw lessons from a comparison of Benares and Jerusalem, our investigation could use either location or religion as the axis, and the other as the variable.

To begin by using location as our analytic axis, we know that both cities have been holy sites for more than two millennia. However, in each case the religion that marked the city as a holy birthplace has since been replaced as the predominant religion of the region, not by just one successor, but by a series of later religions. This phenomenon should direct our careful scrutiny to the successor religions in each particular locality, if anything is to be learned about locality and religion.

If, however, we take religion as our primary axis of analysis, different issues are highlighted. The religious content of Buddhism and Christianity is of course entirely different. Nevertheless, the relationships between these faiths and their respective places of origin are strikingly similar. In other words, both religions migrated away from their birthplaces and flourished elsewhere. This points us toward an examination of the dynamics of religious migration and dissemination.

It appears that Benares and Jerusalem are following the same model, in giving birth to a religion that subsequently migrated to several other areas, and in playing host to several successor religions. It might be possible to use these similarities as the key to developing a thesis on the displacement and dissemination of religion in human history.

Hypothesis of corresponding stages

The similarity of phenomena in Benares and Jerusalem, or in North India and the Levant, is not sufficient ground to derive a more broadly applicable thesis. But at least it is a starting point, and if we proceed logically through the following steps, we might be able to arrive at such a general thesis. First, we must propose a preliminary hypothesis based on what we know from our comparison of Benares and Jerusalem. Next we should test this working hypothesis to see whether it is applicable to other cases from around the world. If it is applicable, the hypothesis becomes a thesis; if not, appropriate modifications should be made. Finally, after the viability of the thesis has been established, we will of course have to inquire why such a thesis could be created – in other words, what has made it possible?

To begin, let us consider what sort of hypothesis we might propose to explain the successive displacement of religions in a given locality such as North India or the Levant. In North India there were three shifts, from Brahmanism, to Buddhism, to Hinduism. In the Levant too, three different religions were predominant in succession: Judaism, Christianity, and Islam. These factors suggest the following two hypotheses.

First, the three stages of religious succession in North India correspond to the three great religions of the Levant. That is, Brahmanism corresponds to Judaism, Buddhism to Christianity, and Hinduism to Islam.

Second, this pattern of three successive stages of religious displacement is not limited to North India and the Levant, but can be found in other areas as well.

Taking these two hypotheses together, we could dub it our 'hypothesis of corresponding stages.' Let me pause for a moment to clarify what I mean by 'stages' and 'correspondence,' although I feel it is safe to leave until later a description of the details of correspondence.

The use of the term 'stages' is not meant to indicate stages of development in terms of religious doctrine. Although we call Buddhism as the 'second stage' and Hinduism as the 'third stage' of predominance in North India, this does not mean that Hinduism is a more highly developed or sophisticated religion than Buddhism. I could have used the word 'type' instead of 'stage,' but I wanted to emphasize the historical chain of succession from one religion to the next.

The meaning of the term 'corresponding,' in the sense that I intend it, could best be described as performing a similar social function. As I have mentioned, the main topic of this piece is the relationship between locality and religion. Locality is shorthand for the society and ecology of a place. So when I say that two religions 'correspond' to one another, I mean that they play similar social and historical roles in their respective localities. I do not necessarily mean that the two faiths are similar in doctrine or practice.

Lessons from stratigraphy

In the geological field of stratigraphy, scientists examine layers, or strata, of the earth. Samples from various strata can be compared to determine the correspondences among different areas as they undergo the process of geological change. Our effort to understand the correspondences between the stages of religious succession in different localities is much the same. Just as the first stratum of region A corresponds to the first stratum of region B in geologic terms, I submit that one can say the first stage in region A corresponds to the first stage in region B in terms of religious history.

In stratigraphy, it is common to use the geological strata of one area as the standard against which others are compared. In my current inquiry, I believe it is possible to use the examples of North India and the Levant as the standard for the phenomenon of religious succession vis-à-vis which other cases can be indexed.

Another instance of standard setting is the use of the four ice ages of Northern Europe as the norm to which others are compared. There are regions whose succession of ice ages does not fit the standard European pattern of four. This is not a problem, because a standard is simply an index of measurement; the particular characteristics of different regions can be described in relation to the standard region. Similarly, I can easily predict that not every case of religious succession will neatly correspond to the three stages of my North Indian/Levantine standard. But we will be able to describe the particular characteristics of other regions in relation to the standard.

The immunity phenomenon

I warned earlier that at some point we would have to explain what aspects of religious history made it possible to establish such a thing as a 'hypothesis of corresponding stages.' Fundamentally, it is the relative infrequency of religious epidemics in the locales under consideration that made possible the development of my thesis. Three religious successions may seem like a great many at first, but considering the very high number of religions over the whole course of human civilization, three is actually quite low. It is in fact startling that it should be so low, until one understands that this result follows naturally from the principles of what we have named the 'epidemiology of the spirit.'

As an extension of the earlier analogy between medical epidemiology and spiritual epidemiology, we can easily imagine the phenomenon of 'religious immunity.' Namely, a society that has been afflicted by a religious epidemic will attain a sort of immunity, which inures it to the subsequent influence of similar types of religion. For a certain period of time, this society will not succumb to the onslaught of another religious craze. However, societal immunity weakens with the passage of time, just as medical immunity does. Eventually the society will become vulnerable to 'infection' when exposed to another religious epidemic. Apparently the effect of religious immunity is measured in centuries rather than in years, which easily explains why a locality might succumb to only three waves of religious epidemics over the three thousand years of human civilization.

At some future point we should also carefully consider what specific social and psychological mechanisms contribute to the phenomenon of religious immunity. In any case, the creative borrowing of analogies from other fields certainly seems to be an effective way of advancing phenomenological research.

Hypothesis of corresponding regions

The 'hypothesis of corresponding stages' was an effort to compare the religious shifts of two locales. We examined the connection between locality and religion by using locality as the axis. In contrast, what happens when we look at the same question by using religion as the axis?

In the 'hypothesis of corresponding stages,' the second religious stage in North India, Buddhism, corresponds to Christianity in the Levant. Despite their significant differences in terms of doctrinal content and practice, Buddhism and Christianity share very similar features in terms of their connection to their localities. Each ended up being virtually eradicated in its place of birth, but was disseminated widely in other regions. Buddhism spread mainly eastward from its point of origin, while Christianity spread chiefly to the west. Within the Old World (that is, leaving out the much later incorporation of the Americas into the known world) Buddhism reached the far eastern extreme of Japan, while Christianity spread all the way to the westernmost parts of Europe.

These two religions underwent various transformations and schisms during the course of their dissemination across widespread areas. Although their migrations were in generally opposite directions, it appears that their historical and geographical fates bear many parallels.

These parallels lead me towards the following hypothesis, which could be called the 'hypothesis of corresponding regions.' We can infer from the historical events that, at the very least, North India and the Levant were parallel in their capacity to launch major world religions. Furthermore, the respective termini of religious dissemination, Western Europe and Japan, correspond to each other. Unfortunately the specific details of the correspondence between Western Europe and Japan must be left for consideration elsewhere.

A comparative theory of religion in the history of civilization

I trust that the preceding discussion has clearly outlined the methods and goals of my research. I will conclude by adding a few further points for consideration.

I have attempted to set out one sort of comparative theory of religion. Generally, doctrine and practice are the two major components constituting a religion. Comparison of these components is an essential part of the comparative study of religion, in that it allows us to see the differences and similarities of the evolutionary process of each religion. However, in addition to studying doctrine and practice – which could be called the internal components of religion – it is just as important to study the so-called external components of religion. In my particular research I deal mainly with these latter, external aspects. This entails an analysis of the relationship between religion and the external environment in which it exists.

It is said that the history of thought is a special precinct within the field of history. This seems to mean that it is possible to study thought independently from other phenomena, and to trace out its causal relationships over the course of history. It bears asking whether the history of religion is the same. Certainly one component of religion is thought, and as long as we stick to the study of that aspect, the history of religion is identical to the history of thought. However, as soon as we broaden our scope to include other aspects of religious history, especially what we have called the external aspects, the history of religion can no longer be regarded as a self-contained precinct. If the topic of inquiry is the relationship between religion and society, then religious history overlaps with social history. In the case of religion and culture, we must include the methods of cultural history. What I have attempted here is an inquiry into religion set in the context of the history of civilization, or in other words, a comparative theory of religion in the history of civilization. It appears to me that the term 'civilization' is the best umbrella to cover the range of related social and cultural phenomena.

In the present work on a comparative theory of religion in the history of civilization I employed a number of analytical methods. These were hypotheses, or derivations, or analogies of the methods of other fields. The next important question is whether the application of the methods outlined here can produce meaningful results in explaining the evolution and distribution of the world's religions. Happily, I can report that these tools have already produced good results, which I will present on another occasion. In this essay I hope I have offered some useful methodological guidelines.

(December 1965)

12 The Ocean and Japanese Civilization

Commentary on Chapter 12

In 1996, a new national holiday known as 'Marine Day' was established on July 20. In observation of the day, the Nippon Foundation has held its International Ocean Symposium each year. The fourth symposium, said to be the final, was held on July 28 and 29, 1999, at the Tokyo Big Site, the Tokyo International Exhibition Center. The theme of the symposium was 'Can the Ocean Save Us?' On the second day of the meeting, I gave a keynote address entitled 'The Impact of the Ocean on Civilization' (Umi to bunmei). This talk was published in the January 2000 issue of *Chūō Kōron* under the revised title 'The Ocean and Japanese Civilization' (Umi to Nihon bunmei).[1] This article was translated into Korean.[2] The official report on the entire symposium was issued by the Nippon Foundation, along with an English translation, in March 2000.[3] For the purposes of this volume, I have kept the title 'The Ocean and Japanese Civilization.'

Introduction

Japan is an island nation surrounded by the ocean. It is composed of several thousand islands in a large archipelago that might be dubbed 'Japonesia.' It is impossible to consider the formation and development of this nation without reference to the ocean. I would like to re-examine the relationship between these islands and the ocean by directing our gaze back over the last several thousand years or more.

You will notice from my approach that I am neither a historian nor an archaeologist. A historian would reconstruct the historical record from his reading of authentic, authoritative documents. An archaeologist would construe the world of the past based on excavated artifacts. Since I am an ethnologist, my work has been to use my ethnographic knowledge to analyze the past as part of the history of human civilization. However, until now the setting for my work has almost always been bound to the landmass of the continents. As a specialist in land based civilizations, I myself cannot predict the outcome of my discussion of the ocean.

In the course of my fieldwork, I have traveled to many areas of the world. Antarctica is the one continent on which I have never set foot. My style of scholarship has been to walk with my own legs, to look with my own eyes, and to think with my own head. Unfortunately it is impossible to walk on the ocean; the best we can do is to view it from the deck of a ship. Nevertheless, in the course of my travels I have developed some ideas on the relationship between the oceans and the continents. Here I hope chiefly to discuss the relationship between the ocean and the Japanese archipelago.

Civilization from the perspective of ecological history

Quite a few years ago, in 1957, I presented my ideas on the history of continental civilizations viewed from the perspective of ecological history. Over the years I received many criticisms of these ideas, both positive and negative, but recently my theories appear to have gained wide acceptance. Until that point, the concept of 'Japanese civilization' did not even exist. We spoke of Japanese culture, but no one used the expression 'Japanese civilization.'

In my definition, civilization is the system consisting of human beings, their devices, and their institutions. Culture is simply the spiritual or mental dimension of this system. On these terms, Japanese civilization is impressive: we could say that we are living the most highly civilized life on earth today. Why, then, do we not refer to Japanese civilization? Why do we speak only of culture?

The beginning of modernization in Japan is usually set in 1868, at the time of the Meiji Restoration. The common conception is that until then, Japan was a terribly backward country. I believe that this is a fallacy. There is much evidence to support the idea that the modernization of Japan began not in 1868 but in the latter part of the sixteenth century. We should re-evaluate Japanese history in light of these observations. Over the course of my career I have had the chance to make a thorough and objective study of the civilizations of the world, and in my estimation, Japan was not (and is not) undeveloped in comparison to any other nation. During my travels around the world I have verified my theory of civilization from the perspective of ecological history in each part of the globe. I believe that Japan as well as the world may be analyzed from this point of view.

To briefly recapitulate my theory for those who are not familiar with it, it is in essence a way of understanding the structure of the 'Old World,' or the clustered mass of the African and Eurasian continents. A vast belt of dry land runs through the center of the Old World, from central Africa, through southwest and central Asia, to northeast Asia. Desert occupies the center of this belt, while on either side are grasslands known as steppes. To the east and west of the dry mid-continental areas lie fertile agricultural regions, roughly symmetrical in shape and location. The dry areas in the middle of the continent are occupied by nomadic groups of various ethnicities, who raise livestock for their living. Over the course of history, these nomadic tribes have repeatedly invaded and destroyed the fertile agricultural areas lying beyond the steppe. Thus a repeated cycle of destruction and reconstruction was characteristic of the agricultural areas near the steppe, such as parts of China, India, Eastern Europe, and the Islamic countries.

There are two regions of the Old World that remained unscathed by the violence emanating from the dry center. These lie at the eastern and western extremes of the Eurasian continent: Western Europe at one end, and Japan at the other. In these areas civilization was nurtured in relative security. The very similar ecological circumstances of Western Europe and Japan caused them to follow parallel paths of historical development. It is these two regions that fostered the development of modern civilization, while regions such as China, India, Russia, and the Islamic world suffered the misfortune of repeated destruction. This inability to sustain steady progress in these places was an obstacle to the development of modern civilization. In my broad overview of the history of civilization, I named the parallel regions of Japan and Western Europe 'Zone One.' All of the rest of the Old World belongs to 'Zone Two.' The countries of Zone Two are what are called 'classic Asian states,' namely the Chinese empire, the Indian empire, the Russian empire, and the Islamic empire. I myself call these four blocs the 'classic continental empires.' In contrast to these empires, only Western Europe and Japan succeeded in becoming modern states. It is true that Japan inherited much from Chinese civilization, especially in ancient times, but these components of Japanese civilization were not the ones that formed the foundation of our modernization. Rather, it was the special ecological environment that became the basis for the development of a civilization entirely different from that of the classic continental empires. Likewise, Western Europe inherited much from the ancient empires of the Mediterranean, but went on to develop its own unique civilization. My thesis is that the similar environmental conditions of Japan and Western Europe resulted in the successful creation of similar civilizations.

The inland sea, an ocean of grass

Previously, I said that my research had focused on continents rather than on the ocean. And yet, a sort of ocean does exist in the midst of continental landmasses as well. One could easily imagine the dry inland areas as a kind of inland sea. At the center of most continents, of course, is the desert, where hardly anything grows. But bordering the deserts one typically finds vast grasslands, or steppes. In eastern Asian, Mongolia is a typical example of wide-open grassland. These vast grasslands are a veritable 'sea of grass.' Indeed, one needs a vessel in order to traverse this grassy ocean: none other than the camel.

During the war, I lived in the town of Zhangjiakou, in the present day Chinese province of Hebei. The character for '*kou*' (mouth) refers to an opening cut through the Great Wall. The Great Wall is an enormous rampart stretching from mountain to mountain across a great distance. It was built to prevent invasions of nomads from the steppes. When one passes through a checkpoint gate to the outside of the Wall, one finds oneself suddenly in the ocean of grass, in other words the steppe. I lived on the outside of the Wall, in the equivalent of a seaport whence began voyages into the ocean of grass. It truly feels there like being at the edge of the sea. Beyond lies the boundless Mongolian steppe, which leads to the Gobi Desert and eventually to the westerly steppes of Ukraine and Russia and on to Hungary. Fleets of desert vessels occasionally emerge from the sea of grass: caravans of several hundred camels descend on the town, signaling their arrival with the pealing of their neck bells. These desert cargo ships carry melons, raisins, and other products across the plains from the west, from as far away as Hami and Turfan. Despite the turmoil of war during my time there, the camel caravans somehow managed to keep sailing through the battlefields. Within a few days of the fleet's 'docking,' raisins and dried melons would appear in the markets of Zhangjiakou. I thought to myself that the end of the town's name should be rendered with the ideograph '*kou*' for 'port' rather than the character for 'mouth.'

It seems that people in antiquity also thought of the steppe as an ocean, which defined the separation between the western and eastern worlds. From ancient times, intrepid people made the effort to connect east and west by crossing this ocean. One of the most well known was the Tang dynasty priest Xuan-zhuang San-cang. Xuan-zhuang traversed the vast steppe to the west of China, then turned south to cross over the Himalayas. After enduring great hardship, he brought a large number of Buddhist sutras back from India. The sutras were kept in the Tang dynasty capital of Chang-an (present day Xian). It is said that this is how orthodox Buddhism was able to cross the sea of grass and spread through China. Xuan-zhuang was the model for the popular Chinese tale *Journey to the West* (*Xiyouji*).

During the Han dynasty – several centuries before the exploits of Xuan-zhuang – the Chinese saw the sea of grass that lay beyond the Great Wall as a kind of outer world full of barbarians. But over the course of the Han period, Chinese (or 'Han') civilization began to spread its roots through the dry inner regions. There were colonies scattered through the closer areas of the steppe, and at oases in the desert. One string of oases led westward through the desert from Lanzhou to westernmost Shazhou, or Dunhuang. These oases drew water from the snowmelt of the massive Qilian mountains, along the fringes of the high Tibetan plateau just to the south of the desert. This geographical arrangement allowed for the formation of oasis states throughout inner Asia, which served as way stations for east-west traffic.

Eventually the oasis routes connected eastern Asia to the Occident, where the ancient Roman Empire was the counterpart to Han China. Thus these two centers of ancient civilization were connected via slender threads across the vast expanse of Central Asian desert and steppe. The sea of grass was both a dividing and a connecting element. Later, with the beginning of viable sea transportation in the early modern period, the world of dynamic connections between East Asia and the Occident began in earnest.

Navigators of the Jōmon period

Let us now turn our eyes to Japan and examine the relationship between the ocean and the formation of Japanese civilization.

I am often asked where the Japanese people originally came from. I usually answer the question with a question of my own: why should we think that they came from anywhere else? Apparently many people think that Japanese originated elsewhere, but I do not see why we should not think that they were here in the archipelago from the beginning. While there is no doubt that over the course of Japanese history some people have migrated here from elsewhere, it is equally certain that some must have lived in Japan since the prehistoric period. Paleolithic sites provide evidence of human habitation of these islands since several dozen millennia ago. Based on this, I believe that not all Japanese came from elsewhere; at least some Japanese have lived here since the Paleolithic era.

There is an archaeological site currently under excavation in Aomori prefecture in northeastern Japan known as the Sannai Maruyama site. It dates from the mid-Jōmon period, about 4,500 years ago. I have had the opportunity to visit this site and its surroundings three times. The archaeological evidence seems to show that many people once lived in the area. I believe that the civilization of these people is directly linked to the Japanese civilization of subsequent periods. Can we not consider these people the ancestors of the Japanese race?

Of course I know that we cannot claim that human beings originated in the Japanese archipelago. Africa is the most likely birthplace of the human race. From there, humans took hundreds of thousands, or millions, of years to cross the Eurasian continent on foot. They may have crossed the ocean somewhere, or they may not have had to. Japan was probably connected to the Asian mainland in prehistoric times, so they might have crossed over on foot.

The Sannai Maruyama site is located in the most remote part Aomori Bay. The findings at the site give clues as to how the people there lived. The many remains of sea products indicate that they subsisted mostly on fish and shellfish, although there are also signs of cultivation of chestnuts and other plants. This evidence seems to refute the longstanding belief that the cultivation of plants in the Japanese archipelago dates only from the Yayoi period. If indeed agricultural cultivation can be traced back to the mid-Jōmon, it would establish a link between this period and subsequent forms of Japanese civilization.

The Sannai Maruyama site has not produced any remains of boats or ships. Nevertheless it is almost certain that the people at the site had some sort of navigational technology, based on the quantity of jade pieces discovered there. The only source of jade in Japan is in Niigata prefecture, along the Hime River tributary of the Itoi River. Somehow the jade from the Hime River was brought to Sannai Maruyama. We cannot tell whether this was in short hops or in one long trip, but it is reasonable to assume that there was knowledge of navigation at that time. Also, ores that are only available on the main islands of Japan have been discovered on the outlying island of Hachijōjima. Thus it appears that the Jōmon people were able to travel a significant distance by boat. There is much evidence pointing to contact with Hokkaidō as well. It seems clear that the role of the ocean was more to connect peoples than to separate them. The marine connection allowed for the dissemination of objects.

Some earthenware that was recently excavated on the island nation of Vanuatu, in the South Pacific, looks exactly like Jōmon ware. Does this mean that the range of Jōmon civilization extended this far? And what should we make of the even more distant discovery of Jōmon-like earthenware in Ecuador, South America? As far as I know, archaeologists have not yet come up with conclusive interpretations. Perhaps it is possible that the Jōmon people navigated the entire Pacific Rim.

The equestrian theory

As I said earlier, some portion of the Japanese people have lived on this archipelago from the earliest times. But a great number of peoples also arrived later from the surrounding areas. In this sense, the Japanese people are a mixed race. Some came from the south, some from the west, and some from the north. It may be assumed that many peoples settled this archipelago.

There is an interpretation known as the 'equestrian theory,' which holds that the Japanese islands were conquered by a group of horseback-riding warriors. This original and intriguing theory was promoted in the early postwar years by the prominent archaeologist Egami Namio. He suggested that a group of northern nomads on horseback invaded Japan and established the

Japanese state. These horseback-riders passed through the Korean peninsula, crossed the Genkai Sea from southern Korea, and arrived in Kyūshū, the southernmost of Japan's main islands. Professor Egami's theory gives specific details, such as the date for the arrival of the equestrians, which he puts during the reign of the tenth Emperor, Sujin. That would make it around the fourth century A.D., by some accounts. Professor Egami posits that the Emperor Sujin was actually the leader of the army of horsemen that landed on Kyūshū.

Professor Egami's theory is very compelling. It is an intriguing attempt to demythologize the origins of the Japanese state by suggesting that it was established by a group of horseback-riding conquerors. Nevertheless, I find the equestrian theory difficult to substantiate. As one whose expertise lies in the area of nomads and herders, I find parts of this theory highly implausible.

One of the key elements of nomadic society is the knowledge of milking technique. In other words, nomads know how to intercept the milk intended for the young livestock, by separating the mothers from their offspring. Another element of nomadic herder civilization is the neutering of male livestock. Neutering renders male herd animals more docile. Without it, they can be as wild as untamed beasts, and large herds of livestock would be impossible to control. Thus the two techniques of milking and neutering are essential for the maintenance of nomadic life. Presumably, these practices would have been introduced to Japan with the conquest of the equestrian invaders. Unfortunately, Japan has no tradition of milking or neutering, despite the presence of domesticated horses and cattle.

Many centuries later, during the Boxer Rebellion in late nineteenth century China, the foreign legation in Beijing was besieged. The Japanese Army was part of the international force that marched to the rescue. When the soldiers from other nations saw the Japanese military horses, they were afraid because the animals were 'like wild beasts.' It seems astonishing that even at this late date the Japanese Army did not neuter their horses, but in their view it was simply not the right way to use horses. As for milking, there are a few records of its occasional practice in pre-modern Japan, but it was not prevalent. Could it be possible that the horse-borne warriors who supposedly invaded Japan did not practice the crucial techniques of neutering and milking? What are horse riders but an extension of nomadic and herding civilization? For this reason, I find Professor Egami's theory difficult to accept.

An alternative theory: the Tungus naval forces

Despite the weaknesses of Professor Egami's equestrian theory, it is a very interesting concept from which we can preserve several useful points. For example, we should certainly take into account the similarity between the military organization of ancient Japan and that of Mongolia. There are also many commonalities between the cultures of Japan and of Mongolia and northeast Asia. My guess – which I would like to substantiate by soliciting the input of experts in the field – is that it was the Tungus, not the Mongolians, who came to Japan.

The Japanese language used to be classified as a member of the Ural-Altaic language group. However, since research has shown that the Uralic and Altaic languages are actually quite different, linguists no longer consider them part of the same family. The Uralic group includes the European languages of Finnish, Estonian, and Magyar, or Hungarian. The Altaic language group includes Turkish, Mongolian, and Tungusic. The language of the Manchurian people is of course a member of the Tungusic group. It is entirely different from the language of their Chinese neighbors.

The Tungus were a northeast Asian ethnic group based in the region familiar to us as Manchuria, occupying what is now the southwestern sector of China's three most northeasterly provinces. The name of the Tungus race is obscure to most people, but one branch, the Manchus, is quite well known. In the early seventeenth century, the Manchu people spread outwards from their homeland in the Manchurian mountains to conquer all of China. They founded the Qing dynasty in 1644, and ruled the powerful Chinese empire for nearly three centuries. The Manchus, the modern representatives of the Tungus, are now counted as one of the fifty-five recognized ethnic minorities in China.

My hypothesis is that some branch of the Manchu people arrived in the Japanese archipelago in ancient times. Unlike the horseback-riding warriors of Professor Egami's theory, who came overland, I believe that this conquering force arrived by ship. Thus I have termed my idea 'the Tungus naval force theory.'

Migration routes and boats

A consideration of my Tungus theory will finally focus our discussion on the sea. I believe that the Tungus people reached the Japanese islands by seafaring vessels. These land dwellers must have learned the art of navigation from the many sailors who plied the large rivers of the inland areas. The major river of southern Manchuria is the Liao, the Tumen runs eastward through the region, and the Manchurian-Korean border is defined by the Yalu. It is not hard to imagine that a group of Tungus who had become skilled in riparian navigation ventured out into the ocean at some point.

The Liao and the Yalu Rivers flow into the Yellow Sea, on the western side of the Korean peninsula, while the Tumen River empties into the Sea of Japan, along the eastern side of Korea. If a naval force of Tungus came to Japan, they could have taken either route. My hunch, though it may seem to be a leap, is that they came via the Sea of Japan. Reasoning backward in history from the later pattern of contacts between the Tungus and the Japanese, the most natural route would have been for them to follow the eastern coast of the Korean peninsula, heading due south until they reached Japan.

The ancient vessels of the Tungus were probably not powered by sail. There was no cotton cloth in those days, although they could have used wooden sails as on junks, or sails of woven grass as on the *yanbarusen* boats of Okinawa. But most likely the boats of the Tungus were powered by oar.

My next hunch, again rather daring, is that when the Tungus approached the shores of Japan, they passed through the Kanmon Straits into the Suo Sea and continued farther south down the eastern coast of Kyūshū to land at Hyūga. I base this speculation on the existence of the ancient tombs of Saitobaru in Miyazaki prefecture. This site contains more than three hundred burial mounds, from which have been excavated clay figurines of boats with six oarlocks on each side. These were models of a type of boat that was rowed by fitting long oars into the oarlocks, not unlike an eight-oared scull. This type of vessel was clearly intended for sea voyages. My contention is that the Tungus made their journey from the inland continent to Japan in vessels like these. By the way, I once saw a model of an ancient Korean vessel of the same type, with a line of oarlocks along the sides, at a museum in Seoul.

From these factors, I infer that the Tungus naval forces crossed the Sea of Japan and established a base in Hyūga. Since the ancient tombs of Saitobaru are estimated to have been built between the latter half of the fourth century and the sixth century, we can put the arrival of the Tungus naval forces somewhere in the earlier half of the fourth century. According to ancient Japanese myth, the Emperor Jimmu led an eastern expedition starting from Hyūga. This expeditionary force was described as a naval force, rather than a land army, which sailed eastward through the Inland Sea to land at Kawachi. There may be some connection between the legendary expedition of Emperor Jimmu and my theory of the Tungus navy. Historians cannot give accurate dates for the life of Emperor Jimmu, but if indeed the legend of the eastern expedition is based on historical fact, it could have been around the fifth century.

Japanese relations with the Pohai state

Early in the eighth century a significant event occurred in the relationship between Japan and the Tungus. In 727, a mission arrived in Japan from the government of the country of Pohai, the successor to the government of the Koguryo state, in eastern Manchuria. The inhabitants of Pohai were unmistakably Manchus, that is, Tungus. They lived by hunting and slash-and-burn agriculture, and it is believed that their state was modeled after the institutions of the Chinese Tang dynasty.

As the envoys from Pohai crossed Sea of Japan en route to Japan, they were swept by the Tsushima current and drifted to the coast of Dewa province in the far north of Japan. There they were attacked by aboriginals known as Emishi, or Ainu, and sixteen of the twenty-four envoys were killed. The survivors, having barely escaped alive, reached the ancient capital of Heijōkyō four months later. This marked the start of diplomatic relations between Japan and the state of Pohai. From the eighth century to the early tenth century, that is, from the beginning of the Nara period (710–794) through the first half of the Heian period (794–1185), some thirty or so missions arrived from Pohai state. These were majestic missions, bearing letters from the sovereign and many gifts.

We do not know the port of embarkation used by the Pohai delegations, but I suspect that they departed from the same place as the Tungus naval forces, several centuries earlier. As I mentioned above, a natural departing point would have been the mouth of the

Tumen River on the Japan Sea, at the northern base of the Korean peninsula. This area was within the boundaries of the state of Pohai at the time. The mission could have assembled its fleet of ships and crossed the Sea of Japan, running parallel to the east coast of the Korean peninsula. According to the historical record, their journey began calmly, but as they neared Japan they were swept eastward by the strong Tsushima current. They knew they would land somewhere in Japan, but they could not know where. Eventually they made a base somewhere on the western side of the Noto peninsula, where they gathered themselves and marched to the capital. Thereafter Noto became their base.

This first mission established official diplomatic relations between the Tungusic country of Pohai and Japan. Apparently, the Pohai mission had come expecting something in return; and a Japanese mission was sent in reciprocation. On a subsequent occasion, the Pohai mission arrived on a dilapidated ship and requested that they be sent back on a new ship made in Japan. These missions came as often as once a year.

The maintenance of diplomatic relations with Japan was part of the Pohai international strategy against the state of Silla, which controlled the southeastern part of the Korean peninsula. Japan and Silla were traditionally enemies, as were Pohai and Silla. Apparently Japan and Pohai formed a strategy to launch an allied attack on Silla from both sides of the Korean peninsula. Thus a military alliance was the dominant component in the early years of Tungusic-Japanese relations.

In later years, relations between Pohai and Japan were characterized more by the large amount of government-licensed trade between them. The people of Pohai brought marten furs, highly prized by Japanese court nobles, and took back Japanese linen and silk (there was no cotton at that time). In addition to the exchange of fur and cloth, the Pohai mission would take back gifts. Among the gifts recorded were 'eleven dancing maidens,' a distressful story, indeed. I wonder what happened to those maidens.

The rise and fall of the Tungus bypass

The scholar Ueda Takeshi has conducted solid research on the diplomatic missions of ancient Pohai, describing relations with Japan over the course of more than two centuries. The two countries maintained such a close relationship that it was as if they spoke the same language. In fact, however, they communicated their intentions through the exchange of poetry written in Chinese. At that time, both countries were heavily influenced by Chinese civilization. Educated people were comfortable enough writing Chinese verse that they even enjoyed literary competition.

Japanese making the journey to China also followed the route to Pohai via the Sea of Japan. Many Japanese monks and scholars used this route to travel onwards to the Tang capital of Chang-an. Relations between Japan and the state of Pohai lasted until the destruction of Pohai by its neighbor to the west, the Khitan state of the Mongol people, in 926. At around the same time, the Mount Paektu volcano erupted, just to the south of Pohai. One theory is that the eruption caused critical damage to the agricultural productivity of Pohai, hastening its demise. Ashes from the eruption of Mount Paektu drifted eastward toward Japan. The remains of these ashes have been unearthed in the northeast Tōhoku region.

In the early part of the eleventh century a group of Jurchen pirates (or Toi, the Korean term used in Japan) attacked and plundered the outlying Japanese islands of Iki and Tsushima, as well as Chikuzen on the Kyūshū mainland. Although the origins of these Jurchen were unclear, it appears they were a branch of the Tungus people. The Sea of Japan has offered a stage for the activities of the Tungus people, for better and for worse. This was the last known episode of contact between the Tungus and Japan.

The role of the East China Sea

The seas along the coast of China have also played an important role in Japanese history. The body of water encircled by Kyūshū, Okinawa, China, and the west coast of Korea includes two seas: the northern portion is called the Yellow Sea, while the southern part is known as the East China Sea. For the ancient civilizations of the Far East, this area functioned as an inland sea, filled with the comings and goings of the surrounding peoples. Japan and China maintained a vigorous exchange across the water, as seen in the succession of Japanese envoys to the Sui and Tang courts. The earliest missions favored the northern route, departed from Naniwa, passing through Kyūshū and heading for the Shandong Peninsula. Later, the route heading due west from Kyūshū to

Ningbo, at the lower reaches of the Yangtze River, became more popular. Much as the Mediterranean Sea was the core of ancient Western civilization, the East China Sea lay at the heart of ancient Far Eastern civilization.

One of the major historical events that took place in this sea was the Mongol invasion of Japan during the Kamakura period in Japan (1185–1333) or the Yuan period in China (1271–1368). The Mongols made two invasion attempts, in 1274 and 1281. In both instances, storms damaged the Mongol fleets, forcing their withdrawal and frustrating the plans of the Yuan dynasty to conquer Japan.

During the first invasion attempt, the bulk of the forces fighting for the Mongols were Koryo Korean troops, while in the later attempt the navy of the southern Song kingdom, under Yuan subjugation, formed the main fighting units. Since the leadership were Mongols of nomadic background, it is possible that they were not aware of the peril of typhoons. But it is not likely that the Koryo and southern Song troops shared this ignorance. The decision to send such a massive naval force during the most hostile season of the year seems to have been the folly of the Mongols. Thanks to the assistance of nature, Japan was saved from Mongol invasion.

Shortly before the campaign against Japan, the Yuan Mongol forces, in the course of their invasion of Europe, defeated the European forces at Liegnitz. Just as all of Europe faced the crisis of a possible Mongol conquest, reports of the death of Ogodei Khan reached the front lines, prompting the Mongol forces to retreat. Thus Japan in the Far East and Western Europe in the Far West escaped imminent conquest at almost the same historical moment. Although this was a coincidence, it strengthens our impression of the parallel histories of Japan and Western Europe.

During the Ming period in China (1368–1644), the number of ships manned by Han (ethnic Chinese) sailors proliferated in the East China and South China Seas. Their ships were junks with sails of wooden slats, such as can still be seen plying the lower reaches of the Yangtze River. It is possible to view the remains of a medieval Ming ship at a museum to the west of Quanzhou. This stately vessel, replete with keel and interior partitions, was salvaged from the deep along with its cargo. Shipping tags indicate that part of the cargo was destined for Japan. The East China Sea indeed played an important role in forming the regional civilization of the Far East.

The seafaring Han Chinese

During the medieval period, bands of pirates called '*wakō*' plundered the ships in the East China Sea. Although the term *wakō* literally meant Japanese pirates, apparently not all of these pirates were Japanese. Many Han people were members of pirate bands, often in the form of private maritime troops, or mercenaries. These Chinese bands also marauded throughout the coastal waters, sometimes coming ashore to plunder the towns. Zheng Zhilong, the leader of one of these private maritime bands, used his base on the Gotō Islands, now part of Japan, to extend his power throughout the East China Sea. He took a Japanese woman for his wife, and their son became known as Zheng Chenggong.

Zheng Chenggong is a featured character in Shiba Ryōtarō's epic novel *Dattan shippūroku* (Record of the Tartar storm), set in the early seventeenth century, during the subjugation of China by the Manchu forces. The Manchus, who where ethnically Tungus, went on to establish the Qing dynasty, replacing the ethnically Chinese Ming dynasty. Zheng Chenggong is also the main character in Chikamatsu Monzaemon's play 'The Battles of Coxinga' ('Kokusenya Kassen'). In this account, the honorary Ming name of Zhu (from Zhu Yuanzhang, the name of the first Ming emperor Hongwu) is given to him in appreciation of his efforts to restore the Chinese throne to the Ming. Thus he became known as Guo-shing-ye, or 'Lord of the Imperial Surname.' In Japanese this is rendered as Kokusenya, which lead to the Dutch pronunciation of Koxinga or Coxinga. As a child, the legendary Zheng Chenggong was called Watōnai, meaning 'not Japanese, not Chinese, but mixed blood.'

In historical fact, Zheng Chenggong led his armed maritime band in pillaging the coast of China. The ruling Qing dynasty had great difficulty subduing his forces, although in the end his efforts to restore the Ming dynasty were a failure. At the height of his power, Zheng Chenggong's influence extended widely over the South China Sea, forming a veritable sea-based kingdom. Nowadays there is a Zheng Chenggong memorial museum in the port of Amoy where various articles and materials related to him are displayed. He was a heroic figure even to the Chinese.

The example of Zheng Chenggong shows the extent to which the Han Chinese had become a thoroughly seafaring people by the early seventeenth century. Indeed, there is evidence to suggest that they had become able seamen even earlier. During the Ming period, a general – coincidentally also named Zheng – led a government fleet to subjugate unruly areas of the southern seas. His expeditions covered the entire region of the Indian Ocean, as far as Madagascar. Taking these factors into account, we must increase our appreciation of the seafaring skill of the Han Chinese.

In the same vein, I would like to mention the historical significance of Arab sailors in the western part of the Indian Ocean. We commonly think of the Arabs as landlocked desert dwellers. But like the Han Chinese, the Arabs were seafaring people as well. The western end of the Indian Ocean is known as the Arabian Sea, the equivalent in the Islamic world to the East and South China Seas. Just as the Chinese seas became filled with the junks of the Han, so the western Indian Ocean was filled with the Arab vessels called *dows*. I think that the role of the *dow* boats in the Arabian Sea is comparable to that of the junks in the Far East.

Japanese communities in Southeast Asia

The Japanese came to play a new part in the ongoing drama of the seas in the late sixteenth century, when many Japanese merchant fleets began to make overseas voyages. Although these fleets were nominally merchant traders, my guess is that they had armed crew on board, following the habit of the time of the *wakō* pirates. The government of Japan –at that time ruled by the shogun –maintained control over the proliferating international trade by issuing licenses to the ships setting sail. These licenses were known as *goshuin*, or vermilion seal, after the large official seal set upon permits to travel abroad. The permits had to be issued for each voyage, rather than being granted permanently to a ship. Only authorized trading ships were allowed to set sail for international waters, after loading provisions and goods in Sakai and other ports. The capital underwriting these voyages came from merchant financiers in Kyoto, such as Suminokura Ryōi and Chaya Shirōjirō. Legend has it that the halberd-topped poles adorning the floats of the Gion Festival in Kyoto were originally the masts of the vermilion-seal ships, rendered obsolete when the Japanese government later instituted a policy of national seclusion.

The vermilion-seal trading ships streamed out of Japanese ports, heading south for Luzon, west to Quanzhou, and southwest past Hainan to reach Vietnam and the Indochinese peninsula. On the

Indochinese coast is the present day city of Da Nang, which used to be called Tourane. Its port is now called Hoi An, but during the epoch of Japanese trading ships it was known as Faifo. Although the Japanese ships docking there were merchant vessels, they were not loaded with the peaceful goods, such as silk, that had been typical of the ancient trade with Pohai. Weapons were the main item. These early modern Japanese merchant fleets were what we now call 'merchants of death.' At the time, Vietnam was torn by fighting between north and south. The Japanese ships docked at the midpoint and sold weapons to both sides. Japanese armor, swords, and weapons were reputed to be highly effective and sold for good prices. Evidence of the Japanese presence at Faifo remains even today, in Japanese gravesites and even in people who claim Japanese ancestry.

Following the coastline southward from Vietnam, Japanese ships reached Cambodia. Another settlement of Japanese was located at the town of Oudong, to the west of the capital Phnom Penh. At the magnificent Cambodian temple complex of Angkor Wat, one can see a Japanese signature scribbled with a calligraphy brush on the inner wall of a temple. The name is Morimoto Ukondayū Kazufusa, from Hishū, along with the date Kan'ei 9, or 1632. This Morimoto may well have been a resident of Oudong. The sight of the splendid temple made him think that he had arrived at the Jetavana monastery known as Gion Shōja. His mistake was understandable, as printed illustrations of Angkor Wat, with the notation 'Gion Shōja,' were popular in Japan at that time. It is probable that many Japanese visited Angkor Wat in the early seventeenth century.

Continuing westward, the next major settlement of Japanese was at Ayuthia (present day Ayutthaya) in Thailand, or Siam. Ayuthia, located up the Menam River to the north of present day Bangkok, was the old capital of Siam. Nothing remains of the Japanese community, which was destroyed during the conquest of Ayuthia by Burmese forces borne on elephants.

There is a legend about a Japanese adventurer named Yamada Nagamasa, who was said to have been active in Ayuthia. Some years ago, Thailand requested aid from Japan to establish a museum about Ayuthia. The Japanese residents of Bangkok wished to erect a memorial hall to Yamada as part of the project, but the Thai side refused, saying he was not a true historical figure. Now there is an impressive museum, but no mention of Yamada Nagamasa. His true identity remains unknown: he is said to have been from Shizuoka prefecture, but then again he may be a total fabrication. One theory says he was a creation of the famous hero Shimizu no Jirochō.

Finally, there is a historical record of Japanese mercenaries serving the King of Arakan, an independent kingdom in the western part of Burma, present day Myanmar. Contemporary documents state that the Japanese warriors are brave and skillful fighters, but also very arrogant.

A phantom battle in the Bay of Bengal

Thus the trading fleets of the late sixteenth and early seventeenth centuries made contact with the peoples of Southeast Asia and extended Japanese influence all the way to the Bay of Bengal. There were Japanese warriors as far west as Akyab in Burma, backed up by a sizable and growing Japanese community not far to the east in Ayuthia. At around the same time, just across the Bay of Bengal, armed fleets from Western Europe had reached the port town of Calcutta and the French settlement of Chandernagore.

I often wonder what would have happened if these opposing movements – eastward for the European sailors and westward for the Japanese – had continued. Even though I know that such historical 'what ifs' are rather pointless, I take great pleasure in imagining what might have been. As it happened, the Japanese government began to close off the trading routes to the south, until by 1639 the policy of national seclusion, or *sakoku*, was fully in place. But if Japan had not implemented the national seclusion policy, if the Japanese had continued their outward advance, what might have occurred? I sometimes imagine a clash in the Bay of Bengal between the Japanese and the British fleets – what I have dubbed the 'Phantom Battle of the Bay of Bengal.' Of course this battle never took place. With the implementation of the peculiar policy of national seclusion, overseas Japanese either withdrew, or else lived out the rest of their lives in Southeast Asia, never to return. The Battle of the Bay of Bengal never took place, and the clash of British and Japanese forces was deferred until the 1940s.

By the beginning of the seventeenth century, both Japan and Western Europe were in the midst of a great age of exploration. If Japan had not instituted its policy of national seclusion – in other words, if her outward push had continued – she not only might have colonized parts of Southeast Asia, but also might have headed eastward across the Pacific towards the coast of California.

The early British and French colonies were just being founded in North America at that time. Sooner or later the westward movement of the Europeans would have come up against the Japanese settlers, perhaps with a clash in the upper reaches of the Mississippi River. The territory lying west of the Rocky Mountains might have been ceded to Japan. In this way I amuse myself with historical fantasies.

A western Pacific league of co-longitudinal nations

In conclusion, I would like to present my recommendations for the future orientation of Japan in the international community. History has shown that our pursuit of relations in the westward direction, that is, toward the continental landmass, has met with nothing but failure and tragedy. We began life as a maritime nation, and our most productive international activities, beginning with the Tungusic naval forces mentioned above, have involved ships. Japan is not by nature a continental power, so attempts to establish deep ties with continental regions cannot yield positive results. I believe we should learn from these lessons.

The first known historical instance of a failed continental expedition was the Battle of Hakusukinoe in 663. The allied forces of Japan and Paekche engaged in a fierce river battle against the combined Silla and Tang forces. The Japanese side was thoroughly routed, and it appears that very few Japanese made it home.

A second example of failure, again on the Korean peninsula, was Toyotomi Hideyoshi's ill-considered expedition against Korea. Why on earth did he attempt this invasion? I think it would be hard to find another example in world history of an expansionistic war as meaningless as this one. Hideyoshi's base of operations was Nagoya Castle in present day Saga prefecture, in Kyūshū. Looking north from the top of the mountain there, the Korean peninsula would have been visible in the far distance. Hideyoshi may have watched as the ships of his loyal retainers set sail, hoisting their family crests. I cannot help but wonder what he was thinking as he launched the expedition. This was a clear war of invasion, without any cause other than Hideyoshi's orders to seize Korea. After the lords and soldiers had terrorized the region, the only after effect was a deep sense of rancor toward Japan. Nothing whatsoever was accomplished.

My final example of a pointless tragedy resulting from our continental military expeditions is the sequence of the Sino-Japanese, Russo-Japanese, and Japan-China Wars from the late-nineteenth to the mid-twentieth century. Again, nothing good, and a great deal of bad, resulted from these conflicts.

Although it is important for Japan to have amicable relations with the continent to its west, it is best for us not to become deeply involved. As soon as the involvement becomes deep, the results are unfortunate. The East Asian mainland, indeed the entire continent, is not a simple place to understand. The classical continental civilizations of Asia are filled with all manner of human vices – vices may be too harsh a word – and the complex karma of human interactions. It is not a place that a naive people like the Japanese can effectively master. This lesson has been driven home to me during my travels throughout Asia.

I suggest that as a nation, we should turn our attention in the direction of the ocean rather than the continent. Since the ocean was our original home, let us return there. Our goal should be solidarity with the many other island nations of the Pacific Ocean. Instead of thinking that our neighbors lie along the same latitude, to the east and west, we could join in league with other countries along the same north-south longitude. We should seriously consider forming a group of Pacific island nations, including Indonesia, Micronesia, the Philippines, Papua New Guinea, Australia, and New Zealand.

Of particular importance among these nations is Australia. Modern Japanese civilization in its current form could not exist without the steady supply of iron, aluminum, and natural gas from Australia; nor could Australia thrive without Japan's steady demand for its resources. Australia and Japan have a symbiotic relationship of mutual prosperity. It is for reasons like this that I suggest we should stop thinking about westward involvement with the continent, in favor of a co-longitudinal league of western Pacific nations stretching from Japan to Australia. I believe this is the proper orientation for Japan as we consider our destiny in the coming century.

(January 2000)

Comments

An Ecological View of History: Japanese Civilization in the World Context was one of the most significant works of world historical theory in the postwar period. This volume consists of eleven articles by Professor Umesao Tadao, all originally published more than ten years ago.[1] Indeed, some of the earlier pieces are nearly twenty years old. Nevertheless, upon reading them today, they seem in no way stale or outdated. Whenever I read the neatly organized and persuasively argued ideas of the author, who began his career as an ecologist, I am drawn as always by the power of theory. Thoughts that I myself had sensed only vaguely are here set out in a theoretical framework with all the specificity and objectivity of natural science.

Professor Umesao developed his initial idea for this comparative study of civilization in 1955. It was a period when Japan had begun to regain its place as a responsible member in the international community after its postwar recovery. At that time the author was affiliated with the Department of Biological Sciences at Osaka City University. The locale that originally inspired this work was the Southwest Asian region including Afghanistan, Pakistan, and India, which Umesao had visited as a member of the Kyoto University Karakoram-Hindu Kush scientific study expedition. I should note here that this expedition was the first postwar multidisciplinary research effort, which led the way for later Japanese research expeditions abroad.

At that time, the interpretation of Japan's modernization was a central concern of scholars in the humanities and social sciences. In Japan we now consider the debate on modernization to be a thing of the past, but at the time it was alive and current. Moreover, the debate was predicated on the use of the Western European developmental model as a measure of Japan's stage of modernization. In this discourse there was no mention of India or the Islamic world, much less Southeast Asia, as possible subjects for comparison. It seemed that the track laid out for the discussion of

Japan's development ran strictly alongside the course of the Western European nations. Of course there were a few people not bound by this extreme Euro-centrism, but even they tended to view the world in terms of an East-West dichotomy, as evidenced by the widespread use of terms such as 'Asian-style constraints,' 'Asian-style stagnation,' and 'Asian-African solidarity.' This language reflected the assumptions of a prewar worldview.

These limits on the discourse on Japanese modernization were not without reason. The century of Japanese history from the Meiji Restoration (1868) until the present has been precisely the history of the effort to turn Japan into a modern nation on par with those of Western Europe. To all intents and purposes, modernization was synonymous with Europeanization. Not to put too fine a point on it, Japan was far too preoccupied with her furious hundred-year sprint towards European modernity to pay attention to India, Southeast Asia, or other places.

The epoch defined by the European model as the acme of all aspirations drew to a close after the Second World War, with the emergence of non-European nations as players in the international scene. At around the same time, Japan recovered from the war and began once more to participate in the world. This was the situation in 1955.

It is quite symbolic that the ideas in *An Ecological View of History* were born at this time. Umesao's concept of the arid continental 'Mediant' lay completely outside the range of interests of most Japanese scholars, who, as he writes, tended to be conservative. The proposal of this novel concept propelled Umesao into the vanguard of this era.

It would be problematic to assume that Umesao's theory gave us a crystal ball to see the future. The descriptive content of the work is distinct from the circumstances of the conception of the theory. Among the articles in this volume, the chapter 'An Ecological View of History: Japanese Civilization in the World Context,' published first in *Chūō Kōron* in 1957, presents Umesao's theoretical concepts in a systematic manner. The piece 'Travels in Southeast Asia,' published the following year in the same journal, presents further refinements to the theory. At the outset of 'An Ecological View of History,' Umesao stated that his thesis was a response to the challenge posed by Arnold Toynbee's Western European centered theory of civilization. However, in Japanese academic circles Toynbee's theories were in any case never accepted as received wisdom, despite his visit to Japan. Thus Umesao's ecological approach to the history of civilization was perceived instead as a bold challenge to Marxist and other progressive theories of world history. But leaving aside for now the story of Japanese reactions to his work, I would like to compare and contrast the theories of Umesao and Toynbee as they relate to civilization.

Toynbee's *A Study of History* is a voluminous work that contains an enormous amount of historical knowledge. This mass of information makes it difficult to detect the underlying theoretical framework, but in essence Toynbee is proposing an ontogenetic model of civilization. His theory postulates that the history of all civilizations follows a pattern similar to a biological life cycle of birth, growth, and death. In contrast to Toynbee's comparison of civilizations to the individual biological life cycle, Umesao takes as his model the development of a whole biological population. We use the phrase 'unable to see the forest for the trees,' but Umesao's position could be dubbed 'seeing the forest rather than the trees.' While an individual tree may die, the forest as a whole has a life cycle above and beyond that of individual specimens. Moreover, the forest as a whole undergoes biological transitions from, for example, a young thicket of mixed growth to a mature forest of tall trees. Naturally, the mixture of species and the speed and pattern of succession vary from forest to forest, depending on the conditions of origin, environment, and so on. The condition of the forest could also change with the introduction of foreign species.

As an ecologist, Umesao's thinking differs greatly from Toynbee's. While the ontogenetic model accounts for the particular characteristics of each different civilization with the rubric of 'individuality,' the collective model situates each civilization within its environment, which is a more scientifically prescribed sphere. The categorization and placement of civilizations are defined in terms of global science. This makes possible a framework for the theory of civilization more universal and thus more anthropological than Toynbee's. Furthermore, biological collectives do undergo historical change (or 'succession' in the language of the field), although of a different sort than individuals. With Umesao's model, it was possible to discern laws of history that hewed to the conditions of civilization while also taking into account outside influences. The ecological model of civilization contained many elements that seemed to promise a theory of great flexibility and applicability.

Umesao's model for a theory of civilization is superior to Toynbee's. Yet in Japan, where work in the theory of civilization was not widely popular, no one seriously discussed the significance of Umesao's theory in terms of its position in the field of civilization theory. Instead, 'An Ecological View of History' was perceived as a covert challenge to scholars of historical theory, which is not quite the same thing. Below, I will describe why Umesao's work was seen as such a challenge.

It is well known that in postwar Japan, the Marxist theory of progressive stages of development has been the cornerstone of work in historical theory and historical interpretation. In 'An Ecological View of History,' Umesao urged historians to revise the unquestioned assumptions of Marxist theory. His claims that modernization did not necessarily mean Westernization, and that developmental stages came in diverse forms, provoked the theorists of formal developmental stages who saw history through the lens of Western Europe. Meanwhile, Umesao's ideas were also upsetting to those who believed that the foundations of theory should be for the sake of real world practice. These people positioned Japan as a part of Asia, always a step behind on the developmental scale. On one hand, Umesao's idea of distinguishing Japan from the rest of Asia, categorizing it instead along with Western Europe in his so-called Zone One, implicitly rejected the 'real-worldedness' so valued by the pragmatists. On the other hand, Umesao's work was helpful to those seeking insight into the concept of European-Japanese parallelism described in the comparative theories of feudalism by scholars such as Max Weber and O. Hintze. It also gave a global perspective to theories of Asian autocracy and stagnation. The impact of Umesao's theory was tremendously effective in shaking up the prevailing theories of history.

Although many scholars of historical theory have read Umesao's work, there has yet to be a serious response to his challenge. In Japan, most of these scholars have put their enthusiasm into importing the work of American and European theoreticians, rather than facing challenges from scholars within their own country. A further problem was that many of Umesao's contemporaries were simply unable to grasp the meaning of the ideas that he derived from ecological studies. They avoided his challenge by suggesting that 'An Ecological View of History' rested on the kind of environmental determinism that was an extension of Watsuji Tetsurō's theories on the link between climate and culture. The fact that Umesao's ideas were expressed in such a straightforward, accessible style may have provoked the disapproval of academics with a preference for complexity and detailed conjecture. Be that as it may, the significance of Umesao's proposals has not diminished in the ensuing twenty years, thanks to their fine theoretical framework, breadth of vision, and a viewpoint entirely different from that of Weber or the Marxist historians, not to mention Watsuji.

Although the reactions sparked by 'An Ecological View of History' were varied, there was one group that welcomed it seriously and attempted to further develop its ideas. This was the research team headed by Imanishi Kinji of Kyoto University's Institute for Humanistic Studies. Some of the results of the discussions held by this group are noted in the Commentary section of Chapter Three. We must count the impact of these derivative analyses as part of the influence of Umesao's work.

After presenting the basic framework of his theory in 'An Ecological View of History,' Umesao further developed his ideas in later articles. Umesao defined civilization as the fusion of society and culture, in other words, the overall design of all the elements of daily human life. Thus his methodology closely resembled that of social and cultural anthropology. The chapters in this volume indicate the progressive enrichment of his work on comparative civilization through a succession of opportunities for anthropological research trips to the Middle East, Southeast Asia, and Africa. I should point out that the later development of his theories went beyond the perspective of anthropology. This is evident in his comparative treatment of higher religion and bureaucratic structures, which were not typical subjects for anthropologists. In particular, his 'Methodological Notes on Comparative Religion' is distinctly non-anthropological, treating a subject usually in the province of the sociology of religion. While the subject itself was sociological, Umesao derived his analysis from the epidemiology of infectious diseases.

Umesao wrote the comparative religion article while conducting anthropological research in East Africa. Upon his return to Japan, he left his position in the Department of Biological Sciences at Osaka City University and took charge of a joint research group in the Social Anthropology Research Section at Kyoto University's Institute for Humanistic Studies. In this capacity, he transformed himself from an ecologist to an anthropologist. The joint research topic was the comparative social anthropology of civilizations. Members of this research group published original theses developed from the model postulated in 'An Ecological View of History.' Umesao himself has also continued to publish articles further exploring various facets of comparative civilization. This volume, however, is limited to those works Umesao published when he was still at Osaka City University.

'An Ecological View of History' provided one of the seminal postwar theories of the history of the human race which, to borrow the words in his 'A New World Map of Civilization,' attempted to depict the history of the human race rooted in its localities and set in the context of the flow of global history. Recently, Umesao has transformed himself again to become Director General of the National Museum of Ethnology. He is working on ever more direct and undistorted ways of depicting the human race. It is an occasion for celebration that *An Ecological View of History* is being issued as part of Chūō Kōron's paperback series, in order that it may be appreciated by many new readers.

Tani Yutaka (September 1974)
Kyoto University

Notes

Preface

1 Shiba, Ryōtarō (1969–72), *Saka no ue no kumo,* 6 vols, Bungei Shunjūsha.

2 Nishida, Kitarō (1911), *Zen no kenkyū,* Iwanami Shoten. There are two English translations: *A study of good,* Printing Bureau, Japanese Government, 1960; and *An inquiry into the good,* Yale University Press, 1990.

3 Natsume, Sōseki (1905–07), *Wagahai wa neko de aru,* Nihon Kindai Bungakkan, 1968. Originally published 1905–07. English translation: *I am a cat,* Tuttle, 2002, and earlier versions.

4 Watsuji, Tetsurō (1935), *Fūdo – ningengakuteki kōsatsu,* Iwanami Shoten. There are two English translations: *The climate: a philosophical study,* Printing Bureau, Japanese Government, 1961; and *Climate and culture*: a *philosophical study,* Greenwood Press, 1988.

5 Tanizaki, Jun'ichirō (1943–48), *Sasameyuki.* English translation: *The Makioka Sisters,* Knopf, 1957.

6 Doi, Takeo (1971), *Amae no kōzō*, Kōbundō. English translation: *Anatomy of dependence,* Kōdansha, 1973.

7 Nakane, Chie (1967), *Tate shakai no ningen kankei,* Kōdansha. English translation: *Japanese society,* University of California Press, 1970.

8 Umesao did not intend this treatise to be an introduction. The *Josetsu* (Prolegomena) part of the title was supplied by the journal, not by him.

9 Umesao, Tadao (1995), 'Introduction to an ecological view of civilization', *Japan Echo,* Vol. 22, pp. 42–50. Umesao, Tadao (1986), 'Japan as viewed from an eco-historical perspective', *Review of Japanese Culture and Society,* Vol. 1, No. 1, pp. 25–31.

Umesao, Tadao (2000), 'The ocean, the impact on civilization', (lecture: July 1999), International Ocean Symposium (ed.), *The Ocean, Can She Save Us?*, Tokyo, The Nippon Foundation.
10 Umesao, Tadao (1989–1994), *Umesao Tadao Chosaku shū (Collected works of Umesao Tadao)*, Tokyo, Chūō Kōronsha.

Chapter 1

1 Kihara, Hitoshi (ed.) (1956), *Sabaku to hyōga no tanken* (An Expedition to Deserts and Glaciers), Asahi Shinbunsha, March.
2 *Results of the Kyoto University Scientific Expedition to the Karakoram and Hindukush*, 1955, Kyoto University.
   • Vol. I. Yamashita, K. (ed.) (1965), *Cultivated Plants and Their Relatives.*
   • Vol. II. Kitamura, S. (ed.) (1960), *Flora of Afghanistan.*
   • Vol. III. Kitamura, S. (ed.) (1964), *Plants of West Pakistan and Afghanistan.*
   • Vol. IV. Ueno, M. (ed.) (1963), *Insect Fauna of Afghanistan and Hindukush.*
   • Vol. V. Imanishi, K. (ed.) (1963), *Personality and Health in Hunza Valley.*
   • Vol. VI. *The Zirni Manuscript* (1961).
   • Vol. VII. Matsushita, S. and K. Huzita (eds.) (1965), *Geology of the Karakoram and Hindukush.*
   • Vol. VIII. Kitamura, S. and R. Yosii (eds.) (1966), *Additional Reports.*
3 Umesao, Tadao (1956), *Mogōruzoku tanken ki* (An account of an expedition to the Moghol tribe), Iwanami Shinsho Ao han 253, Iwanami Shoten, September. Compiled in *Umesao Tadao Chosaku shū* (Collected works of Umesao Tadao) (1989–1994), Vol. 4, *Chūyō no kuni guni* (The countries of the Mediant).
4 Umesao,Tadao, (supervisory ed., photographer) Iwanami Shoten Henshūbu and Iwanami Eiga Seisakusho (eds.) (1956), *Afuganisutan no tabi* (Travels in Afghanistan), Iwanami Shashin Bunko 202, Iwanami Shoten, October. Text only compiled in *Chosaku shū* (Collected works of Umesao Tadao), Vol. 4, *Chūyō no kuni guni* (The countries of the Mediant).
5 He later published the results of his research in: Schurmann, H.F. (1962), *The Mongols of Afghanistan: An ethnography of the Moghols and related peoples of Afghanistan*, Mouton & Co.

6 Umesao, Tadao (1962), 'Kaibaru tōge kara Karukatta made (From the Khyber Pass to Calcutta)', Vol. 2, *Indo kara nessa no kuni e* (From India to the countries of the burning sands), *Sekai no Tabi* (Travels around the World), Chūō Kōronsha, January, pp. 65–158. Text compiled in *Chosaku shū* (Collected works of Umesao Tadao), Vol. 4, *Chūyō no kuni guni* (The countries of the Mediant).

7 Umesao, Tadao (1956), 'Nihon wa Ajia no koji da – Indo, Pakisutan, Afuganisutan no tabi kara (Japan is Asia's orphan: from my travels in India, Pakistan, Afghanistan)', *Chisei*, Vol. 3, No. 2, February, Kawade Shobō, pp. 174–189.

8 Translator's note: As the author uses the terms *tōyō* (the East, or the Orient) and *seiyō* (the West, or the Occident) in conjunction with *chūyō* (the 'Mediant' as defined in the section 'The "Mediant"'), this translation has followed this convention.

9 Translator's note: As defined in this section, 'Mediant' (*chūyō*) is the term for the region between the Orient, or the East, and the Occident, or the West.

10 Yasuda, Tokutarō (1955), *Man'yōshū no nazo* (The mystery of the Man'yōshū), Kappa Books, Kōbunsha.

Chapter 2

1 Umesao, Tadao (1956), 'Afuganisutan no yūbokumin (The nomadic tribes of Afghanistan)', *Mainichi Shinbun*, February 13.

Chapter 3

1 Umesao, Tadao (1957), 'Bunmei no seitaishikan josetsu (An introduction to an ecological view of history: Japanese civilization in the world context)', *Chūō Kōron*, February issue, Vol. 72, No. 2, Issue No. 822, pp. 32–49.

2 Katō, Shūichi (1957), 'Kindai Nihon no bunmeishiteki ichi (The place of modern Japan in the history of civilization)', *Chūō Kōron,* March issue, Vol. 72, No. 3, Issue No. 823, pp. 32–49.

3 Katō, Shūichi, Tadao Umesao, and Yoshie Hotta (1957), 'Bunmei no keifu to gendaiteki chitsujo (The lineage of civilization and order in the modern age)', *Sōgō*, Tōyō Keizai Shinpōsha, June issue, Vol. 1, No. 2, pp. 24–35.

4 Takeyama, Michio, Shigetaka Suzuki, Junzō Karaki, Tetsurō Watsuji, and Yoshishige Abe (1957), 'Sekai ni okeru Nihon bunka no ichi (The place of Japanese civilization in the world)', *Kokoro*, June issue, Vol. 10, No. 6, Heibonsha, pp. 18–38.

5 Takeyama, Michio (1957), 'Nihon bunka o ronzu (A discussion of Japanese culture)', *Shinchō*, September issue, Vol. 54, No. 9, pp. 46–68.

6 Nihon Bunka Fōramu (ed.) (1958), Nihon bunka no dentō to hensen (Tradition and transition in Japanese culture), Tokyo: Shinchōsha.

7 Takeuchi, Yoshimi (1958), 'Futatsu no Ajia shikan (Two historical views of Asia)', *Tokyo Shinbun* (evening edition), August 15–17. Later in *Takeuchi Yoshimi hyōronshū* (1966), Vol. 3, *Nihon to Ajia* (Japan and Asia), Tokyo: Chikuma Shobō.

8 Ueyama, Shunpei (1959), 'Rekishikan no mosaku – Marukusu shikan to seitai shikan o megutte (The search for a view of history – concerning the Marxist view of history and the ecological view of history)', *Shisō no Kagaku*, January issue, pp. 27–39. Also, Ueyama, Shunpei (1961), 'Marukusu shikan to seitai shikan (The Marxist view of history and the ecological view of history)', *Kyōto Daigaku Shinbun*, July 3. These articles were later included in Ueyama, Shunpei (1964), *Dai Tōa Sensō no imi – gendaishi bunseki no shiten* (The meaning of the Greater East Asia War – perspective on analysis of modern history), Tokyo: Chūō Kōronsha.

9 Ōta, Hidemichi (1959), 'Seitaishikan to wa nani ka (What is an ecological view of history)', *Rekishi Hyōron*, Shiseidō, March issue, No. 103, pp. 1–8.

10 Kawane, Yoshiyasu (1960), 'Nōdo sei ni tsuite no oboegaki – iwayuru "Sekaishi no kihon hōsoku" hihan no kokoromi (Notes on the system of serfdom – an attempt at a critique of "The basic laws of world history")', *Nihonshi Kenkyū*, No. 47, March, Sōgensha, pp. 54–64; No. 49, July, pp. 50–70.

11 For example, see Kōuchi, Saburō (1964), 'Seitaishikan to shin sekai zō (The ecological view of history and the new world image)', *Nihon Dokusho Shinbun*, April 20; also Iida, Momo (1964), 'Bunmei no seitaishikan shūsetsu (Conclusion to an ecological view of history)', *Tōhoku Daigaku Shinbun*, November, later included in Iida, Momo (1965), *Taishū bunka*

jōkyō o koeru mono (What goes beyond the conditions of mass culture), Shōbunsha.

12 For example, see Fujioka, Yoshinaru (1965), 'Pāsonaritī no shinka (The evolution of personality)', pp. 19–40; Nakao, Sasuke, 'Nōkō bunka no yōso to areraizēshon (Elements of farming culture and allelization)', pp. 57–64; Sasaki, Kōmei, 'Yakihata nōkōmin no sonraku no keitai to kōzō – Tōnan Ajia, Nanbei no jirei o chūshin ni (Configuration and structure of villages of slash-and-burn farmers – based mainly on examples from Southeast Asia and South America)', pp. 79–128; et al. All of the above in *Jinbungakuhō*, No. 21, Kyōto Daigaku Jinbunkagaku Kenkyūjo, December.

13 See Ueyama, Shunpei (1962), 'Hikaku shi hōhōron shiron (Historical treatise on methodology of comparative history)', part two of *Rekishi bunseki no hōhō* (Methods of historical analysis), San'ichi Shobō; also Ueyama, Shunpei (1961), 'Burujoa kakumei to hōkensei (The bourgeois revolution and feudalism)', *Rekishigaku Kenkyū*, April; later included in *Dai Tōa Sensō no imi*, Chūō Kōronsha, August 1964 [see note 8 above].

14 See various essays in Kawakita, Jirō, Tadao Umesao, and Shunpei Ueyama, (eds.) (1966), *Ningen – jinruigakuteki kenkyū* (Human beings – an anthropological study), *Imanishi Kinji hakase kanreki kinen ronbun shū* (Collection of essays in honor of Dr. Imanishi Kinji on the 60th anniversary of his birth), Vol. 3, ChūōKōronsha, August. In particular, see in this volume Tani, Yutaka, 'Kansō chiiki no kokka (States of the arid region)', pp. 15–72; Ueyama, Shunpei, 'Shakai hensei ron (Social formation theory)', pp. 73–99; Iinuma, Jirō, 'Sekai nōgyō shijō ni okeru kodai sōchi nōhō no ichi (The position of ancient methods of early farming in world agricultural history)', pp. 101–138; Tsunoyama, Sakae, 'Sangyō kakumei ron (Theory of industrial revolution)', pp. 139–179; Kawakita, Jirō, 'Chibetto bunka no seitaigaku teki ichi zuke (The positioning of Tibetan culture in terms of ecology)', pp. 289–342.

15 Uemasao, Tadao (1964), 'Bunmei no seitaishikan josetsu (An introduction to an ecological view of history: Japanese civilization in the world context)', reissued, *Chūō Kōron*, October issue, Vol. 79th year, No. 10, issue No. 924, pp. 340–358.

16 Toynbee, Arnold J. (1946), *A Study of History*, abridgement of Volumes I–M, by D. C. Somervell, London: Oxford University Press.
The Japanese translation was issued as parts 1–3 (1949–1952); these were published in volume form.
- Toynbee, Arnold J., *A Study of History*, trans. Rōyama, Michio, Ikuzō Abe, Matsuji Hasegawa (1956), *Rekishi no kenkyū* (complete), Shakai Shisō Kenkyūkai Shuppanbu.
The second part of the Somervell edition was issued in 1957.
- Toynbee, Arnold J., *A Study of History* (continued), trans. Hasegawa, Matsuji (1958), *Zoku – Rekishi no kenkyū*, Shakai Shisō Kenkyūkai Shuppanbu.
Both parts were published later.
- Toynbee, Arnold J., *A Study of History*, Somervell, D.C. (ed.), trans. Hasegawa, Matsuji (1963), *Rekishi no kenkyū (I)*, Gendai Kyōyō Bunko, Shakai Shisōsha.
- Toynbee, Arnold J., *A Study of History*, Somervell, D.C. (ed.), trans. Hasegawa, Matsuji (1963), *Rekishi no kenkyū (II)*, Gendai Kyōyō Bunko, Shakai Shisōsha.
- Toynbee, Arnold J., *A Study of History*, Somervell, D.C. (ed.), trans. Hasegawa, Matsuji (1963), *Rekishi no kenkyū (III)*, Gendai Kyōyō Bunko, Shakai Shisōsha.
- Toynbee, Arnold J., *A Study of History*, Somervell, D.C. (ed.), trans. Hasegawa, Matsuji (1964), *Rekishi no kenkyū (IV)*, Gendai Kyōyō Bunko, Shakai Shisōsha.
- Toynbee, Arnold J., *A Study of History*, Somervell, D.C. (ed.), trans. Hasegawa, Matsuji (1964), *Rekishi no kenkyū (V)*, Gendai Kyōyō Bunko, Shakai Shisōsha.
17 Toynbee, Arnold J. (1948), *Civilization on Trial*, London: Oxford University Press.
- Toynbee, Arnold J. (1948), *Civilization on Trial*, trans. Fukase, Motohiro (1952), *Shiren ni tatsu bunmei* (Vol. 1 and 2), Shakai Shisō Kenkyūkai Shuppanbu.
18 Katō, Shūichi (1956), *Zasshu bunka – Nihon no chiisa na kibō* (Hybrid culture – Japan's small hope), Mirion Bukkusu, Kōdansha.
19 For example, see Coulborn, R. (ed.) (1956), *Feudalism in History*, Princeton University Press.
20 On theories of ecology, see Imanishi, Kinji, et al. (eds.) (1959), *Seitaigaku taikei* (Outline of ecology), 6 volumes

(incomplete), Kokon shoin; in particular, regarding succession of plants, see its Vol. 1, Numata, Makoto (ed.), 'Shokubutsu seitaigaku 1(Plant Ecology 1)', April.

21 For example, since the 1920's, studies on 'human ecology' have been published by urban sociologists in the U.S., such as R.E. Park, E.W. Burgess, and R.D. McKenzie. See a critique of these in Alihan, M.A. (1964), *Social Ecology: A critical analysis*, Cooper Square Publishers.

Chapter 4

1 Umesao, Tadao (1957), 'Shin bunmei sekai chizu (A new world map of civilization)', *Nihon Dokusho Shinbun,* No. 881, January 1.

2 Umesao, Tadao, (1957) 'Shin bunmei sekai chizu (zoku) (A new world map of civilization, continued)', *Nihon Dokusho Shinbun,* No. 885, February 4.

3 Siegfried, André (1955), *Aspects du XX Siècle*, Hachette (*Gendai – Nijūseiki bunmei no hōkō*, trans. Sugi, Toshio, Kinokuniya Shoten, June 1955).

4 Siegfried, André (1951), *Voyages aux Indes*, [publisher unknown] (*Indo kikō,* trans. Honda, Ryōsuke, Iwanami Shoten, March 1955).

Chapter 5

1 Umesao, Tadao (1957), 'Seitaishikan kara mita Nihon (Japan in ecological history)', lecture, Annual Meeting of Institute for the Science of Thought (Shisō no Kagaku Kenkyūkai), July 7, Kanda Gakushikaikan, Tokyo.

Chapter 6

1 Umesao, Tadao (1962), 'Betonamu Raosu jūdan ryokō (Trip traversing Vietnam and Laos)', *Sekai no tabi,* Vol. 8, *Chūgoku Tōnan Ajia,* Chūō Kōronsha, pp. 385–420.

2 Umesao, Tadao (1964), *Tōnan Ajia kikō* (Southeast Asia travelogue), Chūō Kōronsha. Paperback edition: *Tōnan Ajia kikō* (volumes 1and 2) (1979), Chūkō Bunko, Chūō Kōronsha. Compiled in *Chosaku shū* (Collected works of Umesao Tadao) Vol. 6, *Ajia o miru me* (Eyes on Asia).

3 Umesao, Tadao (supervisory ed.) (1958), *Tai gakujutsu chōsa no tabi* (Thailand: scientific study trip), Iwanami Shashin Bunko 275, Iwanami Shoten.

4 Umesao, Tadao (supervisory ed.) (1958), *Indoshina no tabi – Kanbojia, Betonamu, Raosu* (Trip to Indochina: Cambodia, Vietnam, Laos), Iwanami Shashin Bunko 276, Iwanami Shoten.

5 Kira, T. and T. Umesao (eds.), *Nature and Life in Southeast Asia*, Vol. I (1961), Vol. II (1962), Vol. III (1964), Fauna and Flora Research Society, Kyoto.

6 Umesao, Tadao (1958), 'Tōnan Ajia no tabi kara (Travels in Southeast Asia)', *Chūō Kōron*, August issue, Vol. 73, No. 8, issue No. 842, pp. 32–48.

Chapter 7

1 Umesao, Tadao (1958), 'Arabu minzoku no meiun (The fate of the Arab people)', *Shūkan Asahi* (emergency supplement), 'Chūtō no kiki (Crisis in the Middle East)', Vol. 63, No. 35, August 6, pp. 20–21.

2 Ukai, Nobushige (1958), 'Chūkintō (The Middle and Near East)', *Mainichi Shinbun*, July 24.

Chapter 8

1 Umesao, Tadao (1958), 'Tōnan Ajia no Indo (Traces of India in Southeast Asia)', *Nichi-In Bunka,* Vol. 2, September, pp. 1–2.

2 Le May, R. (1954), *The Culture of South-East Asia,* George Allen & Unwin Ltd.

3 Murata, Jirō and Akira Fujieda (eds.) (1955), *Kyoyōkan* (Chuyungkuan), Vol. 2, Kyoto Daigaku Kōgakubu, March; in English as: *Chu-Yung-Kuan: The Buddhist Arch of the Fourteenth Century A.D. at Pass of the Great Wall Northwest of Peking*, Vol. 2, Faculty of Engineering, Kyoto University.

Chapter 9

1 Umesao, Tadao (1962), 'Chūyō no kuniguni (The countries of the 'Mediant')', *Indo kara nessa no kuni e* (From India to the

countries of the burning sands), *Sekai no tabi* (Travels around the world), Vol. 2, Chūō Kōronsha, pp. 394–411.

2 Hotta, Yoshie (1957), *Indo de kangaeta koto* (My thoughts while in India), Iwanami Shinsho, Iwanami Shoten.

Chapter 10

1 Umesao, Tadao (1964), *Tōnan Ajia kikō* (Travels in Southeast Asia), Chūō Kōronsha. The paperback edition is: Umesao, Tadao (1979), *Tōnan Ajia kikō* (Travels in Southeast Asia), Vols. 1 and 2, Chūkō Bunko, Chūō Kōronsha. Compiled in *Chosaku shū* (Collected works of Umesao Tadao), Vol. 6, *Ajia wo miru me* (Eyes on Asia).

2 Umesao, Tadao (1962), 'Ajia no tabi kara: 1: Kindaika e no kiseki: Tai (From my travels in Asia: 1: Tracks toward modernization: Thailand)', *Asahi Jānaru*, March 4 issue, Vol. 4, No. 9, 156th issue, Asahi Shinbunsha, pp. 18–22.

   • Umesao, Tadao (1962), 'Ajia no tabi kara: 2: Nashonarizumu no ikisugi: Biruma (From my travels in Asia: 2: Nationalism gone too far: Burma)', *Asahi Jānaru*, March 18 issue, Vol. 4, No. 11, 158th issue, pp. 20–23.

   • Umesao, Tadao (1962), 'Ajia no tabi kara: 3: Bunkatsu no higeki: Pakisutan (From my travels in Asia: 3: The tragedy of Partition: Pakistan)', *Asahi Jānaru*, March 25 issue, Vol. 4, No. 12, 159th issue, pp. 96–99.

   • Umesao, Tadao (1962), 'Ajia no tabi kara: 4: Tanima no chūritsu: Nepāru (From my travels in Asia: 4: Neutrality in the valley: Nepal)', *Asahi Jānaru*, April 1 issue, Vol. 4, No. 13, 160th issue, pp. 84–87.

   • Umesao, Tadao (1962), 'Ajia no tabi kara: 5: Bunkatsu suru Ajia (From my travels in Asia: 5: Divided Asia)', *Asahi Jānaru*, April 8 issue, Vol. 4, No. 14, 161th issue, pp. 84–87.

   All five articles are compiled in *Chosaku shū* (Collected works of Umesao Tadao), Vol. 6, *Ajia wo miru me* (Eyes on Asia).

3 Umesao, Tadao (1962), 'Tai kara Nepāru made (From Thailand to Nepal)', Part 1, *Asahi Shinbun*, February 22.

   • Umesao, Tadao (1962), 'Tai kara Nepāru made (From Thailand to Nepal)', Part 2, *Asahi Shinbun*, February 23.

- Umesao, Tadao (1962), 'Tai kara Nepāru made (From Thailand to Nepal)', Part 3, *Asahi Shinbun*, February 24.

Chapter 11

1 Umesao, Tadao (1965), 'Hikaku shūkyōron e no hōhōronteki oboegaki (Methodological notes on comparative religion)', *Jinbun Gakuhō*, No. 21, December, Kyoto Daigaku Jinbun Kagaku Kenkyūjo (Kyoto University Institute of Humanistic Studies), pp. 1–18.

Chapter 12

1 Umesao, Tadao (2000), 'Umi to Nihon bunmei (The ocean and Japanese civilization)', *Chūō Kōron*, January issue, Vol. 115, No. 2, issue No. 1388, pp. 62–79.

2 Umesao, Tadao (2000), 'Umi to Nihon bunmei (The ocean and Japanese civilization)', *Nihon Fōramu,* Vol. 44, March, pp. 88–104, Seoul Forum.

3 *International Ocean Symposium 'The Ocean, Can She Save Us?'* (2000), (1999 edition), Tokyo, The Nippon Foundation.

Comments

1 Translator's note: This English language volume includes a later article, Chapter 12: 'The Ocean and Japanese Civilization.'

Index